HANDWRITING ANALYSIS:

The Science of Determining Personality by GRAPHOANALYSIS

HANDWRITING ANALYSIS

the science of determining
personality by
GRAPHOANALYSIS

by M. N. BUNKER

founder, International
Graphoanalysis Society

NELSON-HALL nh Publishers
CHICAGO, U.S.A.

1979

New Edition

Nelson-Hall Publishers
111 N. Canal St.
Chicago, Illinois 60606

To
Glenn Robert Wallace

Preface

The system of handwriting analysis know as Grapho Analysis is not to be confused with out-dated graphology.

Grapho Analysis is exact, scientific—the result of more than forty-five years of painstaking research. It is a science, now used throughout the civilized world for both pleasure and profit.

What is the basis of the uncanny accuracy of grapho analysis? The answer is STROKES. The revealing factor is the strokes of the hand-writing and not the letter formations. It does not matter what language the writing is in—even shorthand reveals the writer.

This book explains how grapho analysis identifies character and person-ality traits and tendencies. These are based in the mind, follow the nervous system and inevitably show up in handwriting. A person trained as a grapho analyst can reconstruct the inclinations and the emotions of the writer of any adequate specimen of handwriting. The analyst can, with surprising accuracy, predict what the writer will do and how he will react under certain conditions.

It is, of course, only quite recently that the study of handwriting has been put on a scientific basis. So it is to be expected that some uninformed people are still skeptical. They should be reminded of the wise words of John Stuart Mill:

"Every great movement must experience three stages: ridicule, discussion, adoption."

Contents

HANDWRITING ANALYSIS:
The Science of Determining Personality
by
GRAPHOANALYSIS

CHAPTER **1**

Your Insurance Policy

GRAPHO ANALYSIS GIVES YOU PROTECTION FROM CHISELERS, THIEVES, HEARTBREAK AND MURDERERS. HOW IT STARTED, HOW IT GREW UP, WHY YOU CAN DEPEND ON IT.

You may be one of those readers who dislikes most heartily to take part in a conversation where one person keeps saying, I, I, until he wears out the pronoun. If you are we have something in common from the start, but no matter how I have tried to find a way to get away from this abominable I, it seems there is no way.

My life has been devoted to grapho analysis and to the research that has gone into it. My countless miles of travel, and hundreds of thousands of letters which were employed for many years in testing writers and their reactions is part of this history. However, you will not have to endure any more I's than absolutely necessary to give you the freedom and protection that came to me personally as a result of understanding what handwriting reveals.

● **HOW YOU GET PROTECTION**

When you are promised protection, the word is not idly used. You are protected by knowing people. First, how they feel; second, how they think, and then how they will act because they feel and act in line with how they feel. An instance comes to mind that occurred many years ago.

An old lady who was a very dear friend had a nephew who was the apple of her eye. Depression conditions made it impossible for him to find a job. She asked my help. His handwriting warned me that he was selfish, deceitful, and untrustworthy. However, I owed that old lady a deep debt of gratitude for things she had done, not only for me, but others.

So I made a place for the young chap. He was brilliant. He had ability, but in giving him the job grapho analysis protected me. I knew what to expect, and it was possible to anticipate what was certain to

3

happen. He did all right for several months. Then remittances that were supposed to have reached my office were not recorded. Passing thru his office one day I saw him tear up a letter, drop it in the waste basket, and slip a bill into his pocket.

That evening I searched the waste basket. A customer had sent five dollars in currency but the accounting department did not show the remittance. That remittance had gone into his pocket. However, I was not surprised. He had a family. His aunt had been a friend of enduring worth. If I had fired him, it would have hurt her, and he became a guinea pig by which what I had learned from handwriting could be tested.

Weeks and months went by. There were no major defalcations, just shortages of five dollars, ten dollars, sometimes only a dollar or two a day. Then one day he wrote a letter to a customer who owed close to a hundred dollars. If the remittance were sent directely to him, he would square the books for fifty dollars.

That morning the young fellow and I had a conference. I did not accuse him of being a thief. There was no reason to do so. When he was hired he had given me all the warning I needed, and so if there was any blame, it rested on my own shoulders. But I had tested grapho analysis. He had helped to prove it by dropping letters into the waste basket, taking money, and feeling that he was getting away with it.

● GRAPHO ANALYSIS HAS BEEN PROVED STEP BY STEP

This incidentally is how grapho analysis was tested and proved. Not in one instance but in hundreds upon hundreds of cases. Men and women, regardless of age, race or political or church affiliation. Even after I began teaching my first students the tests went on except we were both conducting them. They were doing it because they were warned not to believe anything they found in their lesson books just because they were in print. They were urged to test and prove every point, which brings us down to how grapho analysis saved one of the early students' life. This particular lady was charming, highly educated, and a steadfast church worker. She headed committees, entertained the pastor at teas, worked on committees under his directions. She was, if you wish to use a Biblical phrase, "full of good works."

Then the long time pastor was compelled to take a long vacation. A new man came to town, and the good church worker took him into her home, her husband exerted himself to support his wife's efforts to make the stranger feel at home. The man was popular, good looking, conducted himself well. Everyone liked him.

Then he wrote a note about a committee to the grapho analyst. That night she told her husband, "He can't come into the house again. I'm going to see my sister out of state while this man is here." She fulfilled her intention, and it was another church member who was raped and strangled. That charming fellow was a sex driven man with good clothes, a fine vocabulary, and graciousness, who was ready to turn into a sex demon when he was refused what he demanded.

● *"KNOW THYSELF"*

So grapho analysis, as you master rules in the following pages, may help you identify a murderer or a thief. One thing is certain. As you examine your own handwriting, you will get a new understanding of yourself. You will suddenly find that some traits you have considered "bad" are not bad at all. Take for instance the lady who wrote me after getting her analysis pointing out that she was proud. "Every night I ask God to help me overcome pride," she said in her letter. You will learn how to recognize pride from handwriting, and you will see what an important trait it is in making your own life happier, and more successful.

You will be sure of one other gain. You will no longer feel there is any value to gossip. You will not need to have what others think about someone to guide you, for you will be able to take a page of handwriting and know how the writer feels, thinks, and acts.

● **YOU CONQUER FEAR OF THE UNKNOWN**

You may find that some of your friends cannot be trusted. This is entirely possible. However, that does not mean that you need to discard them as acquaintances—which, after all, is all they have been. You are not learning to use grapho analysis to set yourself up as judge. You are not learning to analyze handwriting just to find "bad" things in others. Grapho analysis is not a science to use in finding either "good" or "bad" but the truth. For instance, you may think that deceit is always a bad trait. Instead it is merely a trait. It may be used for the good of others, or it can become a dangerous trait. Its value depends on how it is used.

You will gain one other advantage. If you are shy, afraid of people and what they say, you will find that knowing handwriting gives you freedom from fear. The reason is rather simple. The child that fears the dark is afraid because he does not understand the dark. You are timid, afraid because you do not understand people. When you actually know them you will have no reason for fear unless you have done something to injure others. Even then you may have only yourself to fear.

This promise that you will lose fear is a lesson that I learned during the first few years of my research. Audiences from coast to coast now tell me that there could not have been a time when I was afraid. They do not know. As a young man I was timid, fearful, hesitant to use what I knew. I could get along all right in a play or something I had memorized but to stand on my feet and talk off the cuff was unthinkable.

Then one day Albert G. Burns, founder of the Inventors of America, told me to go out and talk to a group of inventors from all parts of America. I refused. I could not. Al Burns looked at me and said. "If you know ànything about it and believe in grapho analysis you can." I talked. He had brought me to a realization that when I knew and understood people there was nothing to fear. So as you go along with your study of these rules you will be gaining knowledge that others do not have. You will understand them, and there is no knowledge as valuable.

● A SCOUNDREL EXPOSED

It gives you unexpected protection. At the start of World War II when air mail was not so common as it is today, a letter reached me late one afternoon. It was from a woman who had been trained in grapho analysis, and it contained a number of sheets of a love letter. "I do not have any right to analyze this writing," she wrote. "It is my daughter's fiance and she wants you to give a thorough analysis. We both feel that because she is my daughter I might be influenced, and this is important."

Examination of the handwriting showed that the writer was a scoundrel, and might easily be a murderer. It was not an opinion. The handwriting revealed the picture as clearly as an x-ray could have done. So the report was made, mailed, as requested, air mail and special delivery.

A few days later another letter brought the rest of the story. The young man was a stranger in the community, but he and the young woman had met, fallen in love, and were to be married almost at once. Then, as a matter of possible curiosity, the daughter let her mother read a letter and the mother was appalled by what she found. Result, the mother and daughter agreed to submit the handwriting to another analyst, and quite naturally selected the mother's teacher. That analysis undoubtedly saved the young woman's happiness, and possibly her life, for shortly after the engagement was broken the police from another state arrested the fellow as a criminal and took him back to the scene of his crimes.

You will get such protection for your life as you learn and use grapho analysis. You will not get it by merely skimming through these pages, getting some of the rules in mind, and confusing others. Study the rules, and the example of handwriting, and then *use* what you learn. For more than thirty years students of grapho analysis undertaking professional training have been advised not to believe what they have found in lesson books just because it is in print. When you learn something, test it, prove it and then you have it even if your books are destroyed.

● ETHICAL USES OF HANDWRITING ANALYSIS

At this point there is one point that must be emphasized. Do not approach the study of grapho analysis just to find out about people. There is a vast difference between learning to understand people, and finding characteristics that you may feel will be juicy bits of gossip. When you examine a handwriting you are certain to find some traits that you do not like, but you are not judge nor jury.

You may find unusual talent for dancing or painting and you may believe the dancing is sinful. That is your right, but you still have the knowledge that the writer has natural talent for dancing. Or you may find evidence that a writer is likely to steal. There are many potential thieves possibly who have never been caught, and possibly some of them have never actually stolen. Handwriting does not reveal that a man has done any certain thing, any more than it reveals that he has cancer or tuberculosis. It does show the individual who, given an opportunity, will steal. But if you know this, and protect yourself against his doing so from you, then you have had protection.

However, learn discretion in keeping what you learn to yourself. If you were a professional grapho analyst you would be bound by a code of ethics as binding as the ethics of any medical man. You should tell the person whose handwriting you examine the truth, but that does not mean telling all of her or his family, and the neighbors. Gossip is one of the most reprehensible things in civilization and has broken more homes than any other single human weakness. Analyze handwriting truthfully, but do not repeat to others what you have found.

● CURING SELF-CONSCIOUSNESS

You will be able to do a vast amount of good. A well known medical man told me this story of how he helped a mother who was his patient. The mother had a son in high school. He was just squeezing by, sometimes was not even making a passing grade. The mother was exceedingly worried, and this worry affected her as a patient. Worry has such effect, you know.

Finally the doctor suggested that she provide him with the boy's handwriting, with the thought that he might find the answer. He did. The youngster was so self-conscious that he did not dare to stand up among the young folks of his own age and tell what he knew. He thought they knew more than he did, and between under-rating his own ability and the self-consciousness he was making his high school days agony, not only for himself, but his mother and his teachers all suffered.

This doctor, who uses grapho analysis frequently in understanding his patients, had a visit with the boy. He showed the young man from his own handwriting that he was equal and possibly superior mentally to some of his classmates. He convinced him that there was no reason for either fear or self-consciousness, then convinced the mother that she could aid by having her son recite to her. When the boy discovered for himself that he knew and was able to hold his own with other students his own age, his problem was whipped. The boy gained, the mother showed better results from her medical treatment, and the teachers found that they had a near-honor student.

● GRAPHO ANALYSIS HELPS PRACTICAL PSYCHOLOGY

Another instance of a similar nature was successfully handled by the credit manager of a big corporation where he used his knowledge to determine the responsibility of customers. This particular credit manager was invited to talk on his experiences before a large business group. After the talk one of the business men pushed forward and asked for a few minutes of the speaker's time. "You may be able to help us with our son," he said. "My wife and I feel that we may have to send him either to a military school, or let the juvenile court send him to a state school. We simply cannot manage him. He's not a fool, but he has outgrown us."

As a result of that few minutes conversation, the father sent the lad's writing to the credit manager. He studied it. Then he asked for the writing of both parents. He studied those two specimens, and then visited the troubled family. It was a long and a serious interview, but grapho analysis had found the explanation of the trouble. Both parents had become involved in many personal and social activities. They were providing a good residence, good furniture in the residence, but they were not making a home for the boy. They were busy attending social functions, bridge clubs, business conferences.

The lad had become a problem because he resented being shoved to one side. He thought his parents did not care about him, but about their social and business lives. He had come to hate and fear them, and was merely striking back. Fortunately the parents accepted the revelations made from their own writing, the boy admitted that was the way he felt. Today that family is well adjusted, the parents are happy and proud of their son, and he in turn is making good and is fond of his parents, whom he now recognizes as something more than a source of money. He has found that they do love him, and he in turn is a wonderful son.

● YOU GET PERSONAL BENEFITS AND SELF-PROTECTION

You may have such experiences provided you study grapho analysis, as you will find it in the following pages. You may be skeptical, and there is nothing that the profession of grapho analysis will like better than for skeptics to be convinced.

This benefit and protection for you is after all the justification for writing this book, and because I began the research and stumbled onto the key that makes scientific handwriting analysis possible, it is necessary for me now and then to talk about myself. Forget that part, will you, and keep in mind that we are both devoting our time to grapho analysis, and what it can do for you in increasing your happiness, your cash in the bank, and your happiness in getting along with people while you earn your living.

You may have noted that I frankly admit that I stumbled onto the key that made grapho analysis possible. Actually the start came simply because I got to Sunday School ahead of time. The little one room school house served as the church, and there was a long blackboard across one end of the building. On this particular Sunday one of the older boys who had graduated from the eighth grade had come back over the week-end and was writing strange symbols on the blackboard.

All of the early arrivals were properly impressed at how those mysterious strokes could mean words. That was my introduction to shorthand, and when I went home after services it was with the deep-rooted determination that if anyone else could make those strange curlicues mean words it would be equally possible for me. Somehow that resolution made when I was eight stuck until I was sixteen and could get my hands on the first shorthand book.

From that time on I studied shorthand. When other young fellows were chasing baseballs I was writing shorthand outlines and loving it. One system followed another until I had managed to learn at least in a passable way almost twenty different systems, and if you are starting to grow grey, you will recall that in the early part of the twentieth century there were almost as many shorthand systems as there are ways of getting a home permanent wave today.

One other subject was essential although I did not know it then. I studied penmanship. Not just ovals, but Palmerian, Zanerian, Ransomerian, and half a dozen other muscular movement systems. One teacher after another must have added a grey hair here and there because of my papers. Only a few weeks ago I ran onto an old letter I had written back in those days, and just at first I thought it was the work of some successful penmanship teacher, until my eye caught one weakness.

I put long finals on almost every word. Very long finals, and the teachers said "No" and meant it. My papers would be all right for a day or two, and then I would slip back into my original penmanship sin, and would get the papers back with red ink strokes slashed across the tails on the words.

● LOVE LETTERS AND CORRESPONDENCE CLUBS

The why of this became a consuming thought. After all they had said, why did I seemingly obstinately continue to add those long strokes which did not belong there? Although I was not very alert mentally, (my handwriting from those days shows that I was mentally about as nim-compoopish as the average, maybe more so) I came up against the problem of finding why I put those pesky tag ends on there. Monkeys had long tails, but I studied myself in the mirror and did not find any more resemblance than there was between other people and the simian.

Was I putting those tag ends on there because there was something wrong with me mentally, or was it because I liked shorthand instead of baseball, and had a morbid fear of snakes? There was nothing else to do. The reason had to be found, and I set out to find it. No young fellow ever wrote more love letters and joined more correspondence clubs than I did in those days. Now and then I found a writer who put on long tails to the words, but their photographs all looked like nice girls, or fairly decent young fellows. When they did it, however, we certainly had one thing in common. What was it?

● TAUGHT 17 SYSTEMS OF SHORTHAND

It was more or less a matter of trial and error, disappointment, and repeated effort until something happened several years later. I had qualified as a shorthand teacher, not of one system but several, but the idea of learning anything about my problem from shorthand never occurred to me at that time—and then I actually stumbled onto the answer.

An employment agency had sent me to teach shorthand in a business college in Shawnee, Oklahoma. About the second day it was plain that I had made a mistake. The head of the school was drunk half the time, indeed he was drunk the afternoon he found that the local business people were talking about running him out of town, and taking over his business school for me to manage. They did get rid of him as a menace to the morals of the town, and I started to Chicago, but stopped in Wichita because I had met a business college man there who looked progressive.

Actually he was just about broke, but there was a little money in my watch pocket and we made a deal whereby I would stay and teach shorthand for at least a few weeks. Possibly he hired me expecting me to stay until he went broke, but that summer he began advertising me as the only shorthand teacher in captivity who could write and teach seventeen systems of shorthand. Those seventeen systems and that advertising was the answer to my question. Students who had been exposed to shorthand in high school or other business colleges, came flocking into school. There were Gregg, and Spencerian and Dougherty shorthand writers. All the shades of the Pitman systems, Benn Pitman, Issac Pitman, and a dozen variations all were enrolled in my dictation classes. All I had to do was dictate, and walk around looking over their shoulders and watch for inaccuracies. It was a scatterbrained bunch for most stenographers will agree that only a handful of people ever write shorthand as it is taught.

● **HERE IS THE BIG IDEA . . .**

It was a dreary afternoon and the Dague Business College had not folded as anticipated. I was dreaming of an editorship of a magazine in Chicago that never materialized, and suddenly back of Frank Gore's chair his shorthand notes hit me squarely. That is, the idea hit me. Frank made his shorthand notes exactly the way he acted. Precise, careful, and almost copybook right. He acted that way. Frank was just as precise as his cousin that I dated out of school. The rest of the class was straggling their notes over the white pages until it was sometimes impossible to determine whether the left to right stroke was intended for an m or n for a curved rather than a straight stroke.

Frank Gore's notes gave me the key to grapho analysis. It was not handwriting that would answer my questions. It was a stroke—an unnecessary stroke, that I had added to my practice pages that had earned those red marks for me. Strokes were what handwriting was made up of, not just letters. For instance, the longhand g had a down stroke, sometimes a backward stroke before the upward stroke was started. The s was made with a circle, but sometimes there was a circle inside of a circle, sometimes two circles. It was strokes, and that is what you will know more about when you complete this book.

From that afternoon the going was fairly easy. After I went into military service there were experiences that were valuable. There was plenty of opportunity to study handwriting as a reflection of people in my organization and slowly and steadily I was arriving at some basic conclusions. There were times when some principle seemed to be verified, and then it would be knocked out entirely by something that had been overlooked.

One question has been frequently asked by people who are given to statistical thinking. It is a question that cannot be answered. There is no record of the specimens of handwriting nor the people who were studied. Certainly not hundreds or a few thousand. One man wrote me once that he had told someone four thousand odd, but I hope no one believed him. His handwriting showed he would not tell the truth, and as he was one of my test cases, long after proving the principles of grapho analysis, he may be interested, if alive, in knowing that he too was a test. Not a test to see if a principle was correct, but rather a test to prove that a certain combination of elemental traits would produce a scoundrel.

● **STUDIED HUNDREDS OF LETTERS DAILY**

As for the number of handwritings and people, there were not hundreds but thousands of them. My daily mail from magazine readers who were kind enough to read the stuff I wrote—and I wrote ceaselessly except when I was exploring handwriting, ran from fifty to two and three hundred letters a day. I read their letters, their confidences, and I studied their handwriting. Frequently our correspondence ran into a dozen or more letters. Every letter I wrote to my distant correspondent was worded to get a reaction. Aside from this the railroads and buses and cars took me over more than a hundred thousand miles, checking on individuals.

You may say, "the man did not have time to do anything else." You are correct. Many of my pieces of fiction and other magazine copy were written on portable typewriters in the caboose of a freight train. Other writing was done late at night. During the day I followed the job that provided my traveling expenses, and gave me a chance to talk to people, get their handwriting, study them, and their surroundings.

One other point was important. My explorations in order to answer my own question about the tails of my handwriting began when I was young. As years went by I was able to follow through ·on cases where I had been puzzled.

If I had been sports-minded there would have been no grapho analysis. If the one and only girl had not married someone alse, there would never have been any grapho analysis.

● **IMPORTANT PEOPLE HELPED**

There is a deep debt that you and I both owe to many very earnest scholars, men and women who had achieved too much fame to want to sign cigarette and liquor advertising who permitted me to study their handwriting, prepare analyses, and then severely criticize them. They did us both a favor. They helped me and as grapho analysis in your hand becomes a tool to make your own life brighter they helped you.

Truly big people are always ready to help. It is the stuffed shirt who does not know and is scared to death that someone will find that he does not. is the only one who scoffs. Really big minds say, "If you have something let us see it. If you are working to achieve something worth while, let us help you."

This does not mean that all of the people who helped were graduates of colleges. Some of them were and had forgotten it. Some had learned in the vast school of life how little they knew.

Even "bad" people, assured of anonymity frequently helped. I shall never forget one scoundrel who, when he learned what I was attempting to do asked me to take his handwriting, and tell him the truth. He sat thru it quietly, and then spent the rest of the night telling me what had happened to him in his life, the little points I had missed, and where I was right.

● *ARE YOU WILLING TO FACE YOURSELF?*

This, my friend, is how grapho analysis has come to you. In the chapters that follow you are going to get a new look at yourself. When you find something you do not like in your own handwriting, face it like the fellow just mentioned. You are not perfect, and when you find things in your writing that you do not like, you can be sure they are there. And you can be equally sure that before you finally lay this book aside, you will have discovered how you can change at least some of the weaknesses, either discarding them, or overshadowing and starving them by building stronger traits that offset them. You will learn how you can change your own writing and change your character.

At this point you may feel like throwing this book down, and saying "I don't believe it," which after all would be foolish. A man cannot disbelieve a thing about which he knows nothing—and before you complete this book you will have learned how to strengthen your own personality by changing your writing. I know. I did it.

When you know how to use grapho analysis and so understand yourself you will also have found the key to changing your own character traits. This discovery of how to change personality came about as a result of demand. Thousands of men and women through the years wrote, "You analyze our handwriting and tell us how we feel, and think, and act, but you do not tell us how to correct our weaknesses. Do this, and you will have helped us more than money or anything else can repay."

With such a challenge a second period of testing began. It was just as tedious, just as heartbreaking as the long search to find the answer to my own question about the tails on my handwriting. However, one thought persisted. If handwriting revealed the traits of character of the individual, would it be possible to change the writing, and eventually change the individual, causing him to gain traits he wished to have, and nullify those he wanted to destroy or remove from his thinking?

That was how the tests began, and in a later chapter you will be given the key to how to make such changes. This book alone cannot teach you all there is to know on the subject. Only a professional grapho analyst can guide you in making some of the more complicated changes, but *you can change your character* by changing your writing.

● *CHANGE IN HANDWRITING CHANGES A LIFE*

The case of Charlie is a striking example of how such changes can be accomplished, and the results. Charlie made a great deal more money than he ever expected to have by getting the franchise for pin-ball machines in army camps during World War II. When he settled up after the War was over he had money, a lot of money he did not know how to handle. Quite naturally he immediately became the saucer of honey around which hovered men with doubtful ideas that they wanted to finance. Charlie invested and invested until he suddenly found himself without funds. His investments were not paying off. His days of being a capitalist were over, with his bank account overdrawn. He had urged that I accompany him on a trip to the city, and we had unexpected car trouble. It was his car and he wrote a check to cover the repairs. That evening I found him in his hotel room writing a suicide note. Under rather severe cross-questioning he admitted what he considered his failure in life. He was whipped and was not only broke, but ashamed.

"I can't go back and face Mary," he said. "She does not know the situation, and she can of course go back to her profession and take care of the children."

As a result of that conversation he started a very simple handwriting exercise, and only a few weeks later breezed into the office to report that he had been made branch manager of a concern where his earnings would mount. He had something he had never had before. He had self-confidence. He had made a few changes in his writing—not major changes, and he had achieved results. You will find out how he did it, before you lay this book aside. You will learn, too, what this simple exercise did for me at a time when I faced great responsibility.

Altogether you will find much in the following chapters that you can use. This is the only reason for writing this book. It is not an easy task, and as I write it there is always the need to omit the pronoun I. What grapho analysis has done for me, and for others, is no more than it can do for you.

CHAPTER **2**

You Show How
You Feel

*ARE YOU A STORMY PETREL, OR A WALL OF
STRENGTH? DO YOU HATE AND LOVE AND
THEN FORGET? ARE YOU A VOLCANO OR AN
ICEBERG? THEIR OWN HANDWRITING RE-
VEALS BILL TILDEN, ELLIS PARKER BUTLER,
ELLA WHEELER WILCOX, FRANKLIN D. ROOSE-
VELT, LOWELL THOMAS, THOMAS DIXON JR.,
AND MANY OTHERS.*

Do you jump at conclusions when you hear a bit of gossip or when you
catch half of a TV newscast? Do you choke up quickly when you listen to
a revivalist or a political speaker when he bears down hard on your feelings?
Are there times when you come down in the morning feeling fit as a fiddle,
then suddenly find that you do not care what happens, the bottom of your
world seems to have dropped out. Then you feel good if someone gives you
a word of approval. Your day brightens up and you feel like going ahead
full steam?

If you find these questions fit your conduct; there is only one handwriting answer. You slant your writing well forward, possibly not as far
as the writing of Warner Baxter, the long time movie favorite. You are
ruled by your feelings. You feel, and show how you feel. Even if you are
not talkative, anyone who knows you, or even a stranger can tell how you
feel by the way you move your head, or the look in your eyes.

The effect of human emotions may be likened to a strong wind. If you
have ever seen a hay field or a field of small grain when swept by a high
wind, you have had a wonderful example of how the strong wind of emo-

tional force will affect an individual who is emotionally responsive. Some people, in fact a great many, are not highly expressive of their feelings. Some men and women can meet the most upsetting situations and keep calm and cool and self possessed through everything. Such writers are identified by their upright or even their backhand writing.

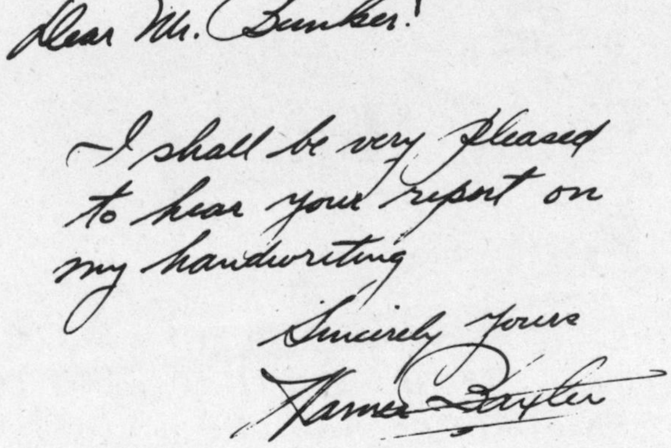
Dear Mr. Bunker!

I shall be very pleased to hear your report on my handwriting

Sincerely yours

PLATE 1. Writing slanted well forward shows you are ruled by your feelings.

However, emotional expression is far more common than you may think. It is common not only in America, but among the Latin races. They feel and show how they feel, their emotional expression ranging from moderate to extreme. No matter how the individual reacts, however, it shows in the handwriting. Take yourself, for instance. If you write far to the right, you are impulsive, and frequently act first and think afterward. If you are calm and self-possessed, you write more nearly vertical, or even backhand.

People show how they feel in varying degrees. For example, it is not possible to say that every warm-hearted person grows hysterical in face of some situations that affect the feelings. This is not true. For this reason it is important that you become familiar with how to measure the degree or amount of emotional expression. You do this with an Emotional Expression Chart, which is reproduced here.

This chart has five lines slanted upward along with one vertical line. One of the slanted lines is made to lean backward, and it is just as important that you understand the value of this slant as any of the forward slanted lines. The forward slanted lines are all used in determining the emotional reaction of the individual writer. The vertical line shows the poise, or lack of emotional expression, while the backward slanted stroke is slanted so that it is extreme, representing the extreme of the slant of backward writing.

You need an actual Emotional Expression Chart for your study. You can make one, either from a small square of glass, or thick plastic. Merely place either the glass or the plastic over the chart illustration here, and trace the chart with India Ink. There is one disadvantage in using a home made chart; the ink is likely to smear, and so your chart becomes messy to use.

EMOTIONAL CHART

PLATE 2. Emotional Expression Chart measures the amount of emotional expression shown in your handwriting.

In order to use the chart effectively you must learn the value of each of the dividing lines, which represents degrees of slant. These rules follow:

1. Writing that is vertical or slants from A to B shows that judgment will rule. The writer will meet emergencies without growing hysterical, and unless the circumstance is unusually emotionally disturbing, without showing any emotional reaction. The vertical writer may be said to be ruled by the head rather than the heart. However, writers who slant their writing to come under or close to B are not totally lacking in expression. They may feel deeply, but they do not show how they feel.

2. Writing that slants from B to C will be quick to respond sympathetically or in a mild way to emotional situations. They are not plungers, they do not impulsively break into a conversation, or act without some thought, especially if there is a matter of importance under consideration.

3. Writing that slants from C to D is evidence of a promptly and very expressive individual. Such writers will usually show traces of tears when speakers tell a particularly heart-rending story. They act promptly, and very often act or speak solely on impulse, and without thinking.

4. Writing that slants from D to E is evidence of extreme emotional response. These are the writers who are whirlwinds as sales-

men, lecturers, actors, writers, and in similar fields. They sweep everything before them, and then suddenly, and to themselves frighteningly, go sour or find that they cannot produce. This is true because they burn out emotional force, and are temporarily exhausted emotionally. It is a striking thing about such writers that even a minor surprise of a favorable nature will revive the emotional expression which is so vital to their relationships with others.

5. Writing that slants to the left of center is just the opposite of emotional expression. It reveals the writer who is not even judicial, but one who pulls back into self. He cannot be judicial, but instead is affected by self and self-interest, past normal self-interest. This rule is general, and you will learn about the exceptions a little later. There is nothing difficult about recognizing the exceptions, so you can accept this rule as it is written, in a majority of cases.

These are the rules, and it is highly important that you get them clearly in mind. It is even more important that you learn how to use your emotional chart on the writing itself, so that your determination of the individual's emotional nature will be accurate. Throughout the steady growth of grapho analysis use through the years, two young men have devoted enough time and study to it to become profesionally skillful. One of these, Glenn Wallace, prepared the following explanation of how to use the emotional chart that will make it easy for you:

"In the first lesson of the General Course you are told that your Emotional Chart is for use in measuring the slant of the UP-STROKES of handwriting. FOR MEASURING THE UP-STROKES OF HANDWRITING.

"Your first reaction was probably this: 'Where do I start on the up-stroke and where do I stop?' This is simple. Most up-strokes start up from the base line of writing. Some do not. The only up-strokes you can effectively measure are those starting from the base line. Thus you have your starting point. The up-stroke continues to go up until it either turns to the left or right, turns down or stops. In other words, when the up-stroke stops going *up*, you stop measuring it.

"The lesson goes on to say that any up-stroke can be measured. This is true, although individual students find it easier to measure some strokes than others. The main point here is that you should never base the slant of any writing on a single up-stroke. Measure several strokes and consider all your findings. Some writers vary the slant of their writing. Some will have up-strokes that are almost exactly the same slant all the time.

"When you first start determining slant of handwriting it will be necessary for you to use your chart. Later, after you have had considerable practice, you will be able to place a page of writing on the palm of your hand, hold it at arm's length, and accurately determine the slant. Keep this in mind and after you have measured several handwritings, start holding the writing on your palm and see if you can determine what the slant will be—then measure it and check yourself.

"Here you have the word 'trade' with the up-strokes properly marked as they should be measured.

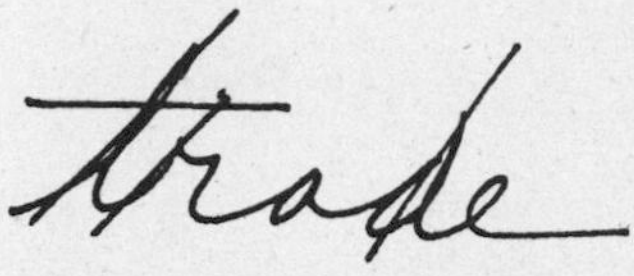

PLATE 2A. Measuring the up-strokes for emotional expression.

"Once again—the rule is very simple. You start where the up-stroke starts up from the base line and stop measuring it when it stops going up. You should easily understand the marking of this specimen.

"However, all up-strokes are not made in the same manner in which those in the first specimen were executed. Some writers make their up-strokes part of a large loop. The principle is still just as simple.

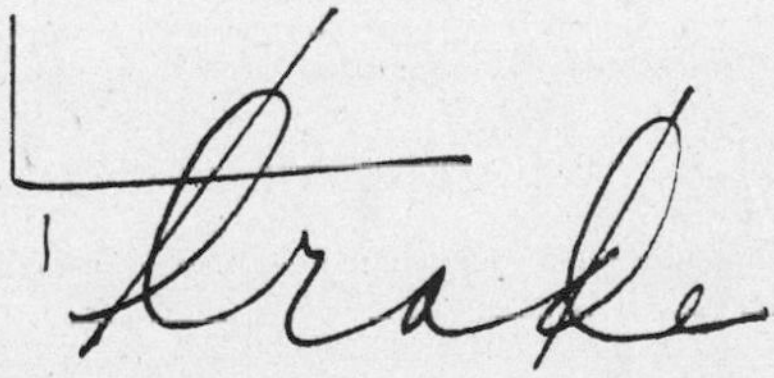

PLATE 2B. Measuring the up-stroke of looped letters.

"You pay no attention to the curve of the stroke. You start where the stroke left the base line and started up, disregard the loop, and stop measuring where the stroke stops going *up*.

"Following this you have several illustrations showing specimens with various and varying slants—all clearly marked to give you a good understanding of how to use your Emotional Chart.

"Every up-stroke is not marked in the specimens that follow. The variety is included here to help you see the variations that may occur."

Follow Wallace's rules for use of the chart. They are simple and you do not need help in learning how to use it. One thing is certain, you cannot hope for accuracy without it.

● *GRAPHO ANALYSIS IS A WORKABLE TOOL*

When you have used the chart on familiar writing until you know where to place it, the next thing to do is consider your objective. You are

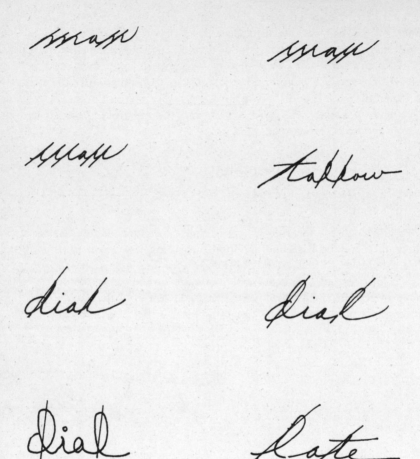

PLATE 2C. Variations in up-stroke letters for use as practice with your Emotional Expression Chart.

not merely learning to measure handwriting. You are learning to analyze and measure handwriting in order to understand people, hence, people are your final interest. In order to accomplish this, there is no way better than to get acquainted with famous names in history—and then get out the old letters from aunts and uncles, possibly some of them may have been puzzles to your family. Further, you are learning these rules to *use*, not just to play with, or to occupy a few spare hours.

You have a workable tool, one that you can depend on, but until you put it into actual use you may be like one of the early students of grapho analysis. She knew her rules. She knew what handwriting revealed about a writer, but when it came to actually applying it and depending on what she knew, she failed to do it. Like many other women, she was ready to consider giving up her career and become a housewife. Then she met a man. He was nice, gracious, considerate, and he loved her. That was the thrilling thing about it. His interest in her was something that increased every day, and then he asked her to marry him.

She had his handwriting. It revealed that he was not only a scoundrel, but a dangerous character as well, but she laid the handwriting aside. After all, she had studied grapho analysis, she knew it worked, but she had not applied it. So she married him. She did not dispose of her property, but when he suggested a trip across the country, she went along. It was her car, because there was no reason for them to own two cars. They would be together from then on.

However, as they drove across the long miles from the east to the west coast, the law was just behind them. They arrested the wonderfully nice man for murdering other wives who had been the apples of his eye, and the dream of his life. He had murdered them. The woman who had not applied her knowledge of grapho analysis had some terrifying days, and a great deal of adverse publicity in popular detective magazines, but she was not murdered. However, she had learned her lesson, and during many years that followed, used what she knew. She finally married, but not until she had analyzed her friend's writing.

So use what you learn as you learn it, step by step. Look for the emotional responsiveness of the writer, first. Then you will learn to follow that with how the individual thinks which you will cover in the next chapter. Now let us look at some people who have made headline in America, and study how they will act emotionally.

Place your emotional Expression Chart on plate 3. Follow the instructions for placing it carefully, and you will find the writer, Hamlin Garland, was very expressive of feelings, actually an extremist. This meant that he felt intensely, showed how he felt, and lived as he felt. This means that he would act before thinking, would speak or talk on impulse based on how he felt at the time.

Although he lived a great many years ago, you now can understand him, and further, you will be able to reconstruct something of how he wrote—for he was a famous fiction writer. What kind of fiction fits a highly emotional personality? Ask yourself the question and then consider. High emotions may be turbulent, quarrelsome, but you can take my word for it

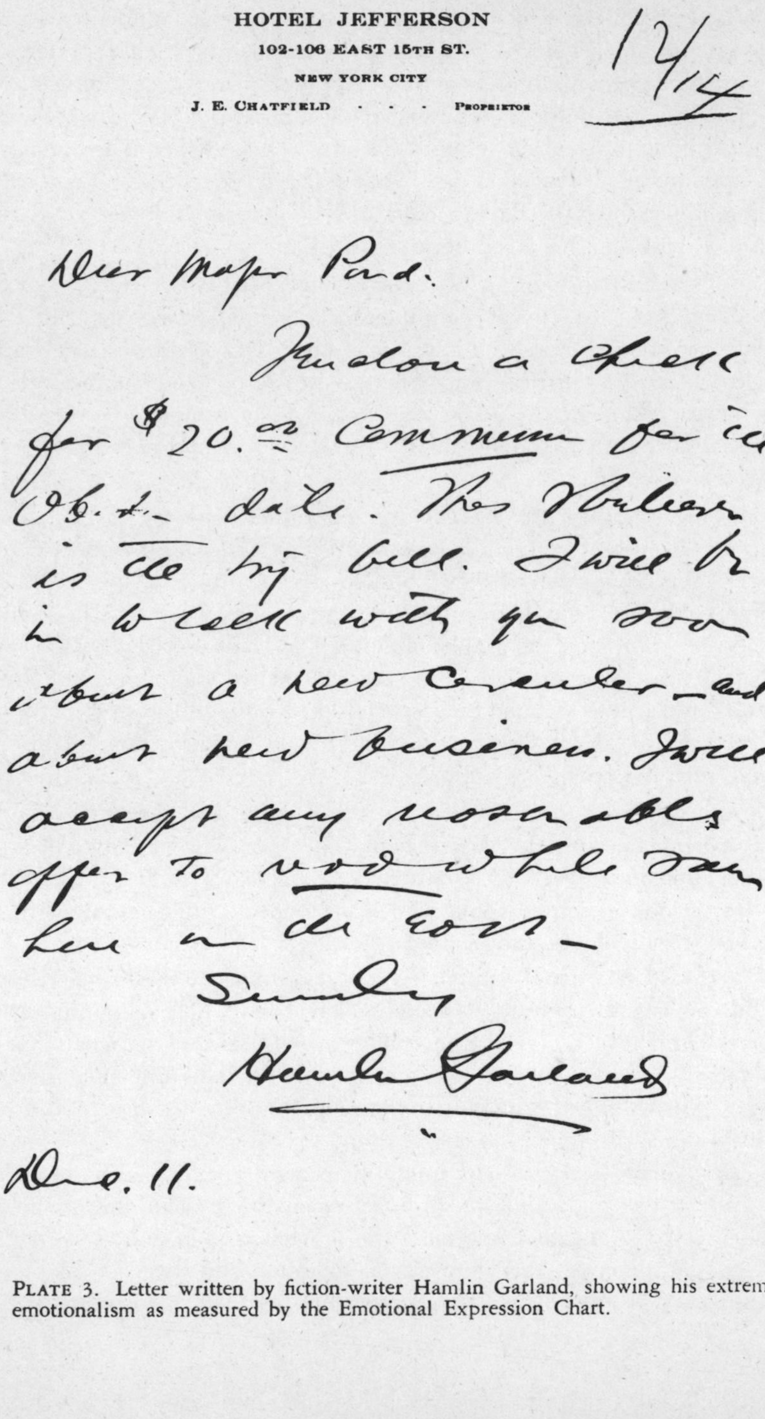

HOTEL JEFFERSON
102-106 EAST 15TH ST.
NEW YORK CITY
J. E. CHATFIELD · · · PROPRIETOR

[handwritten letter]

Dear Major Pond:

Enclose a check for $20.00 Commission for the Ob. t. date. This I believe is the big bill. I will be in to see with you soon about a new circular — and about new business. I will accept any reasonable offer to read while I am here in the East —

Sincerely

Hamlin Garland

Dec. 11.

PLATE 3. Letter written by fiction-writer Hamlin Garland, showing his extreme emotionalism as measured by the Emotional Expression Chart.

that he was not a fighter. Instead his writing, as you will come back to it later and study it as you gain more knowledge, shows a gracious gentleman. Friendly because friendliness goes with emotional expressiveness. He wrote as he felt, and his heart rules. Therefore, he could write fiction that would reach the sympathies, and the heart strings of his readers. If he had been a religious writer, he would have been an evangelical writer, but he was not. He was a fiction writer, and fiction and emotionalism, heart appeal, go with romantic fiction.

PLATE 4. Ella Wheeler Wilcox. Talented writer who became very popular and widely read.

He would plunge into a piece of fiction impulsively and every line he wrote had to have heart appeal. He was also an emotional speaker, that would capture his audiences, hold them spellbound, not by what he said, but by the warmth of the way in which he would say it. He was an able man, but his ability was secondary in his speaking and his writing. He felt, and he reached out in written and spoken words to touch the feelings of his audiences.

In plate 5 you have a similar emotional makeup, one who would appeal to the feelings of readers and listeners. Ella Wheeler Wilcox was the most popular emotional poet in the early part of the Twentieth Century. Countless thousands of school boys memorized and delivered her famous verses, "How Salvator Won", in the closing days of school. Ella Wheeler Wilcox was ruled by her feelings. She was talented, a fact about which she was extremely modest. She wrote me on her way to Europe that she had no right to claim talent. "My mother always wanted to write", she said, "and that longing was transmitted to me. Therefore I am merely doing what my mother longed to do but failed to make come true. I've never really worked at being a writer. I feel what I want to say and I say it."

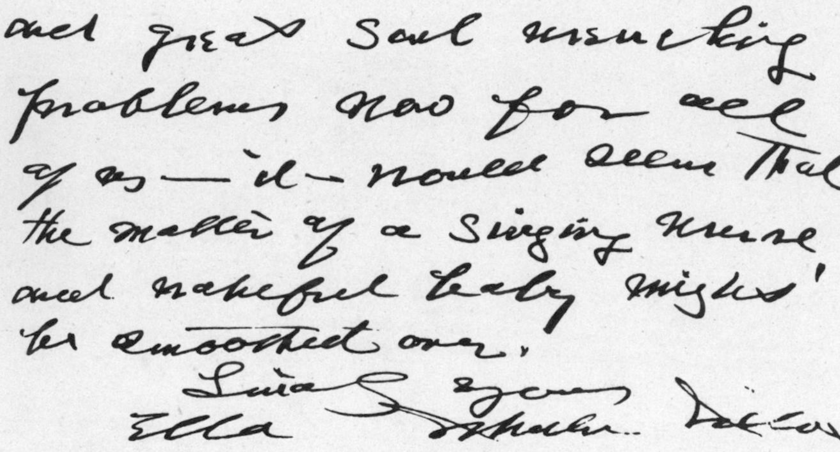

PLATE 5. Handwriting of Ella Wheeler Wilcox gives you clear picture of her personality and of the kind of writing she excelled in.

Just as in the case of Hamlin Garland, who wrote plate 3, she wrote romantic verse and stories. Thousands of those who are grandparents today, were her most ardent fans. However, the point that is important to you is that her letters written back in the early part of the century give you a picture of how she wrote because she wrote as she felt. If you hear either of these names spoken in conversation you will have no need to refer to an encyclopedia to know something about this man and woman. Their writing has given you a clear picture and as you gain new rules you will be able to come back and get better acquainted with them.

You have an entirely different emotional nature in plate 6, which is the handwriting of an internationally famous tennis player. The writing is definitely backhand, which means that he not only looks after himself, and looks at matters without bias, but that he goes to extremes in pulling back into himself rather than showing how he feels. While the other two writers were extroverts, this writing by Bill Tilden is that of an introvert, who is not going to rush in anywhere.

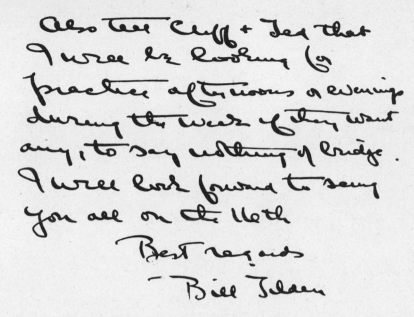

PLATE 6. This handwriting of Bill Tilden is that of an introvert.

The writing in this illustration has a great many heavy strokes, and heavy strokes have their own value in addition to what they reveal about emotional expression or lack of it. Take for example the illustration, plate 7, which is uniformly heavy all the way through. It is not smudged, but heavy. J. Jefferson wrote with pressure on the pen, and left a strong black line from start to finish. This illustration is to particularly emphasize clearly a new rule which you must make your own in order to understand not only how a writer may express his emotional nature, but how strongly he is affected by emotional circumstances. First, however, examine plate 8, where most of the lines are relatively light. Give these two specimens some thought, for one is light, and the other is heavy, although not exceedingly so. Now here are your two new rules to add to the ones you have already had on emotional expression:

1. Heavy writing reveals a writer who soaks up emotional experiences like a blotter. He is greatly hurt or pleased today, and in six months may have forgotten the incident, but the result of his emotional experience today has become a part of his permanent nature. He has absorbed that feeling and will be prejudiced by it long after it has been forgotten as an incident.

2. On the other hand, when the lines of the writing are relative-

ly light the writer may storm, and cry, or bluster around in an emotional tantrum, but when the storm is over, the effect will be gone.

These are important rules. Compare these two handwritings, and the preceding plates and you will find that Ella Wheeler Wilcox in particular was not only expressive of how she felt at the time, but that she carried her feelings over, creating a great reserve of feeling that added to her immediate reaction to an emotional situation. When you have extremely expressive writing, and great depth of feeling the expression becomes intense. It is like a hurricane in its effect on the writer as well as those around him or her.

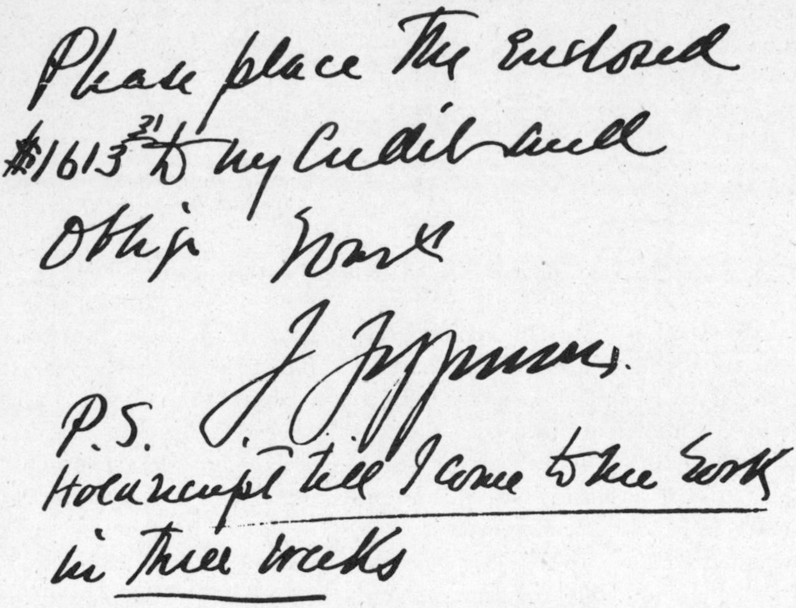

PLATE 7. Actor Joseph Jefferson's handwriting introduces a new rule.

● **THE PROBLEM OF INTROVERTS AND EXTROVERTS**

Joseph Jefferson was one of the great stage performers of fifty years ago. He put feeling into his acting, the same expressive feeling that made Gary Cooper famous and that made little boys sit on hard plank seats and applaud their hero, William S. Hart. Both Cooper and Hart won their spurs as actors by their ability to portray emotions on the screen, while Jefferson was confined to the legitimate theatre.

You have undoubtedly gathered by this time that all highly expressive emotional people are fundamentally actors. They feel, and they want to stir feelings in others. They appeal to the emotions of others. They love it, even though they do not recognize this fact about themselves. This creates a problem in thousands of family arguments when one member of the family slants the writing far forward, and the other is a vertical or backhand writer. They look at things differently, and neither understands how the other faces life.

During the courtship the strongly emotional one looks at the calm poise of the backhand writer—although they pay no attention to the writing, and find strength there, but later that strength becomes a bore for the expressive one. On the other hand, the calm, self-possessed part of the team who was fascinated by the warmth, and emotional fire of the expressive one frequently becomes less fascinated. After that there is conflict. The two who might easily still be in love grow farther and farther apart, simply because neither understands the emotional structure of the other.

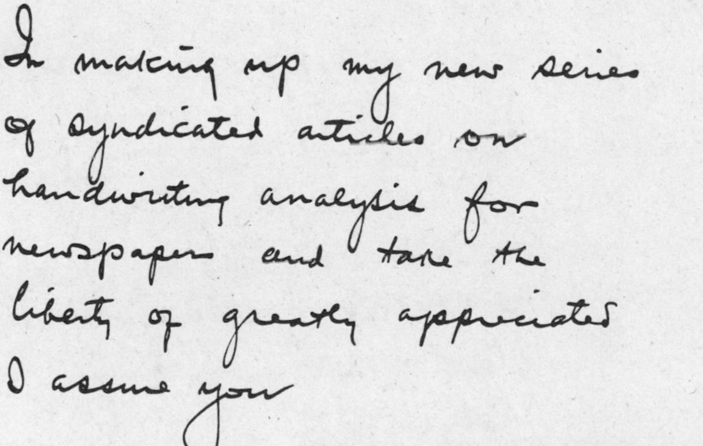

In making up my new series of syndicated articles on handwriting analysis for newspaper and take the liberty of greatly appreciated I assure you

Ellis Parker Butler

PLATE 8. Cool, controlled type of personality shown in this writing of author Ellis Parker Butler.

Bill Tilden could not be as expressive as Ella Wheeler Wilcox, or Joseph Jefferson. His writing shows he felt as deeply, but not in a way to show it, whereas the poet and the actor could never be as calm, and unexpressive as the tennis player.

When you become familiar with these two distinct approaches to life, you have the key, not the total solution, to many social, family and business problems. Such problems may exist in your own life, and in this case, these rules may help you more than many hours spent with a psychologist, for grapho analysis is a branch of psychology—a growing branch which is gaining more and more recognition solely on its merits.

The vertical writer whose pen-strokes are heavy may love just as deeply and sincerely as the most expressive man or woman can ever do, but it is not possible to show it.

Plate 8 was written in 1927 by one of America's great humorists, the famous author of "Pigs Is Pigs" which is still a classic of humor writing.

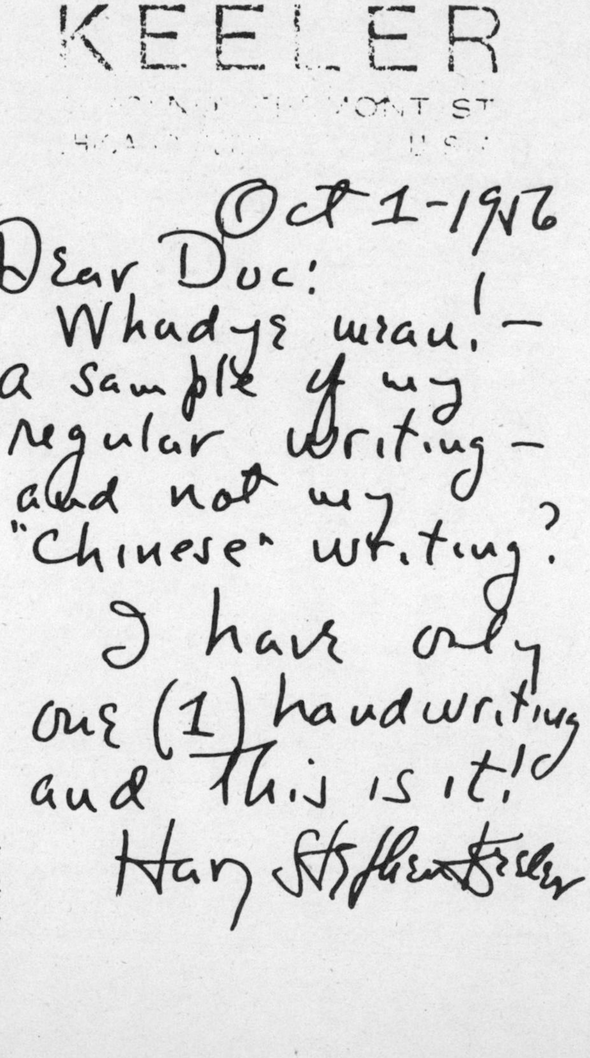

KEELER

Oct 1-1956

Dear Doc:

Whadye mean! — a sample of my regular writing — and not my "Chinese" writing?

I have only one (1) handwriting and this is it!

Harry Stephen Keeler

PLATE 9. Strong sense of color, tone and flavor shows up in the handwriting of mystery-story writer Harry Stephen Keeler.

Ellis Parker Butler was cool, collected, as far as his feelings went. His humor was pure humor, never emotional appeal. He never ridiculed, as he might have done if he had been driven by his emotions. He never wrote a line that did not leave the reader pleasantly in good humor. There was such complete freedom of rancor or emotion, that men and women regardless of race, or religion could read and enjoy his keen wit.

A writer whose strokes are heavy revealing depth of feeling, reveals a strong development of a sense of color, tone, and flavor. As an illustration of how this works out, an editor sent me a handwriting many years ago. "This man is a writer, but I would like to have you tell me from his writing what you believe he will write. If it is fiction, what kind of fiction? If it is factual material, what will be his approach?"

You have a specimen of that writer's work in plate 9. After studying it I gave the answer that it was likely to be fiction, because I could not think of any other subject that will permit such a wide range of color in background, and suggested that such fiction would almost certainly be laid in the orient because of the strong color shown in the writing. I had never heard the man's name, let alone having read one of his books, although I was promptly accused of knowing what he wrote because the conclusions from the handwriting were so accurate. The writer of this specimen is Harry Stephen Keeler, who has produced close to a hundred mystery books, filled with intrigue, and many of them laid in the Far East.

When you have become familiar with this last rule covering heavy writing you have learned that such writing has three distinct values, all registered by the weight of the writing; first, the heavy writing shows depth of feeling, the capacity to absorb emotional experiences and make them a permanent part of the writer's personality; second, the capacity for deep prejudices, loves and hates based on the absorbed emotional experiences as they have occurred; and third, that heavy writing is a register of the fact that the writer possesses strong development of the senses, tone, odor, color, flavor. Cooks who have a reputation for preparing dishes with fine flavors will show this natural ability by their heavy writing. Public speakers, and actors, such as Jefferson, and Franklin D. Roosevelt, reveal capacity to use words with telling effect by the weight of their pen strokes.

You may have been one of the millions who sat entranced by Franklin D. Roosevelt's "fireside chats". After he was through speaking it is entirely possible that you did not remember much of what he said, because it was the way he said it that held his audience. It was his tone, his choice of words, the color sense he showed that influenced voters, and also made enemies for him. In all history of America, there has never been a greater emotional actor in the White House, no man with a capacity for a play on words than the man who sold himself to the American voter on four different occasions. There are some who feel that history has since revealed that he betrayed his friends, sold out those who trusted him, but through it all he never failed to get votes because of his capacity to speak over the air and influence millions. If Franklin D. Roosevelt had elected to go on the stage rather than enter politics he would have outplayed Gable, Bill Hart, and all of the other emotional stars.

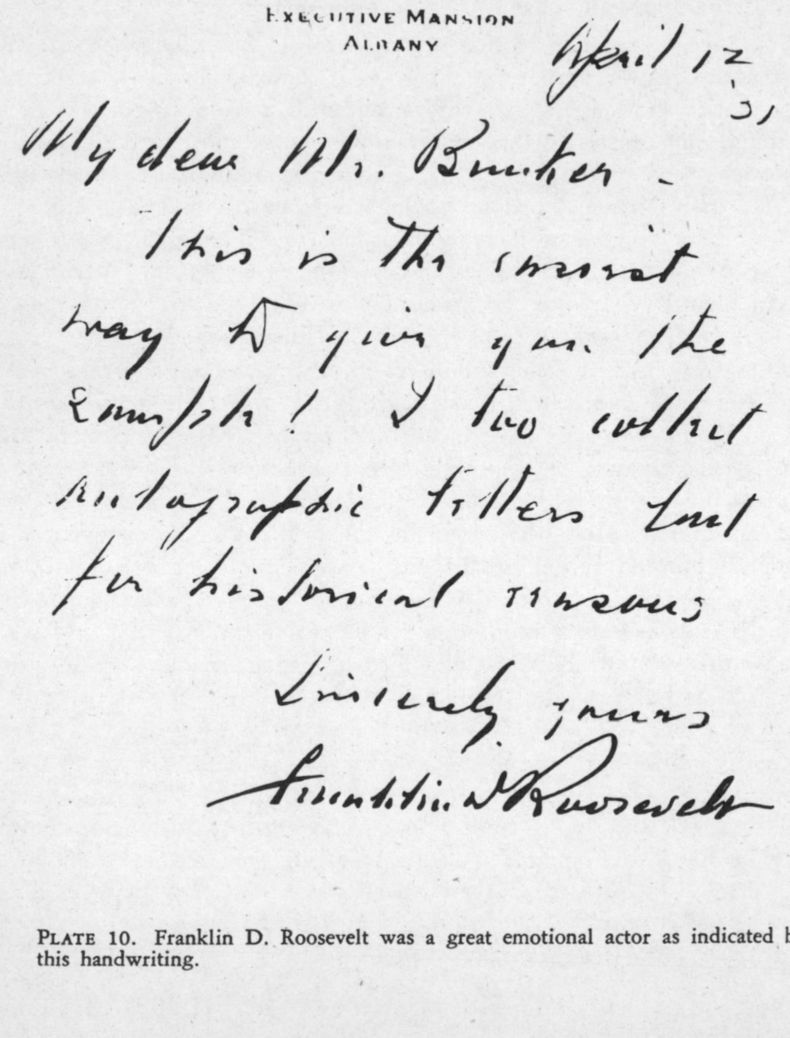
EXECUTIVE MANSION
ALBANY

April 12 '31

My dear Mr. Bunker –

This is the correct way to give you the example! I too collect autographic letters but for historical reasons.

Sincerely yours
Franklin D Roosevelt

PLATE 10. Franklin D. Roosevelt was a great emotional actor as indicated by this handwriting.

PERCY BURTON PRESENTS
LOWELL THOMAS'S ILLUSTRATED TRAVELOGUES:
"WITH ALLENBY IN PALESTINE" AND "FREEING HOLY ARABIA"

My Dear Madame Le Blond

I am sorry you did it give me a chance to place a box at your disposal for last evening. Anytime I can hold a few of my camels for you I will be delighted to do so.

I enjoyed meeting you very much and hope I may have the pleasure many times in the future when I return to London.

With kindest regards,

Very sincerely yours

Lowell Thomas

PLATE 11. The handwriting of Lowell Thomas shows a deep emotional strength that is held in check.

Another great word painter who has held top appeal with the public for many years is the writer of plate 11. Lowell Thomas. As you have listened to him it has not been possible for you to miss the deep, underlying strength he has put back of everything he has said. There is strength in his voice, but it is poised strength, not a helter skelter wind storm. He has never played on the emotions of his listeners, but he has held them by his emotional strength, just the same. Study this writing closely. Every line is heavy in proportion to its size. The writing is vertical to backhand—it is not the writing of a plunger, rather a man who could face great danger without losing his head—calm, enduring, a man whose affections are deep rooted, whose capacity for dislike is just as great. Where Roosevelt was expressive, Lowell Thomas shows a deep emotional strength that is held in check, but not actually controlled. It is a strength that is deep, and lasting.

Finally, here is another specimen of writing of a man whose whole history revealed the effect of emotional prejudice. Plate 12 was written by

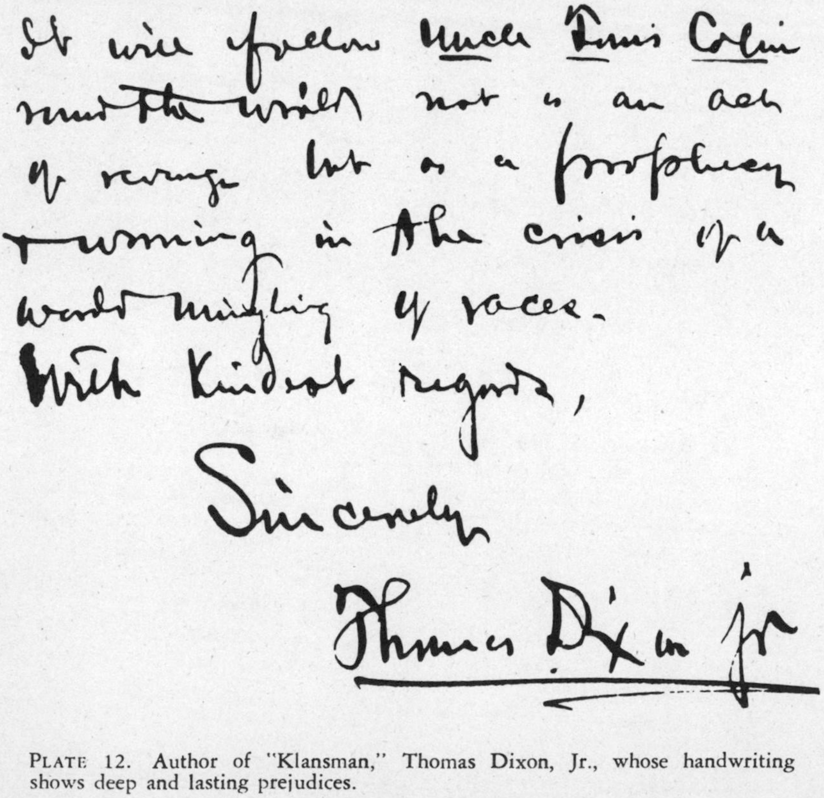

PLATE 12. Author of "Klansman," Thomas Dixon, Jr., whose handwriting shows deep and lasting prejudices.

the famous southern novelist, Thomas Dixon, Jr., whose Klansman and other books swept America during the early part of the 20th Century. This writing is heavy, showing deep emotions which you have already learned mean a capacity for deep and lasting prejudices.

Thomas Dixon reflected the view of the Old South after the Civil War, and his fiction bristled with bitterness. The weight of his handwriting strokes revealed his capacity not only for permanent prejudices or feelings, but it also showed his careful selection of words for strong effect. He was an artist, prejudiced but still an artist who revealed his technique in the depth of his pen strokes.

● *THE CALM AND SELF-POSSESSED WRITER*

You must, after examining these various specimens and considering how the writers worked and lived, have a very clear picture of what to expect from both the deeply emotional writer who is expressive and the one who is not. You must have figured out for yourself that the light line writer may carry memories but not prejudices based on accumulated emotions. This is true. The light writer may storm, and rant or reach a point of near hysteria in the face of tragedy or disappointment, but such individuals, regardless of age, merely have their emotional storm, and it is for-

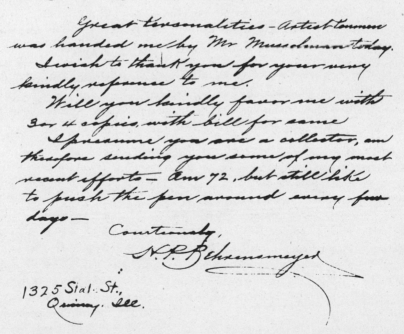

PLATE 13. One of the most famous of penmanship experts, H. P. Behrensmeyer.

gotten. Those who are vertical or backhand writers never have the emotional storms, but remain calm and self-possessed through circumstances that might easily prove the temporary undoing of the highly expressive man or woman.

There is, however, one question that has been asked since the very first class taught in grapho analysis. What about the handwriting of a professional penman? They are trained to write in a certain way. Does their handwriting reveal their feelings, or does the training put a straight jacket on them so that their writing does not reveal their feelings and the way they think?

This is a sensible question. However, it accepts as a fact that all students of Palmerian, Zanerian, Ransomerian and other penmanship manuals stick by the letter formations they learned in school. Even the most loyal of the penmanship enthusiasts will not claim that this is true. Fortunately we have two answers. One is this handwriting of H. P. Behrensmeyer, one of the most famous of all the penmanship experts, whose slant reveals the strong emotional response that won him thousands of friends among the young men and women who attended his penmanship classes through more than fifty years of teaching.

As you study his writing you can recognize the strong emotional responsiveness of the man, and know for sure that you could not be around him for a few days or months without knowing immediately how he felt when he came in touch with any emotional situation that affected or interested him. Mr. Behrensmeyer could not have had the emotional detachment shown in the writing of Lowell Thomas, or Keeler, or Ellis Parker Butler. He simply had to show how he felt because he was built that way. He felt, and he had to show it in the way he walked, the way he talked, by the look in his eye, and in everything he did.

● *HOW SCHOOL TEACHERS USE GRAPHO ANALYSIS*

There is still another answer to this question. If an expert's handwriting revealed how he felt just as if he had not been an expert, can a professional penman learn to analyze handwriting, and with what result? Here is a comment from one of the first professional penmen to study grapho analysis—a woman who has used her skill to assist her husband in selecting personnel in his busines throughout their married life.

"The modern trend in education is toward the development of the individual child. The usual courses in a teacher's training are necessary for successful teaching, yet they are often so theoretical and general as to be of little use when the teacher is confronted with a room full of children; each child a concrete example of the ideology presented as theory during the training period.

"Although teachers are urged to study the child as an idividual, yet they have no way of doing this, except by months of contact and observation. The results are haphazard and too often in error.

"Grapho analysis gives the teacher a scientific and accurate means to analyze and understand the character traits, thought processes, complexes, responses and talents of each child. Negative qualities can be uncovered and turned toward improvement. Positive qualities and talents can be pointed out and encouraged. Thus, these children are often saved years of unhappiness and maladjustment because the teacher has been able to help them understand themselves.

"My knowledge of grapho analysis has been a priceless help to me as a teacher. I have also used it consistently to give me more self-knowledge. This latter has resulted in better health, greater poise and peace of mind, and more ability to help others. I sincerely feel that grapho analysis should be a part of every teacher's education."

EXAMINATION FOR CHAPTER 2

(Correct answers for this examination will be found in the back of the book.)

You can start analyzing handwriting now. Not by guess-work, but by using the tested rules you have studied in this chapter. Each of the specimens included in this test were clipped from just ordinary mail. They are similar to handwritings that you will find in your old correspondence and in the handwritings of friends who may ask you to start telling them what you find.

The questions following each specimen are simple "Yes" or "No" or selective answers. You can answer them correctly if you have learned to use the Emotional Expression Chart. They are no more complex or difficult than you would be asked in a resident class. The questions are very simple, but do not let their simplicity fool you. They are just as important as they are easy to answer, provided you have mastered the rules on emotional expression. You are not likely to make mistakes, but after you have answered the questions under each specimen, you can check your accuracy with the correct answers as they are provided in the back of this volume.

If you find that all your answers are correct, you are honestly attempting to learn to grapho analyze handwriting. On the other hand, when you find that you are missing as many as five of the questions in this or any future test, you should restudy the chapter and specimens until you can see where you made your mistake.

*It is with both sorrow and
ness that I look back over the
few days. I'm sorry because of —*

SPECIMEN A

EXAMINATION

1. . *Does this writing show an impulsive writer?*
       YES_____   No_____

2. . *Will she stop to think things over before taking action?*
       YES_____   No_____

3. . *Will the writer's feelings influence his or her decisions?*
       YES_____   No_____

4. . *Would you expect to find the writer of this specimen always light-hearted?*
       YES_____   No_____

5. . *Will this writer go to extremes in reacting to emotional situations?*
       YES_____   No_____

6. . *Or will the writer's approach to an emotional appeal be indifferent?*
       YES_____   No_____

7. . *Will the writer of this specimen absorb emotional experiences and as a result be influenced by feelings regarding situations that may have been completely forgotten?*
       YES_____   No_____

8. . *If your answer to the above is "No", are you making the determination on the light lines of the writing?*
       YES_____   No_____

*"Truth or fiction" which are at your
disposal. If not available, enclosed
please find stamp for their return.*

SPECIMEN B

9. . *Would you say that the writer of Specimen "B" is more deeply emotional than the writer of Specimen "A"?*.
   Yes_____ No_____

10. . *Or does the heavier writing show a deeper emotional nature?*
    Yes_____ No_____

saw the beauty of old people and ss of children, he listened to their ids, he sorrowed at their partings

SPECIMEN C

11. . *Is there any difference in the way the writer of Specimen "C" and Specimen "D" will respond to an emotional situation?*
    Yes_____ No_____

12. . *What is the difference? Will writer of "C" show feelings more quickly than the writer of specimen "D"?*
    Yes_____ No_____

O.K. for you to use my letter and Photo in any of your Publicity

SPECIMEN D

13. . *If you made the writer of these specimens angry or otherwise emotionally disturbed, which would show feelings more quickly?*
    SPECIMEN "C"_____ SPECIMEN "D"_____

14. . *Examine Specimens "C", "D" and "E" and determine which of the three writers would be most expressive of emotions.*
    "C"_____ "D"_____ "E"_____

many thanks for sending it to me.

SPECIMEN E

15. . *Would you expect the writer of Specimen "E" to have emotions as deep as the writer of specimen "B"?*

    Yes_____   No_____

16. . *Of the five specimens in this test, which writer would be most likely to pile up hurts and then explode in a terrific storm?*

    "A"__ "B"__ "C"__ "D"__ "E"__

CHAPTER **3**

Do you think?--How?

DO YOU THINK FAST OR SLOWLY? ARE YOU A LEARNER OR MERELY CURIOUS. WHAT HANDWRITING REVEALS ABOUT RABBI STEPHEN WISE, NORMA SHEARER, BETTE DAVIS, WINNIE RUTH JUDD, HAZEL GOODWIN KEELER, JOE E. BROWN, W. C. HANDY, S. S. VAN DINE, THOMAS A. EDISON AND OTHERS.

How you think is highly important to your success and happiness. It is equally important that you understand how other people think or understand, because if you possess a keen, comprehending mind it will be easy for you to think that others have your own capacity for understanding, and you may be frequently disappointed. Or, if you think slowly, accumulating ideas from which you finally formulate a plan of operation, you may be fearful of doing business with those who do not seem to think at all, but grasp ideas and formulate conclusions without apparent effort.

● **THREE KINDS OF THINKERS**

Every teacher has had students who never seemed to study but who made better than average grades. Parents and teachers have shaken their heads and muttered, but the boy or girl who did not seem to devote any time to study, but turned in good recitations was still there to be reckoned with. Educators puzzled, when there was no puzzle about it. The students who did not seem to study and still learned merely possessed exceptional comprehension. They could read a book, and because their minds were working very much like sewing machine needles, penetrating as they read, they learned without the slow steady grind of laborious study.

On the other hand the slower student who really has to work to learn is not necessarily slow or stupid. Such students merely think differently, because their minds are geared to a different type of approach. They are

39

slow thinkers with less penetration—less comprehension, but they were still good students.

You may have belonged to either of these groups, or you may be one of those who were not satisfied with what you learned out of a textbook. You had a driving to learn, to find out why, and so you asked questions that possibly even the teacher could not answer.

These three classifications or groups are each important, and each has a vital part of your life and the life of your country. We must have the men and women who think and understand so rapidly that they do not seem to need to study; we must have men and women, young and old, whose desire to learn calls for them to ask questions, to inquire into, to investigate. And we need, just as much, the other group who must take their time to learn, and who are covered by the frequently repeated comment, "It takes a long time for him to get the idea, but when he finally gets it, he knows."

The first thinker is the one whose writing is filled with sharp, needle points. These points reveal comprehension in proportion to the length of the needle points above the line. They are most frequently shown in the *m's, n's, r's* and the upper point of the *s,* but may occur in any stroke combination. Plate 14, which was made especially for this book, shows what to look for.

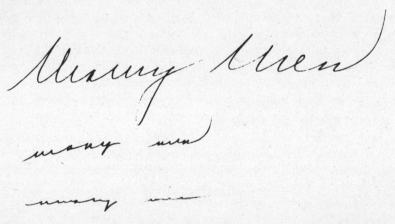

PLATE 14. Sharp needle points reveal a penetrating, comprehending mind.

You will notice these needle points are long, penetrating, regardless of the size of the writing. In smaller writing the needle points are shorter but the writing is smaller. If the points in the second line were found in the writing of the first line, they would not show enough penetration to identify the writer as having a penetrating, comprehending mind. But in each of these lines the points above the line are long, penetrating, very much like a hypodermic needle.

In the third line, however, the points are not penetrating. They do not show penetrating comprehension. Instead, they merely prick the surface. Possibly this will be clearer if I give you the illustration that has been used by so many class teachers of grapho analysis to emphasize and clarify this particular type of thinking.

PLATE 15. Grantland Rice achieved an international reputation as a fine obs rv-ant sports writer. His handwriting contained many penetrating needle points, showing a sharp grasp of his assignments.

If you have ever seen a loaf of bread dough, you know that after setting to raise it forms a tough outer skin. If you press on the dough with a finger, you make a dent, or possibly penetrate the skin, but your finger, or the fork you use, does not penetrate the loaf.

Following are four illustrations that will clarify this penetrating thinking for you. These have been chosen from various walks of life because no matter what a man or woman does, good, bad or indifferent, the individual shows more than ordinary comprehension. You analyze handwriting without outside information. You do not need it and should not be influenced by it.

The first specimen is the writing of Stephen A. Wise, which he sent me many years ago when the very idea of grapho analysis was new. You will notice that he was skeptical. He was entitled to be. There have been handwriting analysts for hundreds of years, people who read a book, or even wrote one, who depend on hunches to make their determinations. You are not doing this. You can understand for yourself without drawing pictures why the sharp points portray a comprehending mind. These strokes penetrate. They are long, and sharp, and like a needle go into a project deeply and smoothly.

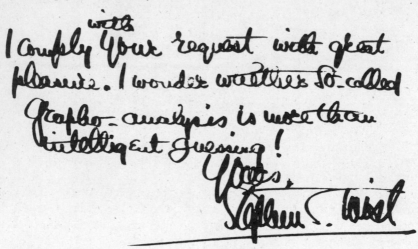

PLATE 16. Handwriting of Rabbi Stephen A. Wise shows an unusual depth of feeling.

The Wise writing is heavy. You already know that heavy writing reveals deep, absorbed emotions that pile up, and in his case there was no emotional expression. Just depth. Rabbi Wise was a doubter, but evidently his analysis must have changed his view, for his secretary wrote that they were amazed and promptly asked me to do an analysis of her own writing.

In plate 17 you have for study one of the long time motion picture actresses who remained a public favorite for many years. Norma Shearer's m's and n's, as well as the last part of the "h" in "wishes" are pointed. She did not have an initial stroke starting at the line and going up to the apex of the small "i's", so these two points must be counted too. The small "r" in "from" is sharp pointed, so that out of about forty strokes, not letters, ten of them are strokes that penetrate like a needle.

Both of these writers possessed the ability to learn without showing great effort. They could walk into a room, and mentally see all of the people there almost at once. They were comprehending, far above that of the average individual.

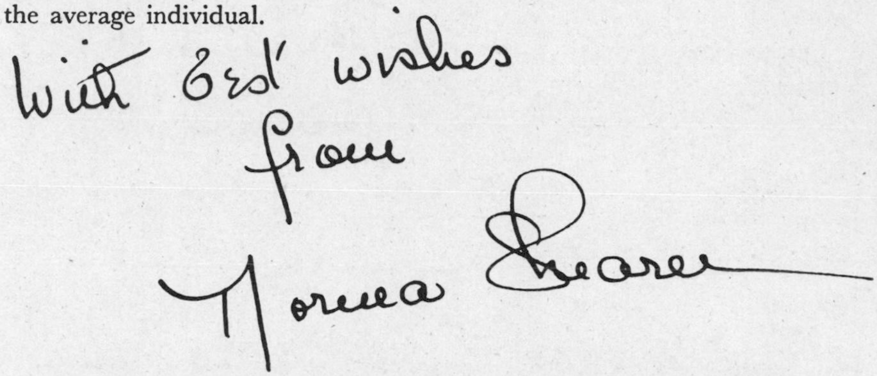

PLATE 17. Notice the pointed m's and n's in Norma Shearer's handwriting.

In case you are a teacher, or supervisor and have children, or adults under your supervision, do not expect them to grasp ideas as quickly as Rabbi Wise, or Norma Shearer. They may need repeated explanations, but when they have finally mastered a subject, they will never lose it. And in mastering it they have accumulated a vast amount of contagious knowledge that will support their final conclusions.

You may say at this point that both are vertical writers, but that was mere chance, just as in the case of Bette Davis. Her publicity agent sent me just one line of her writing, and common sense told me that I should not have attempted an analysis. You may have seen handwriting analysts in public take a signature and analyze it. At least they said they were ana-lyzing the handwriting. Possibly they were telling the truth, but not *all* the truth. You cannot analyze what you do not have. A signature may be long, and in such cases there are strokes enough to identify a limited number of traits, but that is all. It is not possible to make an accurate and complete analysis from a signature or a few lines of writing.

At any rate, Bette Davis found my comments "very true in most re-spects," but that was not an accurate analysis. It was a well deserved re-buke. Very early you may fall into the same trap that caused my error. You have only a scrap of writing, and the evidence that you have all points one way, so you make a statement. If you had examined more writing you might have found other traits that either offset or at least affected those you had found, and the picture would be changed.

This consideration of the effect of one trait on another, sometimes emphasizing it, at other times limiting it, is called evaluation. It is evaluation that makes it possible to pin point even minor traits and their effect on the conduct of any individual writer.

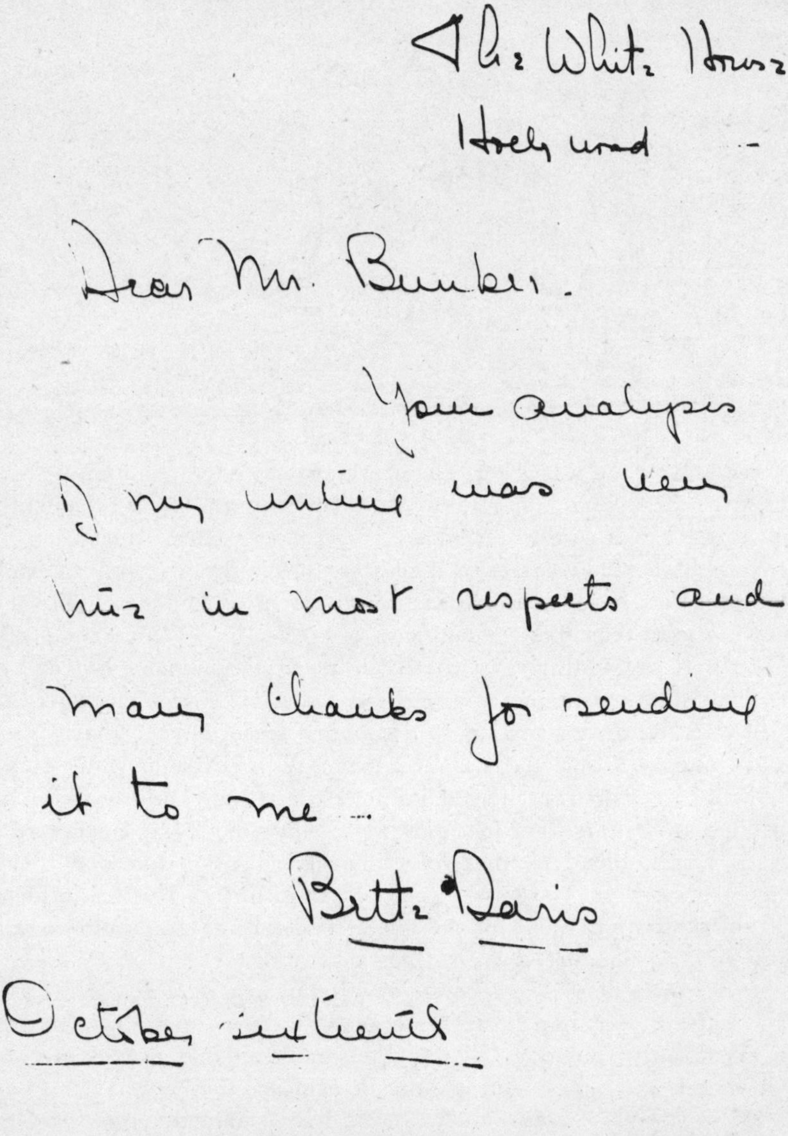

The White House

Hotel used

Dear Mr. Bunker.

Your analysis of my writing was very true in most respects and many thanks for sending it to me ...

Bette Davis

October sixteenth

PLATE 18. Analysis of the Bette Davis signature alone was mostly correct but there was not enough writing for a complete analysis. Then she sent this longer letter.

You will have already noted one marked difference between plate 16 and plate 17. The first is heavy writing, showing deep emotions, strong prejudices, and lasting love or hate, or other emotion. The Norma Shearer writing is not quite as heavy as the Stephen S. Wise writing. It is smaller and the strokes are definitely lighter, but there is depth of feeling here as compared with the writing of Bette Davis.

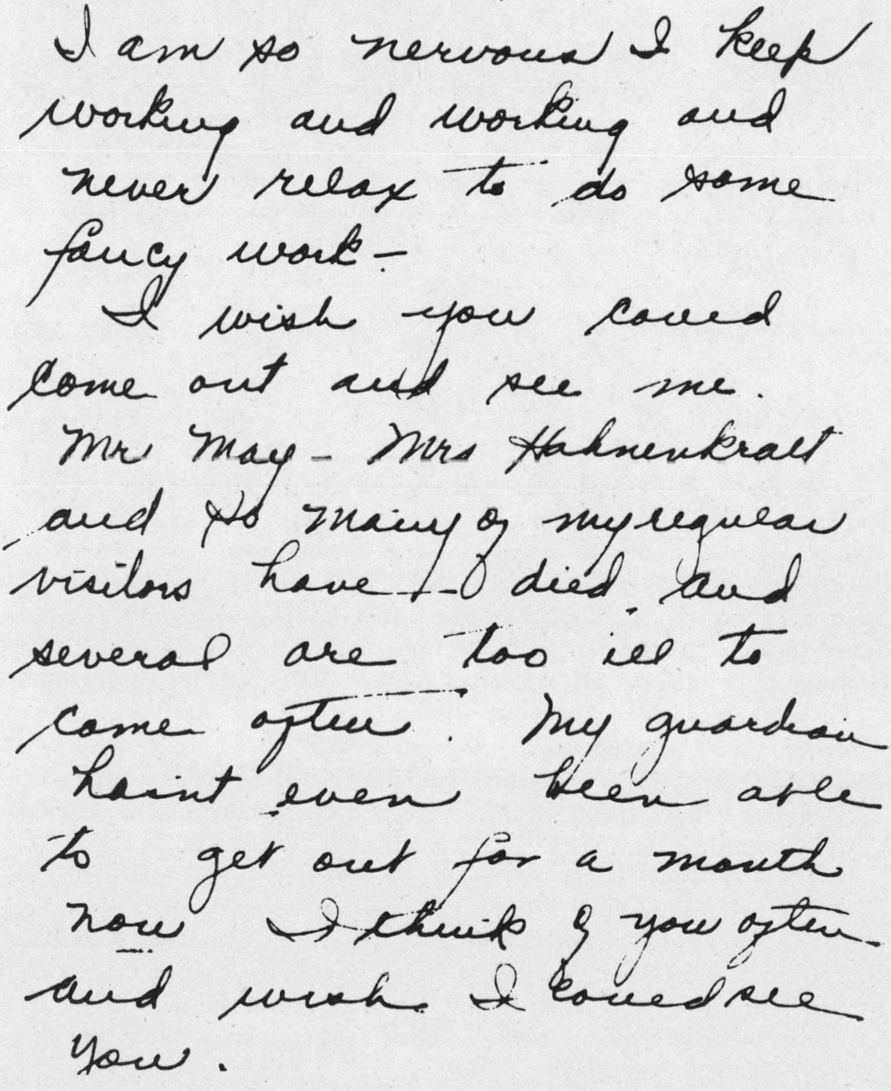

I am so nervous I keep working and working and never relax to do some fancy work —

I wish you could come out and see me. Mr May — Mrs Hahnenkratt and so many of my regular visitors have — died. and several are too ill to come often. My guardian haint even been able to get out for a month now I think of you often and wish I could see you.

PLATE 19. Clear thinking is indicated in the writing of Winnie Ruth Judd, convicted of double murder.

You have two types of thinking in plate 19. In the second line there is a set of two sharp pointed in each word, the n's. In the line above and the line below the m's and n's are made like wedges, or inverted v's. In order to be absolutely accurate, take your pencil, and count the number of needle pointed letters just as you have already done in the four words in the second line, and you will again in the fourth line, and so on throughout the specimen.

This is the writing of Winnie Ruth Judd, who was convicted of murdering two women, and sentenced to the Arizona Penitentiary. She had been a perennial escapee, the efforts having their roots in a mere desire to get away, not to commit another crime. This writing shows that she must have been mentally busy. Penetrating thinkers must have something to occupy their minds. It may be association with people, work they like, hobbies, anything to keep their active minds employed.

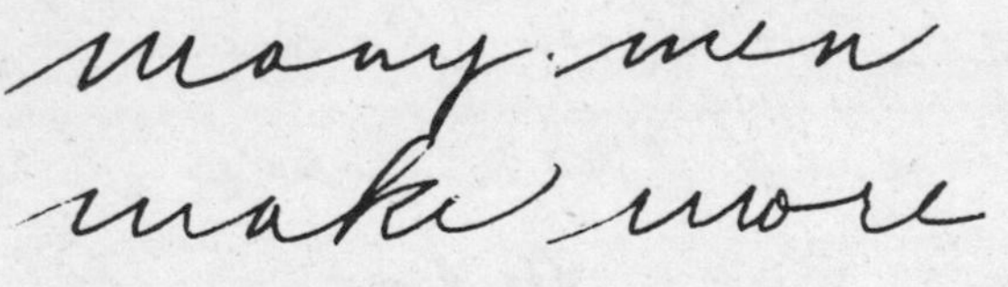

PLATE 20. This kind of writing indicates an intellectually thirsty mind.

In plate 20 you have a specially drawn illustration to show you what to look for when checking for a writer who explores, who seeks knowledge, whose eagerness to dig out facts is primary. Such thinking habits are identified by the stroke combinations that look like the letter v upsidedown. The true investigative mind has a great number of these combinations which may occur in the last part of the h, the m, n, or in some particular letter formation peculiar to the individual writer. Take plate 21 for example. This is a very fine example of an exploratory mind, a writer who is always looking to learn more, and willing to work at it.

This, by the way, is the writing of Hazel Goodwin Keeler, the successful novelist wife of Harry Stephen Keeler, whose handwriting you studied in the second chapter.

Hazel Goodwin Keeler started life as a magazine illustrator. She did good work but illustrating a story does not provide an opportunity to find out about things. Her mind required that she learn, inquire into, and she turned to fiction because she had to dig for background to build successful stories. As you use this principle you find that a great many highly skillful accountants make these inverted v's. Many medical men who are specialists have the same thought habit.

The eagerness to learn is also clearly shown in the writing of the long time motion picture favorite, Joe E. Brown. Some of the strokes in Joe E.

Brown's writing, however, are not exploratory. Some of them, as in "hand-writing" show keen and immediate understanding.

Now, before we go any further with the study of exploratory minds, let us turn back and remember that you are not merly studying hand-

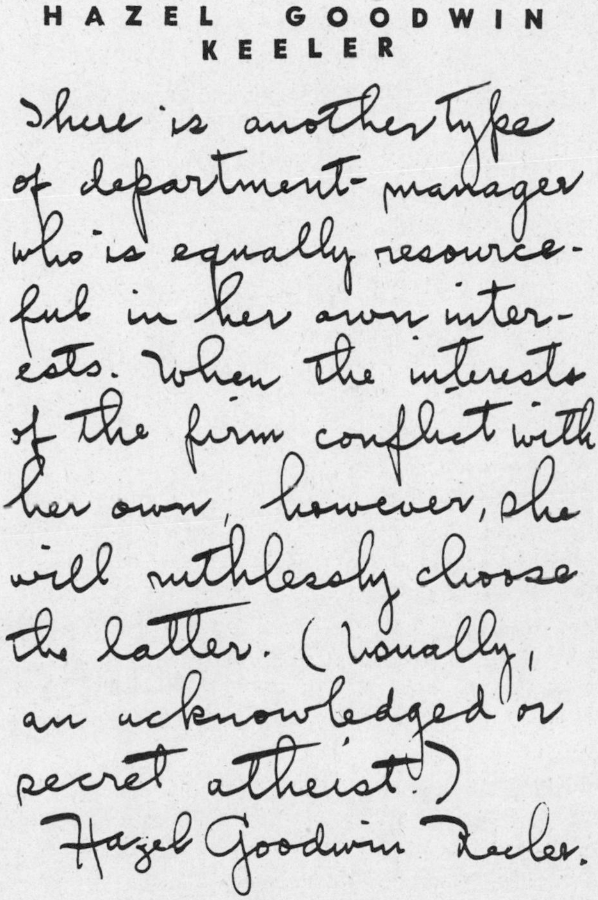

HAZEL GOODWIN KEELER

There is another type of department-manager who is equally resource-ful in her own inter-ests. When the interests of the firm conflict with her own, however, she will ruthlessly choose the latter. (Usually, an acknowledged or secret atheist.)

Hazel Goodwin Keeler.

PLATE 21. Written by one with an exploratory mind.

writing. You are getting acquainted with people just as though they lived next door to you. Examine the Shearer, Davis and Wise specimens care-fully. Ask yourself if these three writers would jump at conclusions, or be curious about your affairs. If you started improvements on your lawn, or in your house, would they be curious to learn what you were doing? On the other hand, could you expect them to read a magazine or newspaper article, and understand it on the first reading if it were highly technical?

If you have considered the poise shown by the vertical writing you know that not one of the three was highly impulsive because they would not jump at a conclusion. There is nothing exploratory in any of these three specimens so you could tear your house down on the inside and they would not bother about it. Further, because all these specimens reveal keen comprehension, the writers would be able to read, see a play, or watch a TV program, and understand it without difficulty.

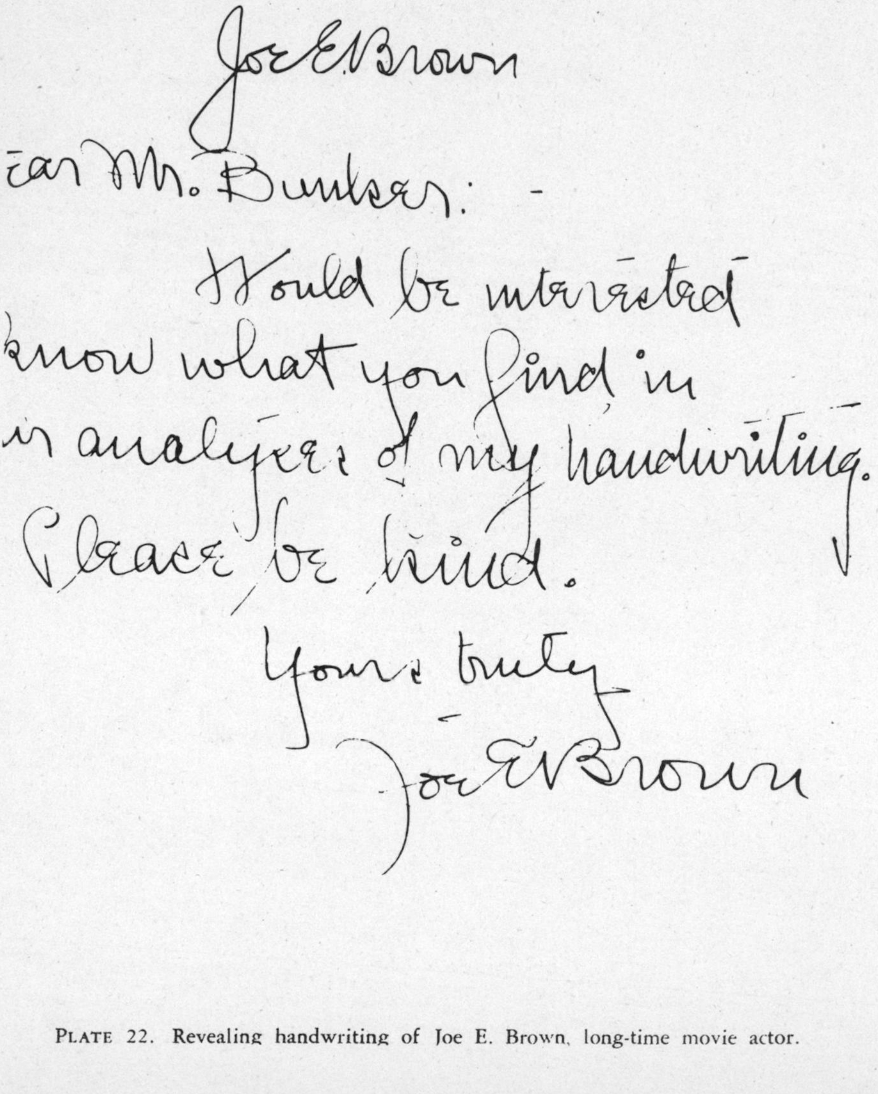
Joe E. Brown

ear Mr. Bunker: -

Would be interested
know what you find in
in analysis of my handwriting.
Please be kind.

Yours truly
Joe E. Brown

PLATE 22. Revealing handwriting of Joe E. Brown, long-time movie actor.

● *HOW TO RECOGNIZE FAST THINKERS*

If either of these three specimens were written by an application for employment and you were handling personnel, either in your own home, or in business, you could safely make a notation, "You will not have to draw pictures to get them to see what you are talking about. They will be a step ahead of many when it comes to understanding." They will grasp ideas readily; they will not have to be told and retold, simply because they possess the type of mind that is frequently described in the phrase, "He thinks like lightning." Business executives frequently puzzle their associates because "they do not take time to think." The associate is mistaken. The sharp or needle pointed writer thinks so fast and so clearly that by the time they know the details of the project they understand it.

Rabbi Wise would understand and more because his comprehension points are longer than the Bette Davis specimen. Her page of writing shows that she would grasp just what was necessary to know. She would not necessarily be interested in understanding any subject fully. Why? Because the comprehension points are relatively short. They penetrate the surface of a subject but they do not probe.

At times Joe E. Brown would think so fast or comprehend so easily that those around him might think he was jumping at conclusions, but his emotional slant is not that of a plunger. He might understand fully and completely but it would be the result of penetration rather than an emotional reaction.

However, plate 22 shows far more desire to explore, and to learn than it does speed of understanding. Joe E. Brown's writing shows that after he had inquired into, had explored enough, he would then be able to comprehend readily solely because he had first accumulated knowledge by exploring.

Another man, famous in the world of entertainment, is revealed by the writing in plate 23. Study this specimen closely. There are a great many upsidedown wedges, and there are also some needle points that reveal great speed in understanding. This is the writing of the grand old man of the Memphis Blues, St. Louis Blues, and Beal Street Blues, W. C. Handy. His compositions were exceedingly popular in the early part of the Twentieth Century and are still familiar to millions of music lovers. Handy built a huge musical publishing venture. He was a musician but he was also a business man, and an explorer. He kept learning, not just music but everything of interest to him. He got the answers, because he wanted to find them. When he had them, he made them part of his thinking, and then his conclusions were immediate. He was equipped with general knowledge, and a new project within the scope of his knowledge would be handled

PLATE 23 & 24. W. C. Handy, composer of "St. Louis Blues" was an alert thinker all his life—this agrees with his handwriting analysis.

promptly. You may have heard the expression, "he sleeps with one eye open," and this fits W. C. Handy, whose musical compositions made him world famous, among all peoples and races.

Your last illustration for study in connection with the learning or inquiring mind is this short specimen written by Dolores Del Rio, when she was at the height of her movie career. Her writing is large, and the inverted v's are long and sharp. If you had a spade digging into the earth

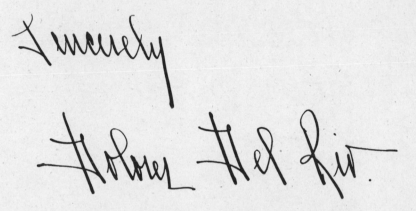

PLATE 25. Written by Delores Del Rio at the height of her movie career.

you would get a lot of soil on the spade, if you dug as deeply into the earth as she did with these sharp wedges. Notice how she makes both the r's and the "s" in Dolores. They are both sharp wedges. Keep always in mind that it is not the letter that counts, it is the combination of strokes. You would not recognize that final "s" as an "s", but as you have studied the examples in this lesson you recognize it as a well developed combination of strokes revealing exploratory thinking.

You have covered a great deal of ground only if you have given attention to the rules and the handwritings that illustrate them. Possibly you will agree that it is time to test your ability to observe, and recognize keen comprehension, and the exploratory mind.

Plate 26 was written by a one-time movie star, David Manners, and is an excellent combination of the two types of thinking—keen comprehension and the exploratory mind. Take your pencil, and check through carefully. How many strokes reveal keen comprehension? How many reveal the exploratory thinker? Some are needle pointed, others are inverted v's. When you are sure on each point, take your pencil and mark the number down carefully because if you were told now where to find the answers you might easily do like many puzzle fans, cheat by looking ahead. Study this specimen and make your own decisions. Keep your count because this simple specimen gives you an opportunity for self-examination.

You are now ready for a study of the slow, carefully, creative thinker who accumulates knowledge, and uses each bit gained much as a mason

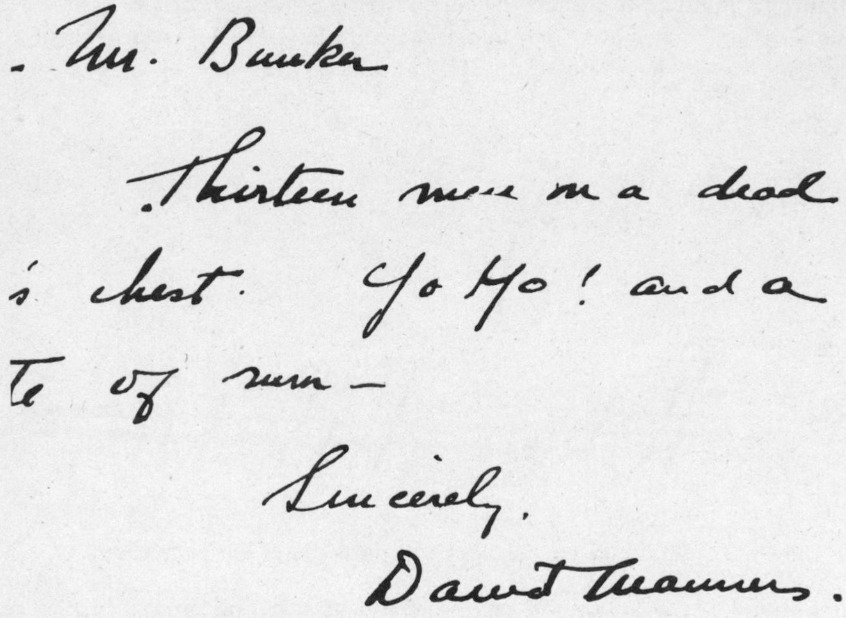

Mr. Bunker

Thirteen men on a dead
is chest. Yo Ho! and a
to of rum —

Sincerely,

David Manners.

PLATE 26. How many of these strokes on the David Manners handwriting reveal keen comprehension?

builds a stone wall. Every item of information or knowledge gained is important, but the writer reaches his conclusions only after accumulation of knowledge. As a result, his handwriting reveals the effect of his building processes. This special illustration was, of course, drawn to give you an idea of what to look for as evidence of the creative mind.

You have an excellent example in plate 28, which is the writing of the

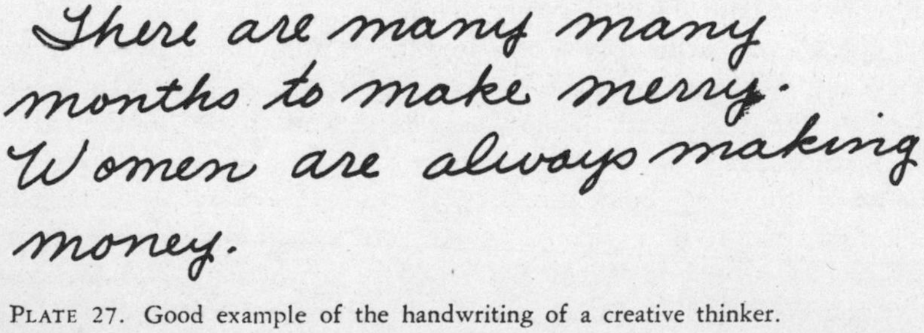

There are many many
months to make merry.
Women are always making
money.

PLATE 27. Good example of the handwriting of a creative thinker.

famous mystery novel writer, S. S. Van Dine, whose books sold in vast quantities in the early 20's, and are still worth reading if you are a who-dunnit fan. Almost all of the m's, and n's are broad across the top.

Van Dine was a slow, careful, cumulative writer. He fitted each word into its place. He created plots, just as carefully as if he had been laying

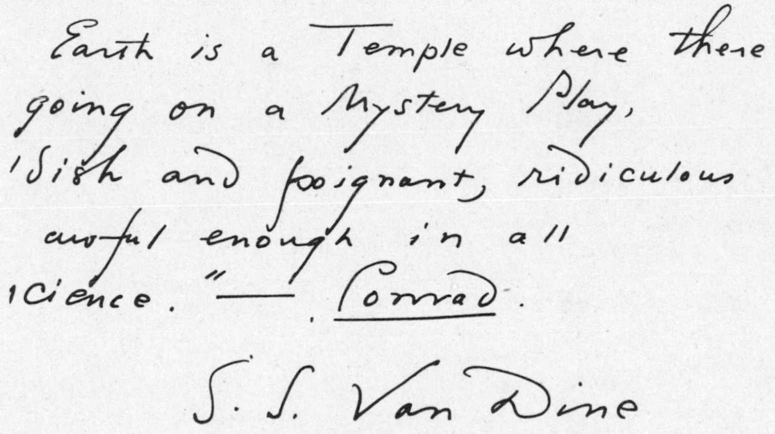

Earth is a Temple where there going on a Mystery Play, 'Sish and poignant, ridiculous awful enough in all 'cience." —— Conrad.

S. S. Van Dine

PLATE 28. S. S. Van Dine who created good mystery stories.

the brick in a patio floor. Each piece had to fit. If he had not been a writer he might easily have been a creative worker, but he would never have been an artist, because this writing lacks many of the qualities that are required for natural artistic creative effort where lines or colors are concerned. We ordinarily think of a builder as one who works with his hands, but Van Dine was a builder with words, and created his stories just as a mason builds a wall. Each part had to fit.

As you read in Oppenheim's letter, he doubted that his writing would reveal his character, his thought habits. He was using a pen for a special purpose, and he did not question whether his writing would reveal him. Instead, he merely doubted. However, he was honest enough not to try to add any funny curlicues to his page. His handwriting showed no love of show, and he was honest, so he submitted his normal, although infrequent handwriting. This was natural for him. These pen strokes show this fact, and when he found that his handwriting had told the truth he was equally frank. He had not believed. He saw what his writing said, about him, and he believed.

Because Van Dine and Oppenheim thought alike they worked alike. It was not a matter of genius, because you are not studying talent just now. Instead, you are learning to understand the thinking habits of each man

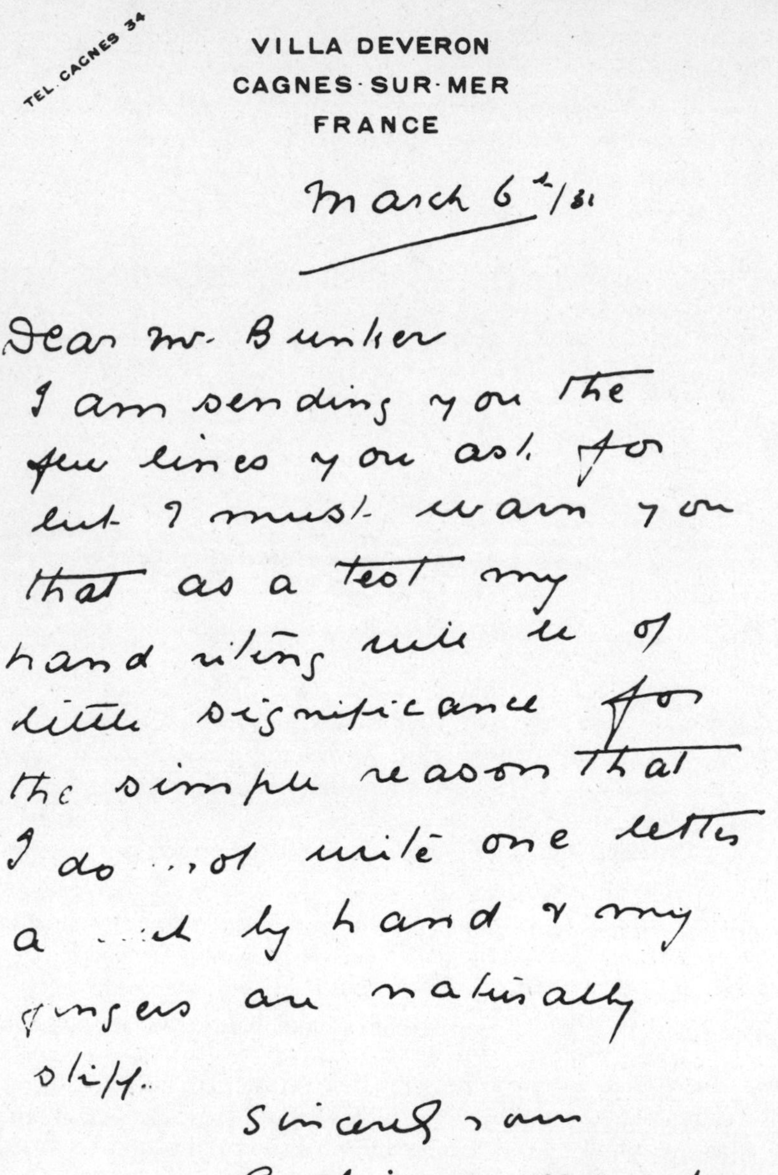

TEL. CAGNES 34

VILLA DEVERON
CAGNES·SUR·MER
FRANCE

March 6ᵉ/31

Dear Mr. Bunker

I am sending you the
few lines you ask for
but I must warn you
that as a test my
handwriting will be of
little significance for
the simple reason that
I do not write one letter
a week by hand & my
fingers are naturally
stiff.

Sincerely I am

E. Phillips Oppenheim

PLATE 29. E. Phillips Oppenheim was a slow, careful, "thinking" writer. His handwriting shows it.

so that you can understand how he wrote, not why. They did not write alike in the sense of what they said, but in the way they said it.

You too will have those who doubt that you can find anything in their writing. Some will laugh, or sneer, but when you know your rules and tell exactly what you find—when you are honest in what you tell from handwriting, you will find most people will admit your accuracy, and you will have gained their respect.

In plate 30 you have an original of Edison's signature. The "m" in Thomas is an almost perfect illustration of the quiet, cumulative or builder type of thinker.

The actual lives of these three men show how perfectly their penstrokes fit their ways of living and working. Edison never hurried. Instead he

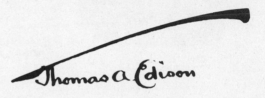

PLATE 30. Perfect illustration of the writing of a creative thinker.

spent endless hours in his laboratory, proving each point before he attempted to produce what his mind had set as a project. Oppenheim was a slow, careful, almost tedious writer, fitting each sentence into its place with mechanical accuracy. Van Dine, too, created rather than wrote books. His writing shows none of the fluidity of thought that is so characteristic of Earl Stanley Gardner, and many other top fiction writers of today.

Plate 31 does not resemble any of these three groups. The reason is very simple. The writer won a contest conducted by movie houses in a great central city. The young chap was sent to Hollywood, where the publicity department had to do something with him, so he was given small parts. Then he was sent on tour. He smiled and told jokes but he had never learned two things, and in a year he was forgotten. He was just one of the fellows who did not think. He breathed, he ate, and slept and played, but outside of a vivid imagination that he did not know how to use, he did not have anything. A "nice" boy, but a lad without any mental cultivation. He was not a fast thinker because he had no mental aliveness. He was not an investigative thinker because he was not interested in learning anything. And he was not a builder or creative thinker, simply because he did not have anything he wanted to build.

● **HOW TO IDENTIFY A NON-THINKER**

This last specimen gives us reason to stop and think. You may easily find specimens of writing that you will examine, and find strongly resemble this page. You will find other traits, because every person is a composite of many traits of character, but when you look for the evidence of thinking you will not find it. However, such situations are not hopeless. A man or woman can change mental habits once they become familiar with the need for change. If this young man's parents and teachers had insisted that he become interested in something while still in school, seriously interested in

PLATE 31. Handwriting showing no desirable traits.

it, there is no reason to think from this specimen that he would not have become aware of the thrill of learning, and doing.

As it was, this handwriting provides a picture of a chap who merely slid along from day to day, not interested in anything giving nothing to life, and getting nothing out of it. When you start the next chapter you will learn how to recognize pride, and you will be able to turn back to this page and find that he was very proud. He was happy when he got his movie contract after winning the contest. He was proud of having won, but when it came to the showdown he had nothing to offer simply because he had not learned to think.

Unfortunately you will find a great many writers who lack ability to think, not because there is something wrong with them, but because they have not been influenced or compelled to think. When they get a job they go through the operations of doing what they are told, or an operation where they can watch someone else, and copy what they have learned by observation, much as animals will do.

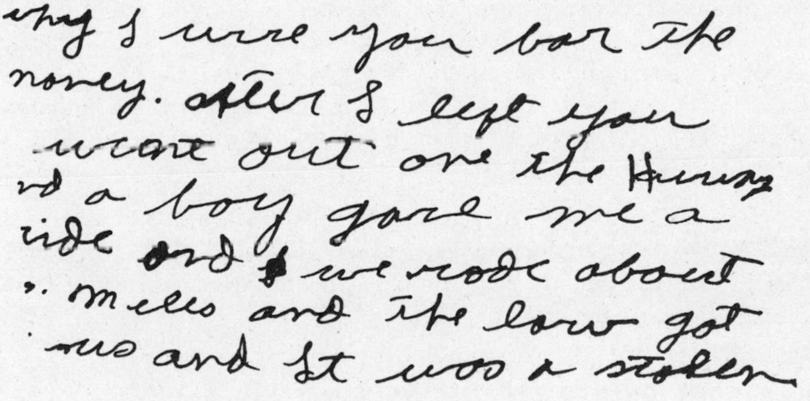

PLATE 32. An analysis shows this to be the handwriting of a "non-thinker."

When you analyze such handwriting there is only one thing you can honestly do. Quietly and firmly urge the writer to become interested in something, some study, some activity where he will have to think to hold his own. It can be done, and inside of a year you will not recognize the writing of a fellow who follows your advice. Right in line with plate 31, here is another, plate 32—a lad who came to me for an analysis very early in the history of grapho analysis.

Jerry was not a bad boy. He was a thief, but it never occurred to him that he should not be a thief. He did not hesitate to pick a pocket, or

wander through a department store and take away a dozen pairs of ladies'
nylon hose when such hose were luxuries. He thought it was smart to roll
drunks, and to disappear. He visited my office frequently, and we had
many long talks. A friend offered to finance Jerry in high school. It did
not appeal to him. He did want a shack by a river where he could swim
every day, and where he could fish. He would go through periods of
ambition, when he would ask to be sent to a farmer's home where he could
work, and when such opportunities came along, he would always take along
a hugh roll of western stories. He read them, and forgot them as fast as he
read them. They made no impression. He did not have a movie hero, nor
a western hero such as the Texas Rangers that he admired, even from a
distance.

He rarely stayed on with a farmer more than two or three days, pre-
ferring to get up in the middle of the night and take off. He did not,
however, steal from the farmer, because he recognized that the farmer was
trying to help him. It was just too much bother to be helped. He did not
have the usual boyish hobbies, and refused to be interested in them for
more than the length of time it took to tell him about them. The last I
saw of him was many years after I had given up the effort to arouse some
sort of mental activity. He had drifted in marriage, and was pimping for
a string of girls. It is probable that he never had a genuine thought in his
entire life.

There are people like that in this world, and you will find some of their
handwriting to be analyzed. You will not enjoy doing it, but there is a
possibility always that you may, by being truthful, arouse a desire to think,
a recognition that thinking is necessary.

● REPORT ONLY WHAT THE HANDWRITING SHOWS

There is one simple basic principle that every grapho analysis student
has had to learn. Do not try to find what is not in the handwriting. And
in cases where you do not find, do not improvise. If you have an active
imagination, or a flair for showing off your knowledge, put a guard on what
you say. Stick to just what you find, and you will gain accuracy, and your
acquaintances and friends will recognize that you possess a skill which they
do not have, and will respect you. Fake your analyses in order to show
what you know, and that is how it will end. They will recognize you as
a faker, and anything you may have learned will go down the drain. Further, tell the truth. You can say unpleasant things tactfully and the force
of the truth will protect you. But before that, know what you say is actually in the handwriting, and you are telling the truth.

EXAMINATION FOR CHAPTER 3

(Correct answers for this examination will be found in the back of the book.)

You can save yourself time, patience, money and happiness by recognizing from a page of handwriting how the writer thinks. When you are working with a stranger whom you must instruct in how to do a job, you can tell from only a few lines of writing whether he will understand readily or must be told over and over again simply because his mental response is so slow that he cannot understand from a single telling.

On the other hand when you can determine, as you can can, that a man, young or old, has an eager inquiring mind you can expect him not only to understand when given instructions, but to seek to learn more.

If you have a friend who takes a long time to accumulate facts before arriving at a conclusion, it will be a real help if you can take his handwriting and recognize this fact. Some people must think out a problem; they must gather facts before drawing a conclusion. They do not think as rapidly or form decisions like one with either keen comprehension or an exploratory mind and is continually striving to learn more.

Assuming that you have studied the illustrations and the rules in this chapter, you should be able to answer all these questions accurately. If you cannot, you should go back over the chapter, read it, study each specimen carefully and you will find where you erred. Then and only then, should you refer to the correct answers in the back of the book.

Specimen F

EXAMINATION

1 . . *This is the handwriting of a famous newscaster. Does he understand or comprehend rapidly or must he take his time to understand a project?*

a. TAKE HIS TIME.   b. UNDERSTAND INSTANTLY.

2 . . *Does he have deep and lasting emotions, capable of hating or loving over a long period of time, or does he go through an emotional storm, and then forget all about it?*

a. DEEP EMOTIONS.   b. SHORT LIVED EMOTIONS.

3 . . *Will he show how he feels or does he possess the poise to face difficulties without showing his feelings?*

a. SHOWS THEM.   b. POSSESSES POISE, DOES NOT SHOW FEELINGS.

4 . . *Does the writer of Specimen "E" in Chapter 2 show keen comprehension or are there times when she comprehends easily and other times when she must think out a project before understanding it?*

     a. KEEN COMPREHENSION ALL THE TIME.   b. SOMETIMES KEEN,
                                                             SOMETIMES NOT.

SPECIMEN G

This is the handwriting of a man who became world famous a generation ago. Although he has been dead for a long time, his name is still familiar to millions of people, proving that the record you leave in your handwriting is as important as the impressions you leave while you are alive. Study the "n's" in these two lines and answer the following questions.

5 . . *Was he comprehending or an exploratory thinker?*
     a. COMPREHENDING.   b. EXPLORATORY.

6 . . *After studying Specimen "B" in Chapter 2, check the proper mental habit.*
     a. COMPREHENDING.   b. EXPLORATORY.   c. SLOW THINKER.

SPECIMEN H

7 . . *Does this writer show the habit of exploring, constantly eager to learn or discover more?*
     YES_____   No_____

8 . . *Why do you say this?*
     a. TOPS OF "M'S" AND "N'S" ARE WELL ROUNDED.

    b. TOPS OF "M'S" AND "N'S" ARE NOT WELL ROUNDED BUT ARE MADE LIKE UPSIDE DOWN "V'S".

9 . . *Refer to Specimen "D" in Chapter 2. Study the specimen carefully, then check below whether the writing showed comprehension, exploratory thinking, or slow and logical thinking, based on accumulated reason.*

    a. COMPREHENDING.   b. EXPLORATORY.   c. SLOW, LOGICAL.

10 . . *Referring to the same specimen, decide which of the following statements most accurately fits the specimen.*

    a. HIGHLY EXPRESSIVE OF EMOTIONS THAT ARE QUICKLY EXHAUSTED, WHILE HE THINKS WITH LIGHTNING SPEED.

    b. OBJECTIVE, DOES NOT SHOW EMOTIONS, AND HAS A VERY INQUIRING AND EXPLORATORY MIND.

    c. DEEPLY AND VERY EXPRESSIVELY EMOTIONAL, ALWAYS EAGER TO LEARN AND INQUIRE INTO.

CHAPTER 4

Your T's Tell On You

SENSITIVENESS, PRIDE, VANITY PURPOSE OR LACK OF IT. THE DREAMER, THE ENTHUSIASTIC, THE INDEPENDENT. WHAT T'S MADE BY JULIA MARLOWE, CRUIKSHANK, ROSE PASTOR STOKES, PAUL WELLMAN, DR. FREDERICK COOK, LORD LYTTON SAY ABOUT THEM. COURT OF LAST RESORT CASE OF THE GUILTLESS WOMAN.

You can get more facts about a writer from the small letter "t" than from any other single letter. For example, you can tell from an "a" or "o" whether a person is frank, deceitful, or given to kidding himself with half truths. A professional grapho analyst will find other values in the two circle letters.

With the small "t" you have a stem. You have a start for that stem, i.e., the stroke that may start from the base line and become part of the stem, but the initial stroke is not necessary. You can have a "t" without a line that starts from the bottom. (See plate 33), A t-stem may be tall or short, and it may be crossed with a bar that is written above the t-stem or just above the small letters in the writing, or again, it may be half way up the stem. The cross bar may be light or heavy, long or short, and finally, there may not be a cross bar at all. The cross bar may not be a bar, but a tied stroke, as in the plate below.

All of these variations provide an opportunity for you to determine the truth about the writer's vanity, pride, sensitiveness, enthusiasm, persistence, ambition and many other very important character traits.

For this reason, it is highly important that you give close attention to these plates. In the top line of plate 34, you will find the t's are exceedingly tall in relation to the height of the small letters. Actually, if you undertake to measure them you will find them three or more times taller from the baseline to the upper tip than the small letters of each of the handwritings. The relation of the t-stems to the lower letters is what counts. For example, if you have large writing, and the t-stems are as high in proportion as in this specimen, then vanity would be shown. Or, if the writing were very small, and the t-stems were still as high in proportion, the vanity would still be shown. These exceedingly tall t's show vanity, or pride gone wild.

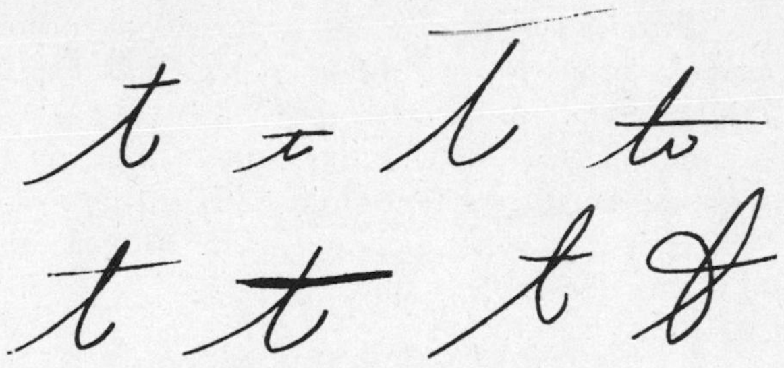

PLATE 33. The small letter "t" is the grapho analyst's most important letter. The "t" tells a lot about the writer.

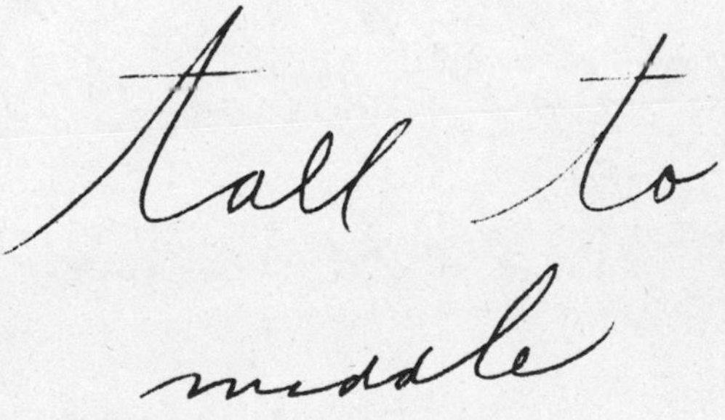

PLATE 34. Showing vanity, or pride gone wild.

● *THE SIGN OF VANITY*

You may know such a writer, and if so, you will recognize how he acts. He feels he is much better on his job, or in his neighborhood than he actually is. He over-rates his importance in any organization. Summed up, he thinks far better of himself than his accomplishments justify. Such writers are vain, not proud.

You have just the opposite in the second line where the t's are very short. The vain writer will do his best to impress those around him with his exceptional ability of past accomplishments, whereas the short t-stem writer is anything but vain. He will not try to impress you with his importance. He will not over-rate what he has accomplished.

There is a very good reason for this. He does not care whether you like what he has done or what he plans to do. He thinks for himself, and will exert himself to sell himself long, either socially or on the job. He is independent. He will think and act for himself, and will take the responsibility for his own decisions. The short t-stem writer is not bothered by customs. He will conform to dress, or other requirements if it is absolutely necessary, but he will be just as ready to ignore these social amenities as to follow them, if it seems important to him to do so—or if it does not seem important to him to conform to them.

Independent writers are independent people. Frequently, they are leaders, cutting across red-tape to get a job done. They are not good "yes" men. Never. Nor do they expect others to agree with them. Independence is shown by short-t-stems, not because they are merely short, but because they are short in relation to the body of the writing.

These two rules apply to d-stems as well. Indeed, all rules that apply to t-stems also apply to d-stems.

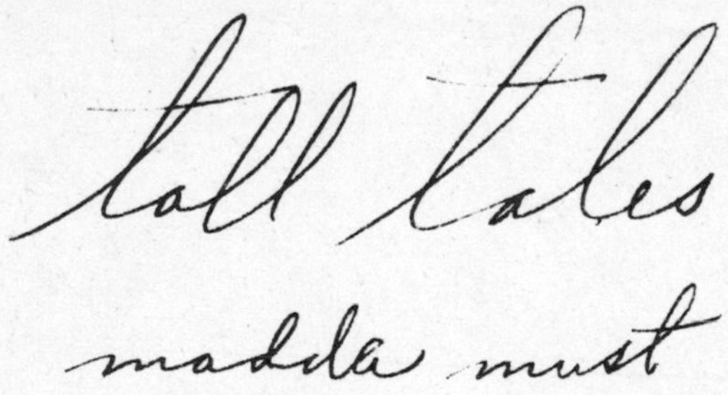

PLATE 35. The loops reveal a sensitive writer.

In plate 35 something has been added to the t-stems, as well as the d-stems. This change makes a difference in the story told by the stems. Instead of a stem standing straight and stiff, you have a looped stem. In the top line the loops are large. In the second line the writing is smaller, and the loops are also smaller—but each is large in proportion to the body of the line of writing. These loops mean that the writer is very sensitive. Such writers are easily hurt. They are slighted when no slight has been meant. They are snubbed when no one has thought of snubbing them. They may not look for chances to be hurt, but as far as their friends and neighbors are concerned, there isn't any reason for them to be hurt.

Where the t's are very tall, showing the writer is vain, the sensitiveness is certain to be more active. In the first place, the writer has put himself into a vulnerable position. He expects others to look up to him, and accept him at his own value. Therefore, when they do not, he is hurt.

On the other hand, the short-stemmed writer, regardless of whether it is a d-stem or t-stem, is not going to be bothered. He may be sensitive, but he casts the sensitiveness to one side, just as he disregards the expectation that he wear a stiff collar when he wants to wear a sport shirt.

● ARE YOU OVER-SENSITIVE?

You will find a great many writers who are sensitive, but very few of them are vain. In fact, more are independent. Most of the people whose writing you will examine as you study these rules will be just men and women who are doing their best to get along in the world, conforming as nearly as they can to common standards of conduct. Few of them will be leaders, and some of those who are independent will lack other qualities of character to make them capable of spearheading a business or other activity. As far as sensitiveness is concerned, it is neither "good" or "bad", although it is a liability. You may find, for instance, sensitiveness in your own writing. If so, why not stop and ask yourself whether you gain anything by being easily hurt. Does it make you any happier to feel that someone has intended to hurt or slight you?

You will not be able to say "yes" to this question and as long as you cannot, why bother to continue being sensitive. You would not actually undertake to carry a fifty pound bag on your shoulders all the rest of your life. You will admit to yourself that it would cramp your style of living, and hurt your personal appearance, yet going through life ready to be hurt or imagining slights is just as silly and useless. The next time you feel that someone has hurt you, slighted you, passed you by, laugh about it, or at least ignore it. Before you know it, the sensitiveness will grow less and you will be happier.

● STORY OF A SUPER-SENSITIVE WOMAN

This matter of useless sensitiveness was brought out by two neighbors of mine. Betty was a remarkable woman. She never gossiped. She never talked about the neighbors. When some inquisitive man or woman in the neighborhood asked her about another neighbor, Betty just did not know. It was an exceedingly admirable trait, just one of many that she had. But she was sensitive. So, when her friend Jo had company, she knew that Betty would not pay the slightest attention to the huge lady who had on a vivid dress. Jo knew this and felt perfectly safe in remarking to Betty "that she might have peeked out of her kitchen and seen the woman." It was an idle remark based on Betty's remarkable record for never spying. It was meant as a joke, nothing more, but Betty rushed madly home and that evening she was all for having her husband put up a dividing fence between her lot and Jo's home.

Of course the fence did not go up. When Jo found out what was going on, she inquired why and was promptly told by Betty that she "had not peeked, and that is was a nasty thing to have said." Possibly it was, but Betty's sensitiveness did not make her any happier, and it did show a weakness in getting along with people that would not be an asset to her, no matter where she lived. First of all, Betty knew her own reputation for not prying. She knew that Jo was not accusing her of prying, but to other neighbors, it left a doubt. It was bound to do so. Was Betty so absolutely free from curiosity about the neighbors or had the joking remark struck home? They were bound to ask it, and Betty's standing as a neighbor would never be the same again, just because she was so uselessly sensitive about something she had not done, and was not accused of doing.

This illustrates the point that sensitive people do not need a reason for being hurt. They are hurt, and that ends it. If you are one of them, and you can get the truth from your handwriting, just remember that other people are too wrapped up in their affairs most of the time to bother to hurt anyone else, and so your hurts are just dead wood.

In plate 36 you will not find vanity, but you will find sensitiveness that is exaggerated. This is the writing of a one-time famous movie performer, and later a TV star. His life had been unhappy, because he had been in an almost constant state of being hurt, or getting over a hurt. You will notice that all of the t's and d's are not looped, but half of them are, and four out of this number are huge loops, showing supersensitiveness. His

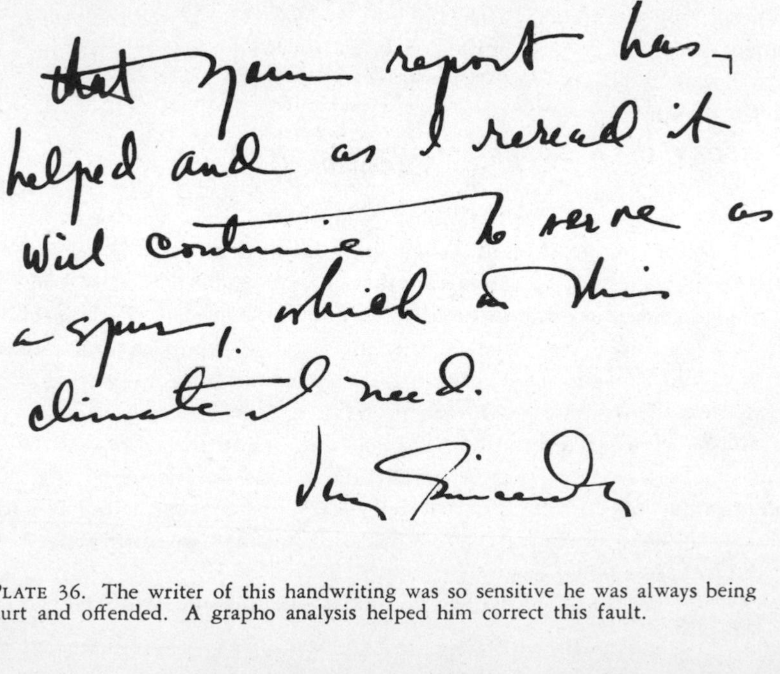

PLATE 36. The writer of this handwriting was so sensitive he was always being hurt and offended. A grapho analysis helped him correct this fault.

handwriting was analyzed during the early part of his career, and he says
that it helped. It did.

He caught the suggestion to get over his sensitiveness and he fought it
earnestly with the result that many of his difficulties were ironed out. You
never gain anything by being easily hurt, and when this man, who is still
famous in the entertainment field, realized that his sensitiveness was a handicap he had the good sense to try to rid himself of it. It worked for him,
and it will be worth your while if your t's and d's are looped, especially with
such huge loops, to stop whenever your feelings are hurt and see how silly
it is.

● WHAT THE IMPORTANT T-BAR REVEALS

When you have covered these rules and made them your own, your
consideration of the small d is done, and you are ready to consider the
effect of t-bars on the facts revealed by this one small letter. T-bars can
be above the stem, or they may be in between, high, or fairly low, between
the top and the stroke just above the level of the small letters. The location
is important.

The t-bar may be long, short or medium in length. They may be
heavy, exceedingly heavy, or very light. It may be written ahead of the
stem or following it, which affects the value as well. Your start, however,
is with the location of the t-bar on the t-stem. In plate 37 there are four
t-bars on the first stem in *trait*. These bars are much heavier than the ones
that cross the second t, and the value is much different. A relatively heavy
t-bar shows purpose, or expresses what so many think of as will power. A
light cross-bar shows a purpose that has less force back of it. The purpose
may exist all right, but the force of the purpose is lighter, and the writer
will be less likely to carry out the purpose that he may have. The light
t-bar does not reveal a clearly defined or strong purpose.

In this plate the bars are all short. They merely represent bars, ful-

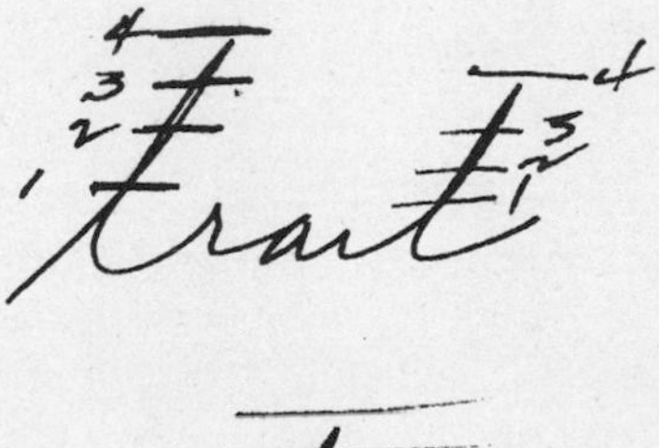

PLATE 37. What the cross-bar on the small "t"
tells you.

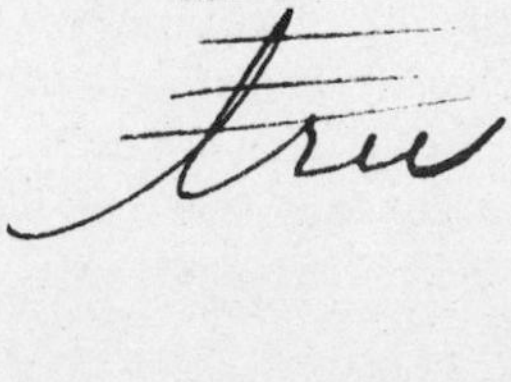

PLATE 38. Cross-bars representing carrying
power, action.

filling a technical purpose as taught in penmanship classes. They cross the stem. They show conformity, exactness, precision. The writer was taught to make them that way, and he complies with what he was taught. However, in the next illustration, plate 38, both t-bars are much longer. They represent carrying power, action. They not only cross the stem but they carry on, they are no longer merely precise t-bars that were made because the copybook showed that it should be crossed. They move. They have carrying power, and in the language of grapho analysis, they represent enthusiasm.

You have undoubtedly known a great many highly enthusiastic men and women. You may be one of them, and you may be sure you are if you find that you make your t-bars long, sweeping. Such writers not only have purpose, but that purpose has life, it is activated, it moves forward with verve, and the quality of influencing others. All of this is increased as the t-bar is made heavier.

However, you must return to plate 37 with its numerous cross-bars in order to understand how the purpose that is shown affects the conduct of the writer. In order to simplify this, you will find the cross-bars numbered 1 to 4. When you find a t-bar written down level or almost level with the tops of small letters you have evidence that the writer undersells himself to himself.

He is not necessarily self-conscious, but he lacks faith in his own ability to make a distant goal. If he were an athlete, going in for high jumping he would never attempt to make as high a jump as he would be capable of doing. He would actually attempt less than half of what he might do if he would exert himself. This is not necessarily a sign of laziness. Instead, it is evidence of lack of faith in his own ability. If the writer were a frog he might have the muscles in his legs permitting him to make a ten foot leap, but instead he would shake his frog-head, and decide that a four foot leap would be safer. And he would make the four foot leap with confidence that he would land safely.

Cross-bar 2 is a normal, healthy condition, but it does not represent that the writer is a long distance planner, i.e., he does not set his purpose far enough ahead so that he will need to exert himself to the limit. On the other hand, the man or woman who puts the cross-bar up near the top of the stem is shooting at a distant goal. He is looking ahead, striving for a more distant purpose. When the cross-bar is heavy, he knows exactly where he is going. When it is light he does not have as clearly defined a purpose, but he still has the distant purpose. The height of the cross-bar determines this, and the heaviness or weight of the stroke identifies how clearly his purpose is defined in his thinking.

The cross-bar written above the t-stem shows a writer who sets his goal, or purpose a very long way ahead. Frequently it is not practical. This is true when the line is light. In such cases the writer is a dreamer, one who sees a distant goal, dreams about it, but does not have a definite purpose to achieve it. He is much like the high school boy who reads the track records earnestly, and dreams of someday equalling them, but does not put in enough time practicing on the track to make his dream come true.

You cannot find a better study of a clearly defined, long distance purpose, combined with enthusiasm than to examine this specimen of Julia Marlowe's writing. Her cross-bars are almost all long. They are heavy, and they are either above the t-stems or just at the upper tip. She was one of the greatest names in American entertainment world for a long, long time, and these three traits so clearly shown in this page of writing undoubtedly were largely responsible for her success. She had a definite goal. She knew where she intended to go. She was enthusiastic about what she was doing, and even though the goal was a long, long way ahead, she intended to achieve it, and did.

Every sales manager is constantly looking for men and women with this combination of traits. Every level of society has room for them. Even if there were no place ready and waiting, such writers will make a place for themselves, so if you have this combination you can consider yourself rich in ability. If you do not have them, you need not lay this book aside and consider yourself hopeless, for in a later chapter you will be given some idea how to develop these qualities.

In many handwritings you will find t-bars at different levels or heights.

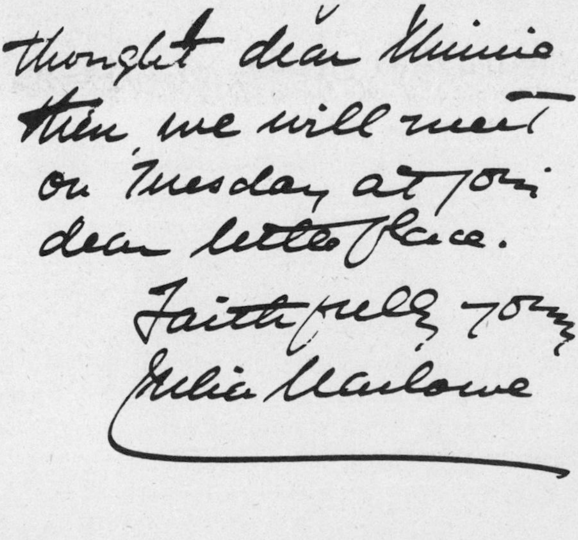
thought dear Minnie
then we will meet
on Tuesday at your
dear little place.
Faithfully yours
Julia Marlowe

PLATE 39. Julia Marlowe's long cross-bars denote enthusiasm.

You do not, however, have any reason to be confused in making your findings. If you were seated at a table, with five adults and four children, you would merely recognize the fact that you had the five adults and the four children at the table. They would not puzzle nor confuse you. In exactly the same way, when you have t-bars at different levels on the t-stems, you have evidence that the writer sets his goal close part of the time and farther away at another.

The writing of George Cruikshank, the famous illustrator as shown in plate 40, has this variation. It shows that in some things he had a distant goal, and in others he was satisfied to make little effort. This is simple enough to understand. His purpose was to be a great illustrator. He did not propose to be a jockey, or a master gardener. He had a goal, and he worked toward that, but in matters outside of his goal he would not make any great effort. However, the weight or thickness of his t-bars show that he always knew where he was going. He had a definite purpose, even when it did not call for any great effort. A man can have a very definite purpose that is easily achieved, and he may be satisfied with his accomplishment.

On the other hand, the writer who has heavy t-bars placed low can accomplish more if he will demand it of himself. Cruikshank's writing is that of a man who was very good in his work, he did not feel it necessary to make an additional effort, and he had no other interests in which he wishes to show accomplishment. Therefore his strong t-bars revealed not only a definite purpose, but contentment with his own fulfillment of that purpose.

Rose Pastor Stokes, the woman who pioneered for birth control, made two distinctly different kinds of t-bars. In this page you find them long, and light, and very, very short. These short ones are especially revealing, particularly in the words, "sketch", "but", "haven't", "got", "regret" and "to". These all show irritability, and in "haven't" and "got" they are slanted downward and have a new value. These two short strokes slanted downward, and made like little arrows reveal that when she wanted something, she wanted it. She expected people to step. She demanded. However, when you consider the whole page, the trait was not a dominant one. She was not going around and demanding all of the time. Instead it was a trait that existed, and, like cash in the bank, could be drawn on and used when she wanted someone to do what she felt should be done.

You have a very similar stroke in the handwriting of John Masefield, the great poet. Almost all of the t-bars in his page of writing are made to the right of the stem, and are sharper arrows in most cases, than in the Rose Pastor Stokes plate. John Masefield revealed by his writing that he demanded.

There is another value in this arrow-like stroke placed to the right of the t-stem. It also means temper, particularly when it is not joined to the stem, and is written alone. Explosive temper, in proportion as the the arrow is heavy or light. Consider the Emma Jo Wengert plate. Emma Jo was suspected of killing a woman. She was arrested. The local authorities felt they had enough evidence to put her on trial for murder. She was tried, and convicted and given a sentence to the penitentiary.

After a period of time the famous "Court of Last Resort" became

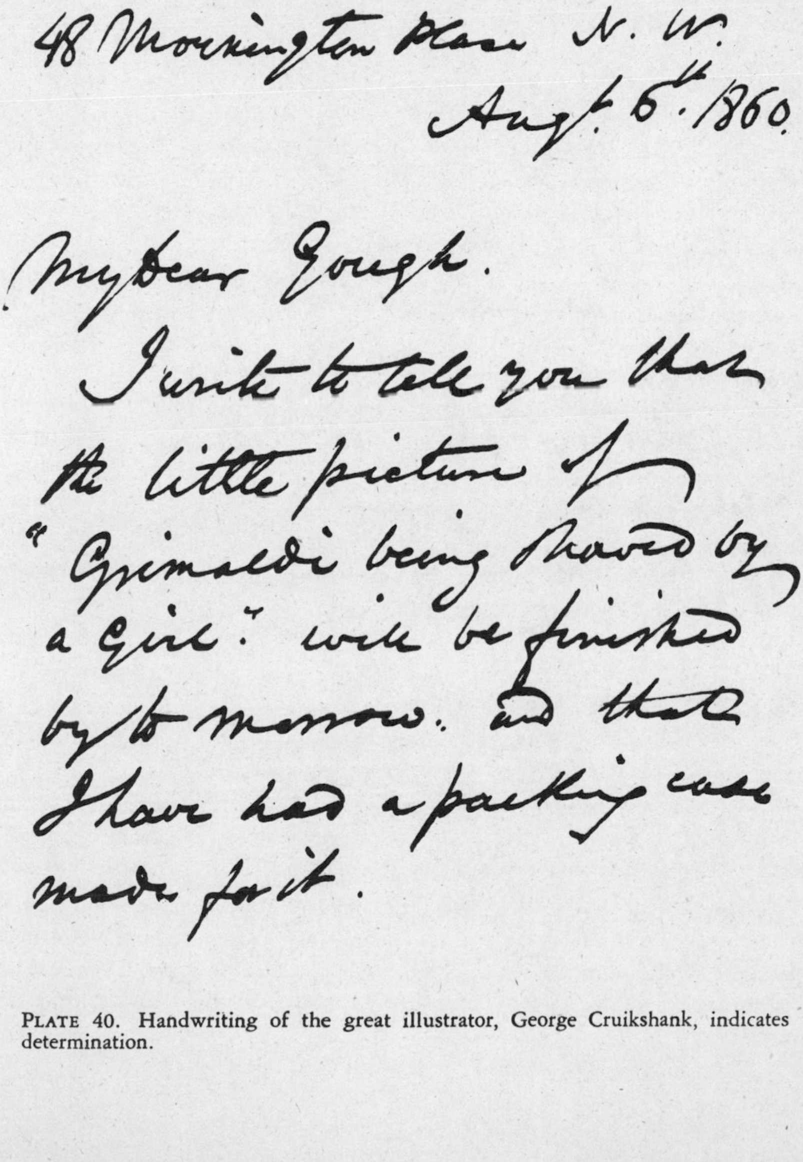
48 Mornington Place N. W.
Augt. 6th. 1860.

My Dear Gough.

I write to tell you that the little picture of "Grimaldi being shaved by a Girl" will be finished by to morrow. and that I have had a packing case made for it.

PLATE 40. Handwriting of the great illustrator, George Cruikshank, indicates determination.

interested in the Emma Jo case. However, before we go ahead with the details of her case it may be better to discuss the "Court" which was set up by Earl Stanley Gardner, the greatest seller in whodunit fiction in America, and Harry Steeger, a New York publisher. As a young man Gardner was a practicing attorney. He defended the underdog. He did not takes cases merely for money, but, like the famous Clarence Darrow, he took cases where he felt justice might not otherwise be done. There is no evidence that he made much of a living until he began writing fiction, and this has undoubtedly made him a wealthy man.

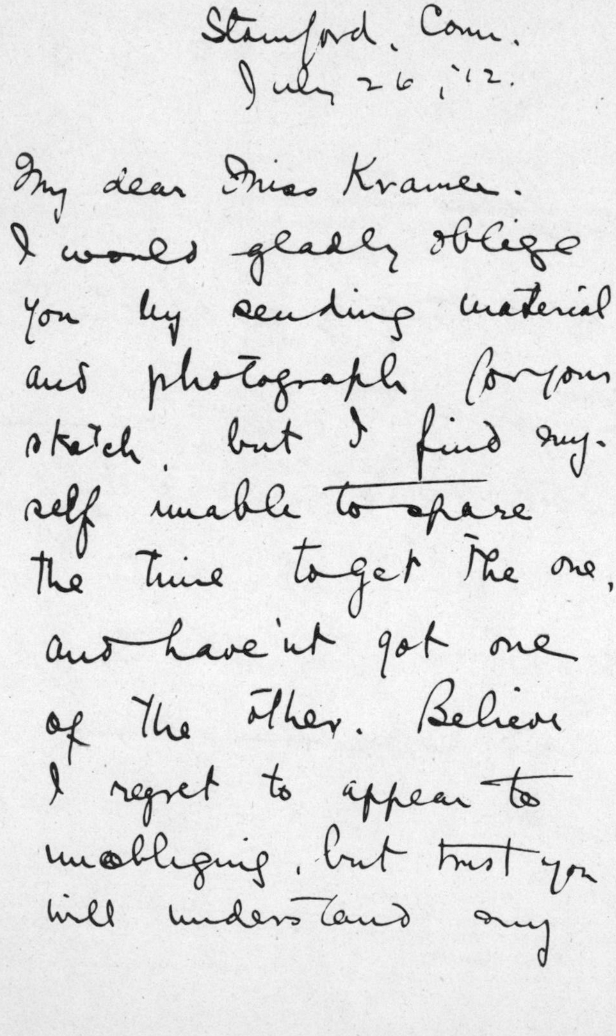

Stamford, Conn.
July 26, '12.

My dear Miss Kramer.
I would gladly oblige
you by sending material
and photograph (or your
sketch. but I find my-
self unable to spare
the time to get the one,
and have'nt got one
of the other. Believe
I regret to appear to
unobliging, but trust you
will understand my

PLATE 41. Short cross-bars in the handwriting of Rose Pastor Stokes shows irritability.

Mr. Steeger was one of the early users of articles on grapho analysis in his early publishing days. I have known Gardner for years solely from his handwriting. He once wrote me that the analysis made from his writing was perfect, which did not allow much for human error. My own acquaintance with Steeger taught me he was absolutely honest, so when the "Court" was established it was natural for me to follow their cases. Emma Jo was one of the early ones. The "Court" which had attracted some of the most famous and able criminologists in America, became interested in the possibility that it was entirely possible that she had not killed the woman at all.

According to the facts, Emma Jo had occupied a room in the woman's home. There had been minor unpleasantness and friction, and Emma Jo had changed her living quarters, but she had not had all of her mail changed. Because of this she visited her first landlady occasionally and picked up mail that had accumulated. It was one of these rare visits when Emma Jo was there to pick up her mail that the woman with whom she had made her home, died. Emma Jo was accused of killing her.

● *IS THIS THE HANDWRITING OF A MURDERESS?*

The experts on the "Court" staff made an extensive study of the case. They found that the woman had died of a sudden heart attack and not

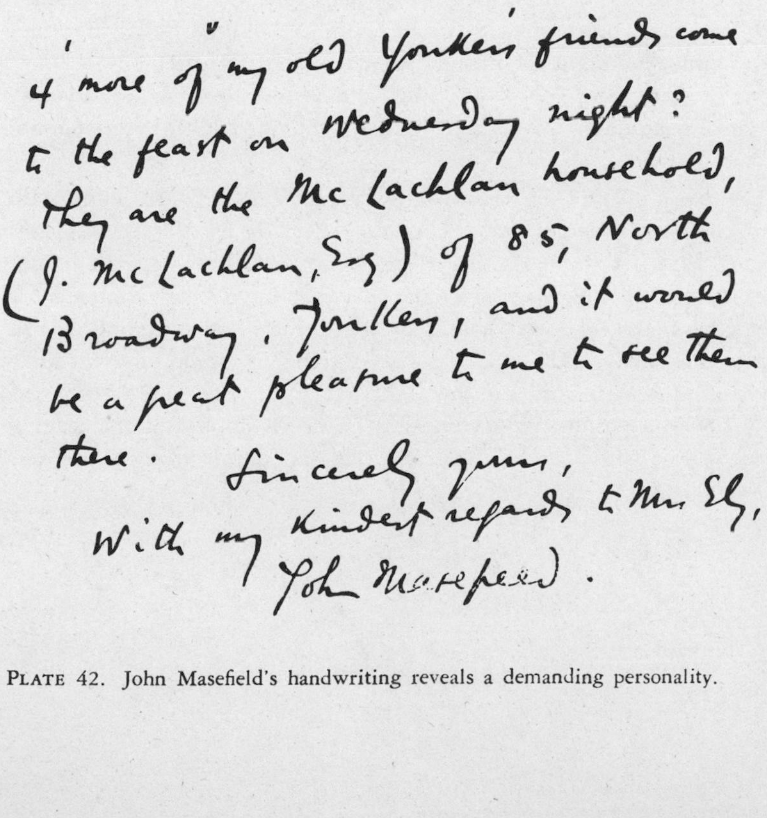
4 more of my old Yonkers friends come
to the feast on Wednesday night?
They are the McLachlan household,
(J. McLachlan, Esq) of 85, North
Broadway, Yonkers, and it would
be a great pleasure to me to see them
there.
Sincerely yours,
With my kindest regards to Mrs. Ely,
John Masefield.

PLATE 42. John Masefield's handwriting reveals a demanding personality.

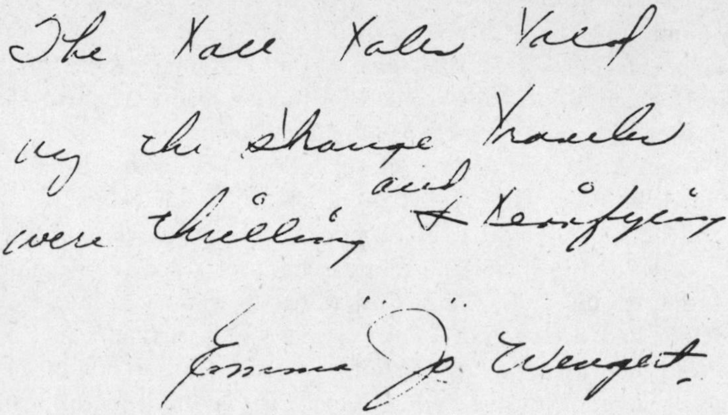

PLATE 43. Notice that some of the t-bars are slanted down in this specimen of Emma Jo Wengert's handwriting.

because Emma Jo had struck her. The evidence was so strong that Emma Jo had not committed a crime that she was freed, and then married her sweetheart who had stood by her all during her trouble. Emma Jo became Emma Jo Wengert, and a free woman.

All of this has a direct bearing on this specimen of writing and what it tells. Look at the t-bars. Some of them are slanted down, but they are light. Emma Jo might, if pushed, demand that you get out of her way. She might stamp her foot mildly, but she would never strike anyone. She was not a demanding woman with force enough back of her demands to ever hurt another.

Compare this set of cross-bars with their downward slant with the plate that follows, and which was made especially for this book. If Emma Jo's cross-bars had been slanted as these are and had been as heavy, the whole picture of the woman's nature would have been changed. These heavy arrows slanted downward as they are, show a demanding disposition, one that does not stand for any delay. Further, as some of them are separated from the stem and on the right side, they mean a nasty, explosive temper. Such a writer might commit a crime on impulse if the writing was slanted well to the right, and the temper and domineering evidence were all three strong.

PLATE 44. The indication of a nasty, explosive temper.

This brings us down to a very important point in the truths revealed about a writer by his handwriting. A trait is nothing more than a trait. It is not necessarily good or necessarily bad. Deceit may be a good thing, depending on how it is used. Some of the most successful salesmen in the country show a high development of the ability to domineer. They benefit financially, although they may not make the most friends. Whether the salesman benefits by being domineering depends on the class of people to whom he sells. If they are not highly intelligent people, they will follow his instructions to sign an application blank. On the other hand, if he sells to people who think for themselves, domineering in dealing with such prospects is a very real handicap. The first salesman, selling to people who are easily influenced, will make sales because his domineering qualities provide the push to get the customer to buy.

● **A PICTURE OF HIGH-PRESSURE SALESMANSHIP**

In the first part of the century hundreds of salesmen made large incomes soliciting for enlarged photographs. They worked the villages and the farming country and they played on the sentimental feelings of the family for grandma or grandpa, who was gone. They would paint a glowing picture of how the pictures belong on the walls of the home, and then they closed by telling the man or woman with whom they were talking, to "sign right here." The prospect almost always signed, not an order that had been read and given consideration, but a form that was provided. As a result they usually found that the promises made by the salesman were vastly different from the actual agreement, and they paid exorbitant prices for the enlargements. However you may look at that kind of selling, it was done, and in that field the domineering salesmen was the one who rolled up the bank account.

The enlarged picture man and his selling is, of course, merely an exaggerated illustration of how a domineering streak in the salesman may help him close orders. Take for example the customer who wants to make a purchase, but is one of those uncertain individuals who keep on wanting, but also hesitating. In such cases the salesman who has some ability to domineer, may be actually doing his customers a favor. He makes up their minds for them.

● **WHAT DOES SELF-CONTROL IN HANDWRITING LOOK LIKE?**

You may have read some of Paul Wellman's highly successful novels. He is an able writer and shows his ability in his writing, but the cross-bars of his t's are the reason for including this specimen now. Study these cross-bars. They are not all alike but a majority of them look very much like an inverted basin. They are curved. In the case of Wellman, the bars are very short, but the length has nothing to do with this rule. When you find the t-bar made like a plate or basin that is upside down, you may be sure that the writer has learned self-control. The curved bars do not show what he has learned to control. It may have been temper or appetite, or some other trait. A professional grapho analyst can pinpoint what has been controlled, but the point you should remember is that the up-curved cross-bar means that the writer has made a conscious effort to gain self-control.

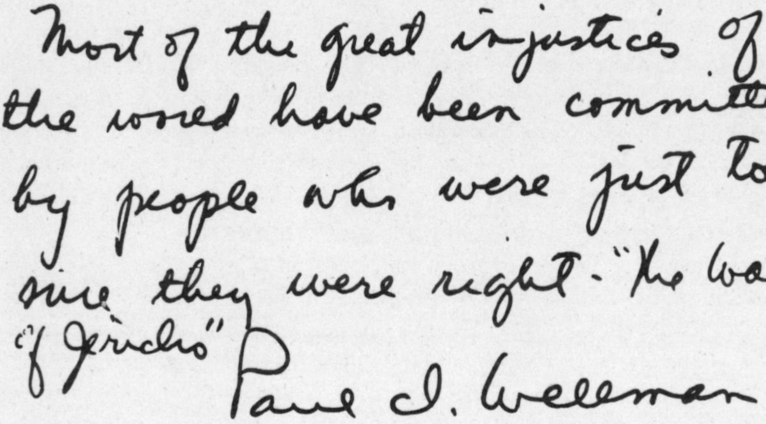

Most of the great injustices of the world have been committed by people who were just too sure they were right. "The walls of Jericho"

Paul I. Wellman

PLATE 45. Paul Wellman, novelist. T-bars made to look like an upside down plate indicate self-control.

There is nothing of self-control in this writing of Frederick A. Cook, plate 46, the man who claimed to have found the North Pole. Dr. Cook was an explorer, and later was active in business. He made a name for himself and then was generally condemned for making false claims. His business ventures were just as questionable, but no matter what history may say about the man, he left some interesting history of himself and his disposition in his writing. A man with contradictions, according to his writing. In the second line he has two t-bars, both of which are written downward, the second sharp like a knife blade. This sharp point means sarcasm, while the first in the "the" is equal in length, and shows both strength and the ability to dominate. The difference between domineering and dominating is the difference in the weight of the stroke. When a t-bar is made and slanted downward, and is as heavy at the finish as at the start, you have a. writer who commands attention. He does not demand it. He does not drive people, but he gets their attention by his positiveness, his general ability, and his ability to take a strong stand on any or every problem. In case the stroke starts heavy, and grows lighter to a sharp point, and is still slanted downward, he is demanding, or domineering. To make this point very clear and avoid misunderstanding, please study plate 46 carefully. In the top line the writing shows a writer who is capable of domination, a writer who has strength of purpose that commands attention, although it does not mean that it commands respect. The writer may be a "bad" man but he has at least one strong trait of character.

The second line shows how the domineering t-bars are made. As you study the difference you will understand the different qualities . The writer who dominates carries through, he does not lose the strength of purpose, while the one who domineers may start with a strong purpose, but it grows weaker, and lacks the carrying power, or the influence of the strong bar that reveals the ability to dominate. The writer who domineers advertises his own weakness to accomplish, and this is the reason that he demand that others jump when he speaks.

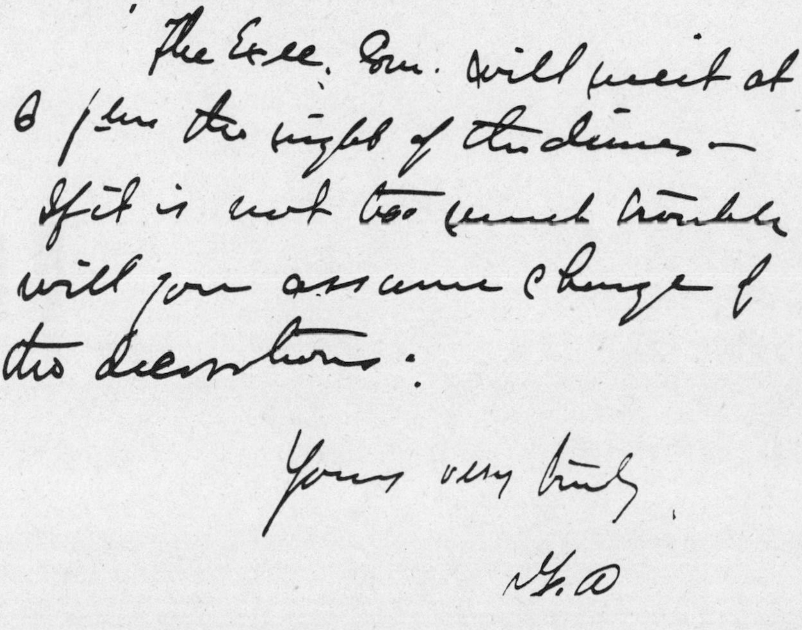
The Exec. Com. will meet at 8 p.m. the night of the dinner — If it is not too much trouble will you assume charge of the decorations.

Yours very truly

F. A. C.

PLATE 46. The handwriting of Frederick A. Cook, explorer, reveals a strong-willed man given to fits of temper.

In the word "too" in the third line, the stroke is made after the t, and is long enough to cover the width of three ordinary letters. This combination shows both strong purpose, and enthusiasm, but its location after the t-stem reveals temper. In the word "trouble" in the same line the bar is written well after the t-stem, and again it represents temper.

So long after Dr. Cook's name has been forgotten by many, his picture stands out clearly as a man who was given to fits of temper, a strong willed man, who could grow enthusiastic, but who had rare periods of self-control. You will find this in the last word in the body of the note. In this case the t-bar is long, strong, or heavy, and it is slightly bowed or curved upward, and then downward as it should to reveal self-control.

● *PROCRASTINATION ILLUSTRATED*

You will frequently find two or three different types of t-bars in a single page. Let us say that you find four long, sweeping t-bars that are made heavy, and that run the length of four or five of the small letters.

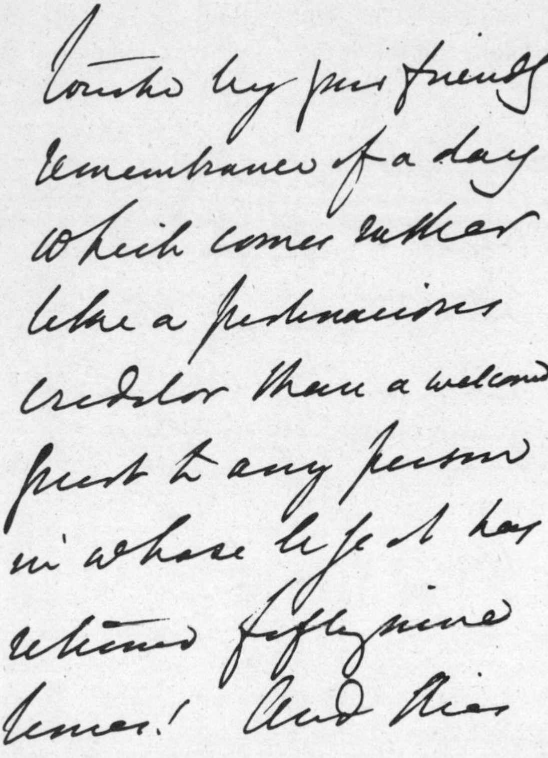
Touched by your friendly
remembrance of a day
which comes rather
like a pertinacious
creditor than a welcome
guest to any person
in whose life it has
returned fifty nine
times! And this

PLATE 47. Showing the enthusiasm, sarcasm and strong purpose of Owen Meredith (Lord Lytton).

These bars mean strong purpose and enthusiasm. Then you find four arrow-like t-bars to the right of the t-stem. These mean sarcasm and temper. The sarcasm is shown by the arrow-like strokes, and the location gives the temper. If, on the other hand, the arrow-like t-bars were written back of the t-stem, you would have an entirely different meaning.

T-bars made back of the stem show procrastination. They are behind, they put off, they lay aside work, promising themselves they will get to it some day, but they are always putting off until another time. In case you found this combination of three different kinds of strokes in a single page of one person's writing your conclusions would be that the writer is occasionally very enthusiastic, and when he is interested in a certain plan or purpose will grow enthusiastic about it. At other times he puts off, delays, or procrastinates and when pushed his temper is aroused, and he becomes sarcastic. It is true that the sarcasm is there when he is procrastinating, putting off, but it is only when he has been forced to do something that he has been putting off that the sarcasm is an expression of temper.

Before you leave this chapter, let us examine one more specimen of handwriting and consider how the writer will act. This is the writing of "Owen Meredith", (Lord Lytton) of literary fame. There are only three t-bars on this page. The first, which occurs in the first line, is not heavy in proportion to the body of the writing, hence it does not show strong purpose. It is long, which reveals enthusiasm and it is written ahead of the t-stem, indicating irritability, or temper. However, the bar does not come to a sharp point, but is uniformly heavy, so there is no sarcasm.

The second occurs in the sixth line from the top, and is short, sharp-pointed like an arrow, and is slanted downward. This shows temper, sarcasm, and a domineering streak. The last t-bar occurs in the bottom line and it is long. It grows lighter toward the finish, and is very long. This combination gives you enthusiasm, sarcasm, and a writer whose purpose is strong but grows less until it fades into the sharp sarcasm point.

It may easily be that when you have read and studied this chapter you will have become somewhat confused. If you are not absolutely sure that you know the value of each stroke as it is illustrated, it will be better to go back and re-examine the various illustrations, and study the rules again. There is nothing more embarrassing than looking at a handwriting, and finding something that is not there, simply because you have forgotten whether a long t-bar means enthusiasm or temper. And if you attempt to analyze a specimen for a friend, you can make some very ridiculous mistakes unless you can recognize the strokes without a great deal of trouble.

● IS HE IMPULSIVE?

Take this plate you have just examined. Possibly you have overlooked the important influence that is shown by the slant of the writing. You know facts shown by the t-bars, but you must now consider the influence of the slant of the writing. Take your Emotional Expression Chart, and determine the impulsiveness, the capacity the writer has for showing how he feels. Will he do so? If so, to what degree? You can make this determination for yourself, and then you tie the emotional response or reactions to the traits shown by the t-bars and you will get a new and clearer understanding of the writer.

This is important for when a writer is sarcastic, and at the same time cool, unexpressive, you can be sure that the sarcasm, or temper is a matter of planned action. It is not an impulsive gesture. Instead, the temper or irritability are the result of a cool, even cold approach, and it is intended.

EXAMINATION FOR CHAPTER 4
(Correct answers for this examination will be found in the back of the book.)

After you have determined the emotional response or lack of it, your next step was to determine how the writer's mind worked, i.e., how quickly he grasped ideas. Or was he a slow, cumulative thinker,—an analytical thinker?

A great many professional analysts look next for the t-bars, because this one letter has such a wide variation of possible values. First it has height or lack of it, both of which are exceedingly important. Then you have the cross-bars which vary in their location on the stem, while some are heavy, some are middle weight, and some exceedingly light. Length is equally important because a long sweeping t-bar has a much different value than a short one. Sometimes you will find two or three different types of t-bars in a single handwriting. This does not complicate the evidence, but it does alter it. Each of the bars has its own value and each contributes to the writer's mental habits and the resulting conduct.

In examining the t-bars the same rule applies as to all other phases of the handwriting strokes. Do not guess. When you start guessing you will make mistakes and mistakes can be costly both to you and the person analyzed.

Remember, when you analyze a handwriting, you are actually looking into the mind of the writer and what you say may change a life.

SPECIMEN I

EXAMINATION

1 . . *Do the t-bars in the above specimen represent enthusiasm?*
    Yes_____   No_____

2 . . *If you answer "No", check the value that you can give the t-bars
    in the following specimen:*
        a. STRONG PURPOSE.   b. SARCASM.

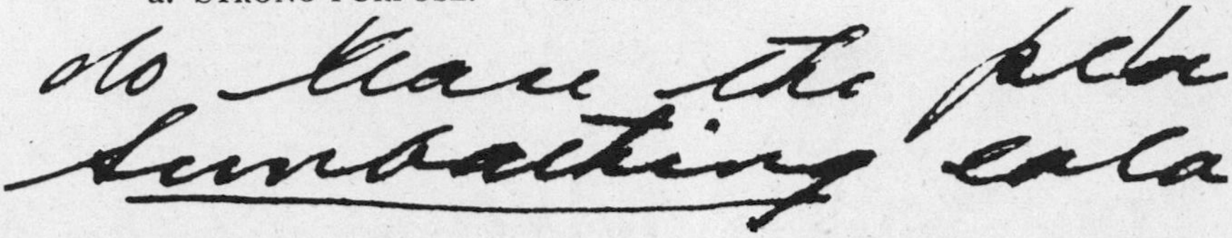

[handwritten specimen]

SPECIMEN J

3 . . *In the following specimen there are three t-bars. Check the
    values that you would give them. Remember, they may have
    more than one value depending on their weight, length and
    location.*
        a. ENTHUSIASM.   b. VISIONARY.   c. STRONG PURPOSE.
        d. WEAK PURPOSE.

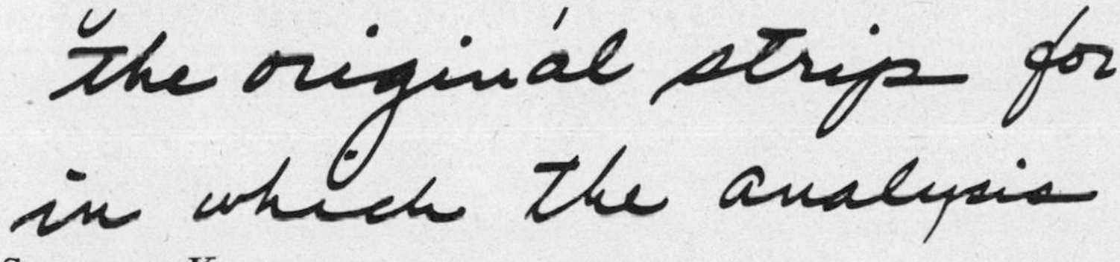

[handwritten specimen]

SPECIMEN K

4 . . *Refer to specimen "G" in Chapter 3. Does this writing show very
    little or a great deal of enthusiasm?*
        a. VERY LITTLE.   b. A GREAT DEAL.

5 . . *Would you determine from the above writing that the writer is
    sarcastic?*
    Yes_____   No_____

6 . . *Give your reasons for the above answer.*
        a. BLUNT POINT AT THE END.   b. SHARP POINT AT THE END.
        c. BECAUSE IT IS A SHORT STROKE.   d. BECAUSE IT IS A HEAVY
                                                    STROKE.

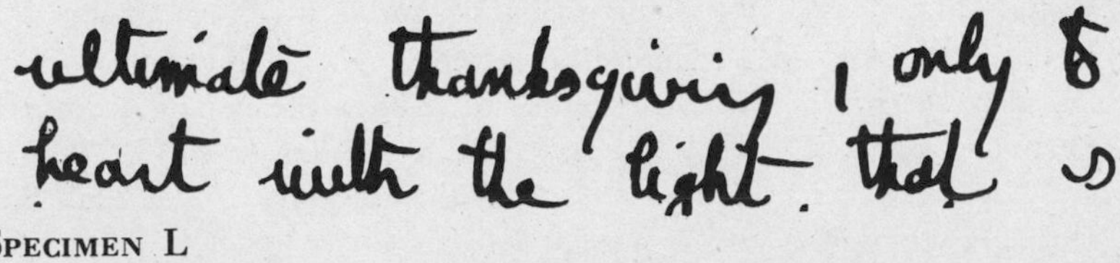

[handwritten specimen]

SPECIMEN L

CHAPTER **5**

You Start Analyzing
Handwriting

AN APPLICANT FOR A JOB—THE CHANGES AN
EAST INDIAN MADE BY COMING TO AMERICA
—THE WOMAN WHO LOST RESENTMENT.
WHAT BEAUTIFUL PENMANSHIP SHOWS.

You have learned enough to start analyzing handwriting. It is true
that you will not be able to tell *everything* about a writer, but you can get
a definite and specific benefit from what you have learned. Furthermore,
until you start using what you have learned, you are getting nothing but
theory, and grapho analysis is not merely theory. There is no room for
guesswork: no maybe this, or maybe that. You have rules, and when you
look at a handwriting for the first time you examine it for the emotional
response. The reason for this is that your writer's emotional expression or
lack of it, his capacity for absorbing emotional experiences and being influenced by unexpressed feelings, or lack of this capacity, affects everything
else you will find.

Let us examine plate 48 just as though you were going to marry the
writer, or going to hire him or her for an important job. When you look
at the handwriting you do not try to determine the sex of the writer, because you cannot. There was a time when our grandparents talked about a
"ladylike" hand, or a "masculine" hand, but it was just a way of saying
that the "ladylike" writer made the letters so they could be read, and the
"masculine" writer sprawled the letters out across the page. If you will turn
back to the page of Ella Wheeler Wilcox's writing (plate 5) you can see
what they called a "masculine" hand in the old days, yet Miss Wilcox was
a womanly woman, as well as a great artist.

● IS SUBJECT EMOTIONALLY RESPONSIVE?

So you do not know the sex of this writer. However, for convenience let us use the pronoun he, to make the matter simple. The writing slants far to the right. Use your Emotional Expression Chart, following Glenn Wallace's explanation of just how to get the exact results. Determine the emotional slant, which you will find shows a high degree of emotional response. He is affected by emotional circumstances, and shows how he feels. He shows it when he is downcast or blue and reacts just as promptly to something that pleases him. This is your basis for the character traits that will be rooted in this foundation and affected by it.

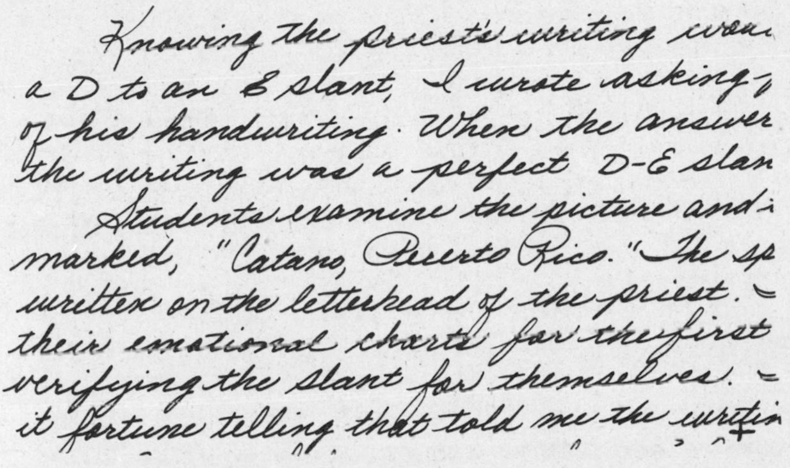

PLATE 48. How can you tell that the writer of this handwriting is steady, dependable and thorough?

The next step is to study the writing to establish how permanently he is affected by emotional situations. These lines are not exceedingly light, neither are they heavy. Therefore, you know that though he reacts promptly, he will not carry any great or lasting effects of emotional storms. He is expressive enough and has enough depth of feeling to be friendly and warmhearted, but he will not hate or love with the seething force of a volcano about to erupt.

● HOW TO RECOGNIZE A SENSITIVE PERSONALITY

Your next step is to consider how he thinks. Many of the n's and m's are more wedge-shaped at the top, than rounded. Take the third line for example. In the word "handwriting" both sections of the first "n" are more nearly wedges than rounded tops. The last part of the "n" in the last syllable is clearly a wedge. The same wedge shape occurs in the word "When". In all cases the "n" and "m" are more nearly pointed than well rounded. Here and there you have definite sharp points of well shaped wedges. None of the points, however, are comprehension strokes. They are not needle pointed, but exploratory, inquiring into, expressing an interest in learning. This interest is not highly developed. If it were, the wedges would be more clearly defined; they would be sharper. However, you have enough evidence to know that the writer is not one to understand immediately because of keen comprehension, and is not a slow thinker for whom you will have to draw pictures, and repeat explanations.

Up to this point you have established that the writer is quick to feel and show how he feels, and that he will be ready to learn. In case you employ either men or women or both, or are active socially you will recognize the importance of establishing both of these facts.

Next, the t-bars are generally short. There is no enthusiasm, and anything that the writer does or says that seems to be enthusiasm is the result of the emotional reaction. The bars are usually at the top, or very close to it. The writer sets his goal a long way ahead. He is not underselling himself to himself. He is shooting at a point in life where he will have to strive hard to make his goal. This is important not only for this fact in itself, but because when a man is working toward a distant goal, and shows the ability to learn, it will be natural for him to try that much harder to learn. The distant goal, about which he does not grow enthusiastic, will be a spur to push him to learn. Some of these t-bars are relatively heavy, so that his purpose in life is clear in his own mind. He knows where he is going.

● *HOW TO SEE DIGNITY AND PRECISION IN HANDWRITING*

Now you are ready for a new principle that affects the small "d". As you examine this specimen you will find that the d-stems are retraced, instead of being looped. A retraced d-stem shows dignity. The writer will do the precise thing, he will dress carefully, learn what customs and conventions require, and will act accordingly. He is not a stuffed shirt, he is not pompous but he is dignified in the way that compels him to do the right thing at the right time as far as possible.

These "d's" are not short and they are not tall. Instead, they are well balanced, therefore, you can be sure the writer is neither exceedingly independent, nor vain. If his "d's" were much taller he would be vain, and then his dignity would become a pompous trait, and he might easily be unbearable as an employee or associate.

The short t-bar indicates precision. There is no waste. Instead the bar is just as long as necessary to make a well balanced t-bar, or in some cases even shorter. So you have evidence of precision, and you can substantiate it by the way he dots his "i's". This a new rule and you should jot it down. The i-dots are well rounded and they are not dashes, nor splotches of ink. These i-dots add, by the way they are made, to the evidence of carefulness, precision. Here is the rule to remember: The closer the i-dots are to the i-stem, the more careful the writer will be about details. He will not do his work in a slap-happy fashion. Because he is ready to learn, he will pay attention when given instructions, he will pay attention to what he is told, and then be careful in performing whatever he has been assigned.

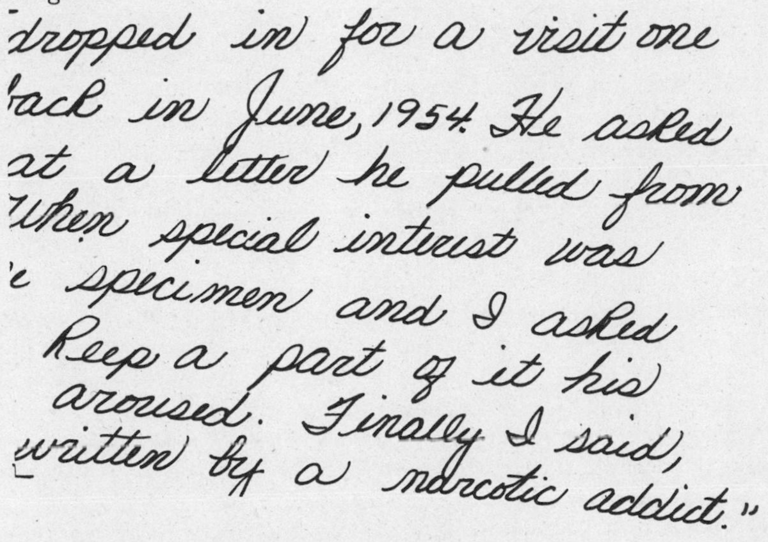

dropped in for a visit one back in June, 1954. He asked at a letter he pulled from when special interest was e specimen and I asked Keep a part of it his aroused. Finally I said, written by a narcotic addict. "

PLATE 49. This fellow plays his cards close to his chest. His characteristics are plainly spelled out in this handwriting sample.

This writer will not be a whirlwind of accomplishment. But he will be steady, dependable, thorough. He will grow on a job that he likes because when he sets a goal in life he has basic intelligence and desire to learn to think, learn and grow.

He does not hide his head and say "I can't", because his t-bars are high enough to show that he is not going to be easily satisfied with his own accomplishments regardless of where he is or what he is doing.

In plate 49 you have a very much different individual. After you have determined the slant and its value from the emotional expression angle, you will be ready to consider the writer's ability to think, form conclusions, and learn. These "n" and "m" tops are well rounded. Some of them are almost flat. One or two exploratory points occur, but the majority of the strokes reveal a thinker who learns only by accumulating impressions, just as a bricklayer uses bricks to build a wall. He arrives at conclusions slowly, and when he knows something, he is sure of it because he has not hurried in forming his decisions. You will find it worth while to compare this page with the signature of Thomas A. Edison for there is striking similarity.

The story is told that Edison's school teachers considered him too "dumb" to learn. Legend has it that he lost his hearing because an irate teacher boxed his ears so sharply that the lad's eardrums gave way, and if you are a teacher you may feel the same way if you have a boy or girl in your classes who makes these broad or well rounded "m's" and "n's". Take heart. They are not stupid, but they do not learn as readily as the mental explorer or the youngster with exceptional comprehension, who does not seem to be spending any time studying.

These t-bars are even shorter than in the preceding plate. They are precise but there is even more significance to their contribution to the picture of this man. Notice how they are right down level with the tops of the lower case or small letters. He is not taking any chances on himself. He has too many of these low t-bars, which mean lack of faith to accomplish a distant goal. He will be careful but, like a frog that could leap ten feet and is satisfied to leap only two because he is not sure of how he will land, this fellow plays his cards close to his chest. He will be thorough but you cannot expect him to do any dreaming, or make much if any effort to achieve a goal in life where he must struggle and work.

● *RETRACED "N'S" AND "M'S" SHOW THRIFT AND CAREFULNESS*
Do not confuse this lack of faith in himself with lack of self-reliance. You will learn a great deal more about self reliance, and how you can build your own, if you lack it, in a later chapter. You will learn also what you can do about changing your own thinking habits, if you are one of these low-bar writers.

This handwriting shows rare ability in some trades and professions, but no matter how much ability he has, he will not use it until he learns that he must believe in himself, that he must raise his sights, and start aiming at a point where he will use all of his ability.

You will recognize the dignity, the conventionality that is shown by the d-stems which are so much like those you have just examined in the preceding plate. Both writers are conformists, they will conduct themselves according to custom, and each is proud, but not vain.

At this point you have another new rule. When "n's" and "m's" are carefully retraced as they are in this specimen, the writer is thrifty, as well as careful. The two traits are great supports for one another, because a man who is careful may be exceedingly generous, but he is going to be thrifty as well. This writer is reasonably generous, as shown by the frequency with which he adds a long stroke after the last letter. He is not extravagant, but he is generous. However, he will not be a waster, and he will accumulate before he gives away.

● *ABILITY BUT NOT MUCH DRIVE*

His t-bars are weak, which means that his purposes are not strong. He is not going any particular place in life, unless someone else starts him on the road, and even then he will not have faith enough in himself to accomplish anywhere near what he might. Talent? His handwriting shows a strong basic natural ability but, after all, ability is not worth much unless the man who has it believes in himself enough to use it.

Throughout the years more than a million people have written me and the organization I have headed. A high percentage of them have been like this chap. They had a good deal of genuine ability, but they lacked faith in themselves, and so did nothing about it. Even after a vocational analysis, they would ask someone else to furnish the push and drive. It is not a pleasant thing to recognize but most people who fail just do not make enough effort to avoid failure, or they misuse good traits because they fail to learn how to use them.

Your next illustration, plate 50, was written by a young lady, who applied for a position in an accounting department. This is a broad term, because almost every community has men and women who handle money, and records for clubs, sororities, fraternities, and church groups. So you can consider that she might have applied to handle such work for you, your club, or if she did not apply, she may have been nominated or sug-

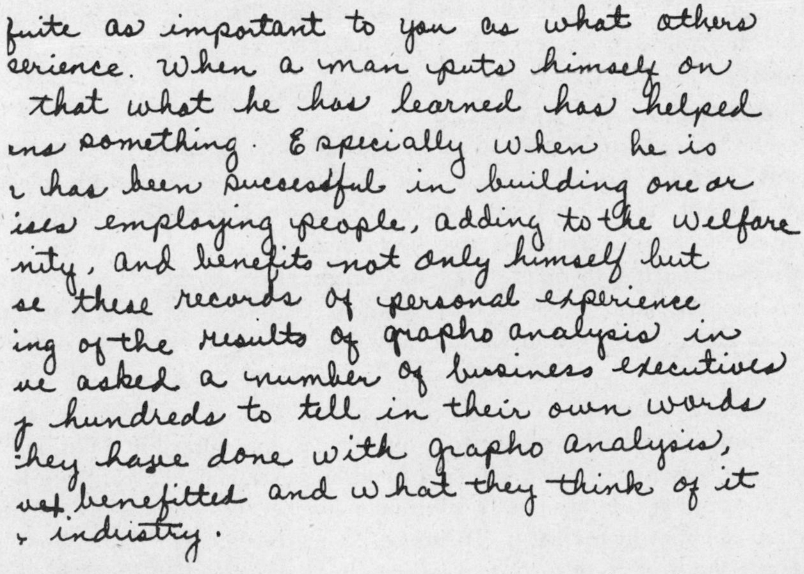

PLATE 50. Small writing shows concentration, the ability to do one thing at a time and ignore intrusions.

gested. From what you already know and what you will learn in this chapter, you can determine many, if not all, of her qualifications for such a place.

Your Emotional Expression Chart shows that she is cool, self-possessed, and does not get excited. She is not a young woman to act, and then think. Just the opposite. Her writing is quite small and this gives you a new rule. Small writing shows concentration, the ability to do one thing at a time, and ignore intrusions. If she were working in your office or your home and could work in a room with others, there could be traffic all the day long, and she would ignore it, giving her attention to the job in hand.

As you check the "m's" and "n's", and the last half of many of the "h's", you find those inverted v's that reveal an exploratory mind. As an accountant she must want to learn facts, and she must know how to keep still about what she knows. You have not had any rule concerning the ability to keep a secret, but as you study this page of writing you will find that a high percentage of the "a's" and "o's" are closed with little loops. They are tied shut, just as you might tie a twine about the mouth of a bag. She will not talk, and talk, and she will not betray confidences. Her t-bars vary in height. Some of them are right down on the top of the small letters but enough are written well up on the stem, to be an indication that she will work to do a better job. Some of them are quite heavy too. She will intend to do a good job. She is thrifty, and yet the finals are quite long. She will save money, save time, and then give freely when there is reason.

● CONCENTRATION REVEALED

The facts you have learned so far indicate a dependable young woman, who is careful. However, look at your i-dots. They are carefully placed, some of them quite close to the i-stem. She not only concentrates, she pays attention to details. You can give her a heavy load of work in an office and depend on her to do it. Or you can give her charge of your church or club books, and go home quite content that she will handle the job without a cent missing, and without any gaps in her records.

Grapho analysis does not foretell the future, any more than it reveals your past, or the past of your neighbor next door. But, looking at this page from what you have learned, you can be quite sure that when and if the young lady marries, she will be a good housekeeper. She will be a good and conscientious mother, and a good neighbor because she has the qualities of character that fit her for it. If she were a teacher and the school building took fire, she would not rush madly down the hall screaming fire, but would march her youngsters to safety, keeping a calm, level head every minute of the time.

A few of her t-stem, and d-stems are looped, but the loop is very small. She will not be sensitive to a point of moody discouragement. Instead, the combination of her poise, emotional balance, and concentration will cause her to pass off the hurts very quickly.

Would you say that the writer of plate 50 has the qualities to make a good bookkeeper and accountant? You need not smile. In the years business firms have been sending me specimens for examination, asking about why an employee has not made good or why he cannot do so, a great many have been submitted that had no more fitness for an accounting job than this page shows. If you concluded on quick examination that he is not adapted to it, you were right.

This is the writing of a young man who was a salesman. Then he became an editor while in the army, and today he is a successful editor because he has found his proper niche in life. One of his greatest assets is shown by the frequent breaks between letters of a word. You had the same characteristic in the handwriting of one of your earlier specimens, a writer who gained international fame. You should go back and check each specimen because you will not have any difficulty locating the right one, and the things you do for yourself in studying handwriting plates and comparing them will increase your facility in using what you learn.

● HERE IS A SHARP THINKER

These breaks identify a sixth sense, a writer's ability to feel situations without being told. It is sometimes called psychic sense, and it is a quality that is found in the handwriting of great interpretative musicians. Notice that the word interpretative is used. A musician who is able to do more than mechanical execution.

Check through on the "m's" and "n's". A great many reveal the exploratory, or learner type of thinking. Also, there are very few keen comprehension strokes. This young man will succeed because he never stops learning. He is constantly looking for new knowledge, and he explores and digs all of the time. You will possibly find it easier to think of the inverted v-stroke that indentifies the mental explorer if you think of an axe that is resting on its heels, with the blade pointing up.

Thus your editor likes his job because he makes a good many of the cross-bars as enthusiastic strokes. When a man gets on a job that he does not like and about which he is not enthusiastic, he almost always leaves it or loses the length of his cross-bars. There is another interesting stroke or letter formation here. The letter "d" does not have any down-stroke to the stem. This formation is an indication of literary ability, not yet brought to its full development. As this young editor goes along he will change his small "d" so that the form resembles a Greek letter called *delta*. This is

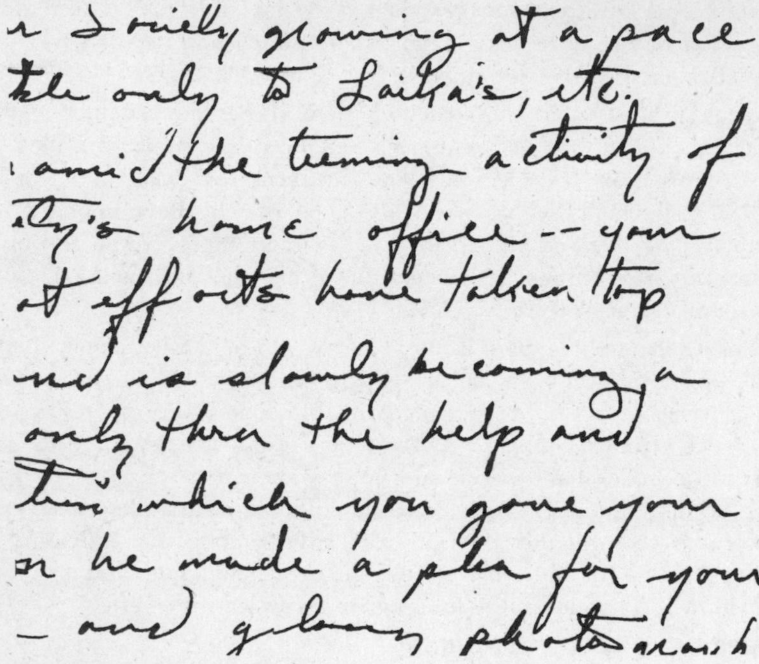

PLATE 51. Handwriting of a professional grapho analyst.

just one of the letter formations that reveals literary talent and about which you will learn in a later chapter.

In plate 51 you have a specimen of writing done by a professional grapho analyst, whose ability to analyze handwriting is very highly developed. When you compare this plate with the writing of the young lady who applied for the accounting job you will find many striking resemblances. Both writings are smaller than ordinary and as you already know, the small writer concentrates.

The exploratory strokes are prominent, and run all the way through the specimen. It is entirely possible that his study and use of grapho analysis has helped him strengthen his desire to find out the answers. All through the years, since the first students in grapho analysis began more than thirty years ago, there has been a ceaseless flow of records from men and women of all ages who have actually changed their ways of thinking as a result of studying how to analyze handwriting.

● **COMPACT WRITING REVEALS A SAVER**

The writing shows close attention to details, by the way the "i's" are dotted. He is thrifty. The letters are close together, just as the parts of the "m's" and "n's" which you have already studied are close together and reveal thrift. Writing that is compact always reveals a natural inclination to save, to not waste.

There is a very pronounced example of the explorer who wants to get the answers about everything in the handwriting in your next illustration, plate 52. Here the wedge-shaped letters are very prominent, and there is no sign of thrift, for each letter stands out clearly, well separated from those on each side. The i-dots are very near the point of the i-stem, and you have

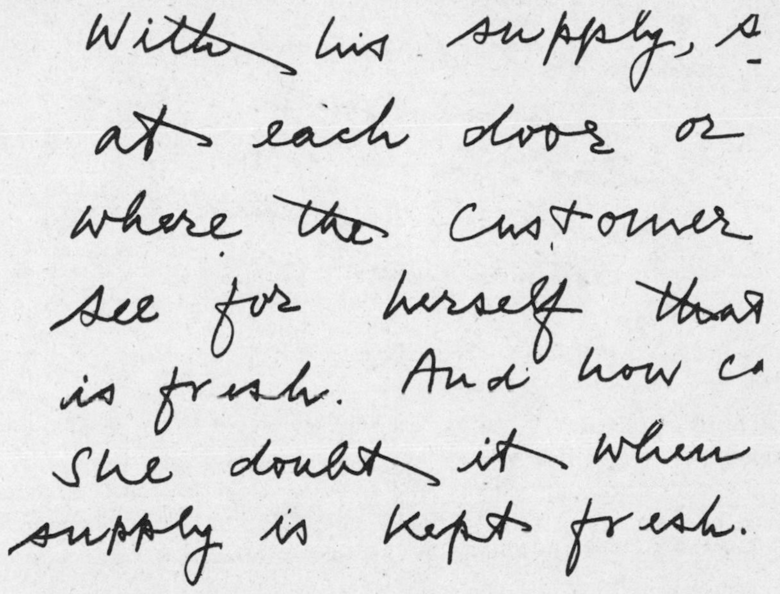

PLATE 52. These cross-bars show enthusiasm and the flourishes reveal showmanship tendencies.

a unique cross-bar for many of the "t's". They are long, which reveals enthusiasm, they are slanted sharply downward and to the right, and most of them are made with a little flourish.

The sum of such cross-bars is enthusiasm, a very mild inclination to dominate, not strong enough to alienate friends, and the flourish reveals showmanship.

As you examine and compare these handwritings, you may ask yourself the same question that many thousands of others have asked from the floor when I have been teaching. "Does beautiful handwriting reflect a beautiful disposition, and does handwriting that is difficult to read mean that the writer is a difficult person to understand, or to get along with?" Certainly not. The most expert professional writers have revealed their principal character traits in their handwriting in spite of years of endless hours of practice, and when they were relaxed their handwriting did not look the same as it did when they were preparing their copybook specimens.

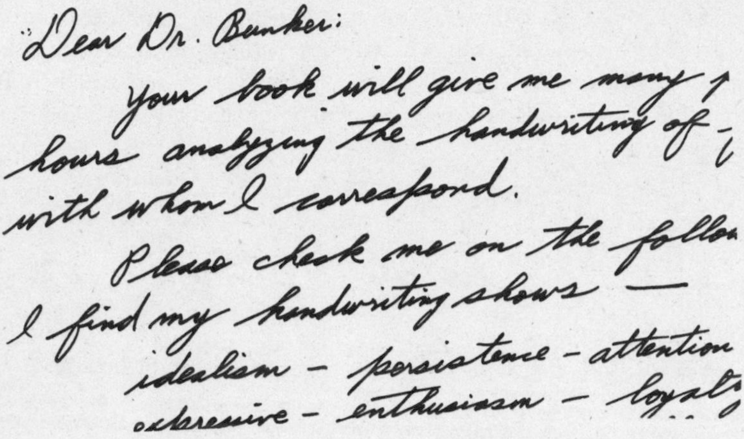

Dear Dr. Bunker:

Your book will give me many hours analyzing the handwriting of, with whom I correspond.

Please check me on the follo I find my handwriting shows —

idealism — persistence — attention ostensive — enthusiasm — loyalty

PLATE 53. The straight, inflexible stroke at the start of the word is a resentment stroke.

This is emphasized by an experience I once had with one of the principal penmen in America, whose name was a household word in the heyday of copy book practice in school. As I mentioned one trait after another he nodded his head, until when I finally said, "You're an ultra conservative and thrifty man." Then he allowed his face to relax into a grin.

"You mean I'm tight?" he said.

He was tight as the bark on a beech. He had accumulated a great deal of money, but both professional and personal friends admitted that he did not spend any whenever he could avoid it.

He had asked the question, and he got an affirmative answer. There was no sense in lying about it, for he knew he was not a spender and if I had tried to explain it away and put it in softer words than I had already used, he would have known that I was not telling the truth. When you analyze a handwriting for a friend or stranger, tell the truth. It is not necessary to say, "You're tight" to a man who does not spend money or time on others, but if you squirm and fidget he will think a lot less of you. It is worthwhile to develop a vocabulary so that you can say unnice things diplomatically. But even though you are a neophyte, tell the truth. It will mean that you gain the respect of the person whose writing you are analyzing.

You may be interested in the fact that the writer of plate 52 was born and educated in India. He was indeed the first teacher of grapho analysis in that country, where he was very successful in analyzing the handwriting of school and college students. Eventually he came to America and this writing is the result of a voluntary change which he made in becoming adapted to American ways. While he was growing into adulthood in his native land, his writing was pinched, and very heavy, expressing his deep emotions, and incidentally, his love for color. Keep this in mind.

When the writing is very heavy it reveals strong appetites for rich foods, brilliant colors, fine odors, and tones. In the case of the Indian whose writing was so compact and heavy, he now writes with a lighter line and with the letters well separated because he is not compelled to be so thirfty. Further, immediately on landing in America he broke out in a rash of brilliant shirts and all of the pent up desire that had accumulated during half a life time in India was satisfied, and his writing showed the change in his character habits.

Your writing will show changes as you make them. You may not do it consciously, for a severe shock, that affects your emotional nature, will cause your writing to change. Intense emotional pressures may be lifted and your writing will change. As I explained earlier, I don't like to talk about myself, but this incident illustrates the point for you. At one time I had a vast amount of problems, serious problems forced on me. A very close friend said to me, "Just look at your writing. Every line shows that you resent imposition. You are just as different as you can be from what you were when I first knew you."

My handwriting showed it. Problems that poured in on me from every side had become so great that I anticipated being faced with another one, and my writing developed the stroke that showed resentment. It took a true friend to point it out, but that friend could not do anything about it, and it took time for me to do something. As I write this book there is not one atom of resentment in my writing. The strokes that show it are all gone, because the cause has been removed.

This can occur in your case, or in the handwriting of anyone else. It is a temporary thing, but strokes change as you change, they come and go, depending on circumstances, but your handwriting in its entirety remains the same. This fact is the reason that you have a later chapter that tells you how you can actually change and strengthen your own ability by changing your writing.

In plate 53 you have an illustration of the resentment stroke. Notice that there is a straight or inflexible stroke at the start of almost every word. You cannot miss these strokes for they are there. This is a warning of resentment against fancied or actual imposition. If the writer is actually being imposed on, the strokes come into the writing because of the resentment that is possibly justified. But in many cases a vivid imagination helps to create a cause for them. The writer imagines she is imposed on, and the resentment grows and grows until someone like my friend has the courage to tell the writer the truth. This will not help when the cause actually exists, but the writer who has imagined the imposition may take stock, recognize that he has no reason to feel imposed upon, and the strokes will disappear.

You will find a striking illustration of what can happen in losing resentment in plate 54. As you check it you will find that this writer is both proud and sensitive. Also her writing slants well to the right; she feels and shows her feelings immediately.

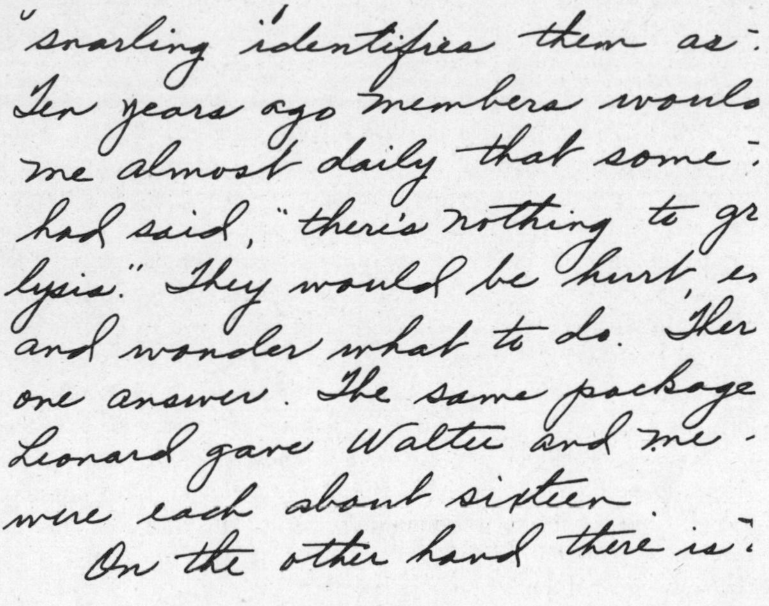

PLATE 54. This writer is both proud and sensitive.

For several years she worked with a woman whose writing was vertical, and very light. Also she was critical, because she felt that everything had to be done precisely the same. She was not an easy person to work with, even for others of equal rank, and this writer was under the older woman's supervision. There was no doubt that she became emotionally upset many, many times. Her sensitiveness was overworked, and before long she was starting to put in resentment strokes that were strong, and occurred before every word. She resented. She expected to be criticized, and she fought back by resenting what she felt was an imposition.

Then there was a change of department heads, and the reasons for the resentment no longer existed, her sensitiveness was no longer stirred every day, and she began losing the initial resentment strokes.

● **YOUR HANDWRITING WARNS YOU OF PERSONALITY DEFECTS**

If you find them in your own handwriting, make every effort to remove the cause—if there is a cause—because resentment grows, and multiplies like weeds in a garden. There is no single trait that can do more to wreck your happiness than feeling that you are imposed upon, and resenting that imposition. It is so easy to start resenting just a little, and the feeling grows, and multiplies and very soon you resent not only the imposition, but you resent what others do, and what they say. In case you are sarcastic you will grow more so, because sarcasm becomes a defense mechanism used to ward off that which you hate so badly.

EXAMINATION FOR CHAPTER 5

(Correct answers for this examination will be found in the back of the book.)

You have already found that you are not asked to answer questions on every principle given in a single chapter. The reason is simple: If you have learned the rules covered by the questions so that you can answer them correctly, it is reasonable to assume that you have been honest in studying all of the rules.

I would gladly oblige
you by sending material
and photograph for your
sketch, but I find my-
self unable to spare
the time to get the one,
and have'nt got one

SPECIMEN M

Never lose track of the basic fact when you guess because you do not know, you can make some very damaging conclusions. No book could be compiled that gave you every variation of letters, so it is essential that you learn to observe. Master these basic rules, and then exercise caution and common sense in applying them.

Many years ago when grapho analysis was first offered to home and resident students there were some who would check the questions and then look for the answers. Months later when they found a handwriting that was a little more difficult than the average they would be confused and made some rather horrible mistakes. It is expected that you are going to study the chapter before looking at the questions.

EXAMINATION

The above specimen is the writing of a very famous woman whose name for many years made headlines in great newspapers and magazines. She made many enemies and possibly just as many friends.

It is included here for you to use in making your first attempt at actually analyzing handwriting; not merely hunting for the use of strokes that reveal individual characteristics.

1 . . *Each of these remarks can be answered easily with a "Yes" or "No" if you have studied and given attention to each illustration used to illustrate a principle.*

    a. HIGHLY RESPONSIVE TO EMOTIONAL SITUATIONS_____

    b. OBJECTIVE, SHOWING VERY LITTLE IF ANY RESPONSE TO EMOTIONAL SITUATIONS_____

    c. KEEN, COMPREHENDING THINKER_____

    d. SLOW THINKER_____

    e. EXPLORATORY THINKER_____

    f. SUPERFICIAL THINKER_____

    g. STRONG PURPOSE_____

    h. WEAK PURPOSE_____

    i. AVERAGE PURPOSE_____

    j. ENTHUSIASTIC_____

    k. NO ENTHUSIASM_____

    l. DOMINEERING_____

    m. THRIFTY_____

    n. CAPABLE OF KEEPING SECRETS_____

2 . . *Would you expect to find this woman becoming hysterical in an emergency?*

        YES_____   No_____

3 . . *In your opinion, based on what you know, how do you rate this writers ability?*

      a. AVERAGE.   b. BETTER THAN AVERAGE.   c. HIGH.

CHAPTER **6**

Mind vs. Muscles

STARTLING DISCOVERY OF THE TALENT OF
FAMOUS MUSCLE MEN—CHARLES ATLAS; THE
ENGLISH ARMY SERGEANT; THE STRONG MAN
WHO MIGHT HAVE BEEN AN ACCOUNTANT;
GEORGE F. JOWETT, SEIGMUND KLEIN, JACK
DEMPSEY; THE STRONG MAN WITH MUSICAL
TALENT. A FORMER MR. AMERICA AND HIS
CODE REVEALED BY HIS WRITING.

"But there is neither East nor West,
Border nor Breed, nor Birth,
When two strong men stand face to face,
Though they come from the ends of the earth."

The Ballad of East and West—KIPLING

SOMEHOW the argument has been going on for years and years; only a doughty man would dare to guess how many. It has been an argument, though, as to whether a big muscled, "strong man" or the steel-nerved athlete, loses mental ability and vitality as his muscular power increases. Dour skeptics have pointed to the record of college football teams and sneered, "they graduate because they play football and win letters, not because they know what is in the books, and what the teachers have tried to give them."

On the other side of the fence there have been supporters of the athletes who have stressed the point that building a strong body is certain to strengthen the mind, and that some athletes are not stupid merely because they have built powerful physiques.

● **BRAINS AND/OR MUSCLE**

These have been arguments, but in order to arrive at facts, it seemed only reasonable to gather evidence and examine it. Invitations were sent

98

to champion swimmers, tennis players, big muscle boys, and prize fighters; scores of them. Physical strength and success was the basis for making the tests, and here for the first time, possibly, they are presented for your consideration, and to provide the answer. The men whose handwriting you will find in this chapter were selected only because of their body building accomplishments, and not from their handwriting, nor for their scholastic records. They are only a very small part of the original evidence which was gathered to get at the truth, but these speciments represent the average intelligence of the entire group.

The specimen in plate 55 has an interesting history. At one time I was editor of the most widely circulated boy's magazine in America. We had a regular section devoted to body building which was exceedingly popular, and the man who wrote this plate was a contributor. He was a professional body builder in India, and he furnished us a feature article now and then, although his principal contribution to the magazine was photographs of Indian athletes. One afternoon in a slack moment I examined his handwriting, and found that he possessed remarkable literary ability or tendencies. You will find them when you study the plate. Notice how he makes his small "g's" like very poorly executed figure 8's. If you ever examine the writing of Charles Dickens, and other famous names, you will find the same figure 8's for the small "g". This does not mean actual literary ability, but it is a fluidity in thinking and expression that is important to a good writer.

After I had analyzed his writing to my own satisfaction I dictated a

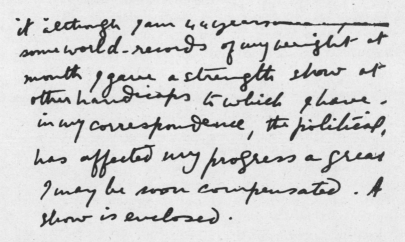

PLATE 55. The small "g" that looks like a figure 8 indicates fluidity in thinking and expression—important to professional writers.

letter to our Indian contributor and told him what his handwriting had shown. Just as quickly as a reply could come back, he confided that he had always wanted to be a writer, and that if his handwriting revealed such ability he was going to make a start.

A few months later he informed me in another letter that he had been writing, and that he found it the easiest thing that he had ever done. You may find these same formations in your own writing. If so, do not scoff and say you cannot write because you probably have never tried to do so. The "m's" and "n's" vary greatly. In some of the words they are made like inverted "v's". Take the word "mu" in the third line from the bottom. On the other hand, in "my" in the second line from the top the strokes are all comprehension or quick understanding strokes. As you examine the entire page you will find many of the inverted "v's" that are not fully developed. Some of them are simply not there at all and when you find "m's" and "n's" made in "am" in the first line, and "strength" in the third line, you have evidence that the writer is merely rushing along without doing much thinking. This is not always a negative trait. Men and women who become very familiar with a subject, and work with it all day long, become so accustomed to thinking or acting in their individual fields that they do not need to give much thought to their jobs. However, such writers owe it to themselves to develop a hobby that will compel them to think, in order to keep the mind awake, and eager to learn.

You will find that this man makes all, or almost all, of his t-bars at the right of the t-stem, and you will recall that this is evidence of temper, or marked irritability. This fellow had been a difficult man to work with until he began writing. It was not six months before the t-bars were back across the t-stems, and the irritability was gone.

● IRRITABILITY SHOWN BY YOUR T-STEM

It has been my experience that a very great many writers who are easily irritated have developed this trait, not because it is something they must have, but in defense when they have not found the natural hobby or profession in which they can be both successful and happy.

Salesmen in particular who are unhappy with the merchandise they are selling, but feel that they must continue in order to live, frequently develop this kind of reaction, and when they finally get into a job they like, it disappears.

You will find the writing of an English physical trainer in plate 56. This writing is interesting because it shows so many traits you have already studied. First, as you know, heavy writing means strong appetites, and also deep emotions. Like the writing of the Indian, the "m's" and "n's" are very short pointed, when there are points. In many of the strokes there is

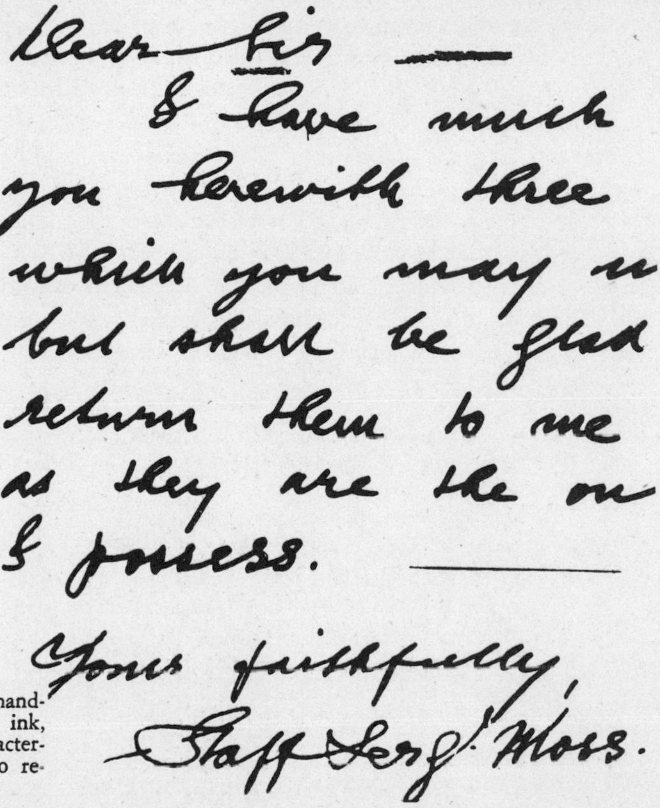

[handwritten letter]

Dear Sir —
I have much
you herewith three
which you may u
but shall be glad
return them to me
as they are the on
I possess. —

Yours faithfully,
Staff Sergt. Moss.

PLATE 56. Heavy hand-
writing, loaded with ink,
brings out a new characteristic you will want to remember.

nothing more than a tiny hump, that really would not penetrate anything. The t-bars are at the right of most of the t-stems, so you have evidence that he was irritable, and quick tempered. However, this page illustrates a new point of character that you may very well remember and use. Almost all of the circle letters are just blobs of ink. The "a's" and "o's", even the "e's" are loaded with ink. You already know that heavy writing shows strong appetites, and these blobs of ink go a little further. They show sex desire that is very strong indeed.

A number of years ago a man who pretended to be a movie scout registered in a great hotel. His signature was little more than a matter of heavy ink, in fact it looked on the hotel register as if he might have written his name with a blunt stick. However, he was immediately popular. Parents with daughters they wanted to get into the movies entertained him royally. Their homes were open to him, and they encouraged their daughters to accept his invitations to dance, and cocktail parties.

● UNCONTROLLED SEX DRIVE

This went along for several weeks, until he was literally the king pin in that resort neighborhood. The next thing to occur was that one of the young women was killed, left strangled and naked by the side of the road. She had fought off his advances and in a mad sex frenzy he had killed her. There was a great hubbub in the newspapers, the hotel where he had registered was greatly embarrassed, and, of course, the grieving parents had no recourse except to help the law punish him. The point that is significant, however, was that he advertised his desires when he registered. If the hotel clerk, or if the parents had taken the trouble to examine his handwriting the young woman would not have lost her life, and others would not have had experiences of which they would be ashamed all through life. Heavy

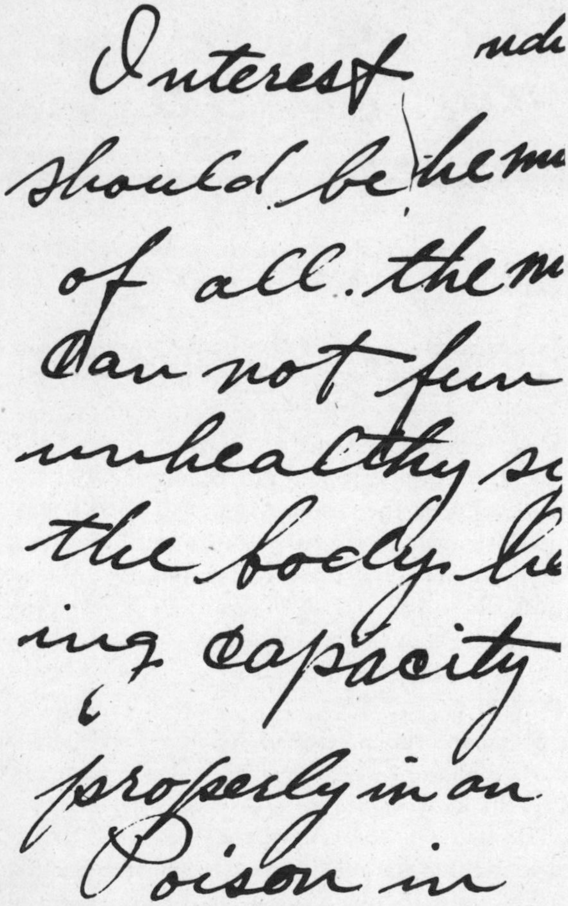

PLATE 57. Handwriting of muscleman Charles Atlas shows initiative, responsive emotional nature.

writing, where all of the circle letters—the a, g, e, and o's are closed—reveal a sex mad wolf, who will not be denied. Such writers will eat rich foods, frequently drink excessively, and are not only dangerous to themselves but to others.

In learning this rule you must also recognize another. A letter that is clogged with ink does not necessarily mean a wolf or sex mad writer. Pens catch lint on some kinds of paper. A single blurred and ink-loaded letter is not a sign of danger. It is only when a page shows this trait repeatedly, where it is in the majority of the circle letters that it should be considered evidence of sex appetites gone wild.

If you read magazines and their advertising you have for many years now seen the advertising of Charles Atlas, whose course in physical development has sold to hundreds of thousands of ambitious young men. Atlas is a trade name, and it has become world famous. Atlas won a contest for the most perfect physique about the time of the Harding administration, and indeed President Harding's death had a very considerable influence on the success of the Atlas course. The course had just been put on the market when Harding went to Alaska and when he died Atlas and Dr. Tilner, who was associated with him at the time, sat up all night getting out literature warning the young and old who had written them, that a strong body was essential, no matter where they worked or what they did.

You will find first of all that Atlas' writing (plate 57) shows a highly responsive emotional nature. It shows friendliness, emotional warmth, and expression. His t-bars are long, showing enthusiasm, and, though they vary in location, the variance reveals an important combination of traits. He is capable of setting his goal a long way ahead but, on the other hand, he also works toward an immediate goal, that he is sure he can reach.

Your attention is called particularly to the letter "p" in "capacity". Compare this with the same letter in the next plate. The Atlas "p" shows initiative, the kind of man who sees an opportunity and takes advantage of it. Atlas did that. He won a contest. He was rated as the world's most perfect man. He could have sat still on that title, and no one would have been any better off. But Atlas said to himself, "here is an opportunity for me to help others. I have built my body and I know how I did it. I can show others, and can help them, and build a business of my own." In other words, he had the initiative, and the purpose shown by his t-bars to do something with the opportunity he had made by building his own body to a high degree of perfection.

In case you are an executive, and you need employees with initiative and purpose, look for "p's" made in this way, along with heavy cross-bars for the "t's". The longer and heavier the t-bars the more enthusiasm, and purpose, and the Atlas letter "p" is a good basis for judging the initiative.

On the other hand, the large p-loops in plate 58 reveal a love for physical activity, sports that call for vigorous use of the muscles of the body. This is the writing of a one-time naval swimming star, but the examination of hundreds of athletes who participated in sports for the pure love of the sport, not merely to win a title, have shown the large p-loops. All three of the "p's" in this plate are large, two of them very large indeed. The writer

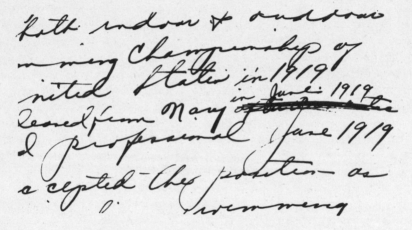

PLATE 58. Large p-loops reveal a love for physical activity.

wrote me that he would rather swim than eat, and it did not make any difference to him whether he got a title. He was happy in the water, and there was nothing he would not attempt in the water. He enjoyed it.

It is true that there have been other prize winners who have not had this stroke, but they have other reasons for achieving success. Some of them have loved the plaudits of the crowd, and were eager to put on a good show. Others worked for financial rewards. There have been a great many prize fighters who have not had these big p-loops, but they have been fighting not merely for the love of it but to win a purse.

● HERE IS AN INQUIRING MIND

There is a much, much different character in the handwriting of Staff Sergeant Moss (plate 56), of the British army who was also a prize winner, but here the "p" is much smaller. But it is not smaller in proportion to the rest of the writing. The swimming star's writing is large and a single word could be superimposed on five or six of the words in Moss' plate. But both were sportsmen for the pure joy of the sport and revealed it in their "p's". This plate shows a man who was constantly on the alert to learn, to inquire into, and to gain knowledge by honestly investigating or exploring.

Even his double "l's" in "shall" are wedge shaped at the top. Some of his circles are closed with ink, but many of them are not, so that you can know he loved good food, and other senuous, but not sensual satisfaction.

There is another trait of character shown in the Moss writing to which you should give attention. In the words "may" and "they" the down-strokes are heavy to the very end. If your friends say that you are a good starter and a poor finisher, this is a stroke that you can profitably cultivate in your own writing. These strong down strokes reveal determination, the intention to go through to the completion of a job.

On the other hand, the writer who makes his down strokes as in plate 59 may be a good starter, but, like an old car climbing a hill, they run out of the drive to get to the finish. These two rules are important. The down-stroke that is heavy shows determination, and the one that starts out heavy and fades out toward the finish shows the same kind of determination—the writer who starts out with a lot of pep, and who does not carry through to the completion of the job.

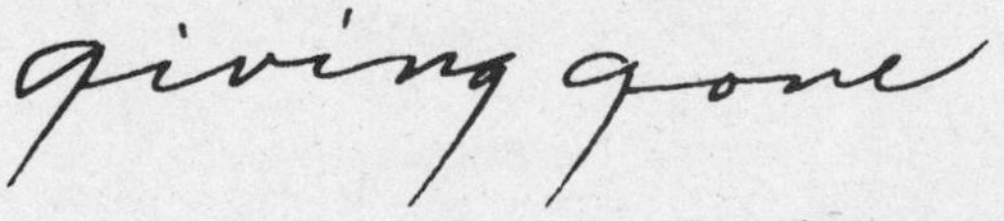

PLATE 59. Heavy down-stroke shows determination but it should not fade toward the end.

Up to this point you have examined the handwritings of five strong men, and three out of the five show an eager desire to learn, and in two of them, you have men who might easily have stood high in a field of scholarship outside of body building. The first one showed talent that the writer had not realized he possessed, and when it was pointed out to him his writing changed, and the "m's" and "n's" sharpened, and he lost the irritability.

In your next specimen, plate 60, you have a handwriting of a man who might have been an accountant. From start to finish the exploratory inverted "v's" are consistent. The writing is small, the d-stems show pride, and the cross-bars of the "t's" are precisely placed, short, showing no enthusiasm, but by their length revealing the habit of accuracy or the opposite of waste of effort.

The "p's" are made with straight stems, so there is no actual love of physical sports. This is actually the writing of one of the most remarkably built business men in the Philippine Islands, a man who after World War II went back to a ruined business and started building again. Mariano G. Antonio's writing is an excellent example of the mentally capable strong man, and even more important evidence that there is no limitation on

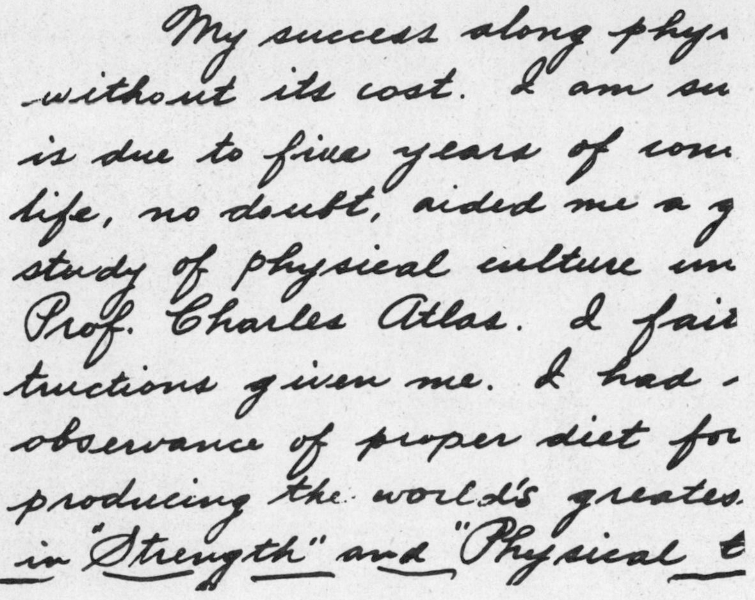

My success along phys.
without its cost. I am su
is due to five years of com.
life, no doubt, aided me a g
study of physical culture in
Prof. Charles Atlas. I fair
tuctions given me. I had -
observance of proper diet for
producing the world's greates.
in "Strength" and "Physical t

PLATE 60. An "accountant personality." Shows attention to detail, organizational ability, accuracy in even little things.

mental development. A hundred years ago his country was dominated by a foreign power that enslaved the people, yet Antonio, in any man's language, would have to be rated brilliant.

With him building a strong body, beautifully rounded muscles, was a business just like selling merchandise. He studied his body needs just as he would study a book on medicine, or a textbook on any other subject. He shows attention to details, organization ability, accuracy in everything he does. His "d's" are short-stemmed, indicating his independence of what others might think or say, a quality of character that he displayed in his years of developing an extensive business at a time when it was not common for a Filipino to strike out on his own.

Incidentally, if you are looking for an accountant in your office, you cannot make a mistake by comparing his handwriting with this plate, because there is no dishonesty here, and the mentality revealed is particularly suitable to that field.

George F. Jowett, whose handwriting is plate 62, was a Canadian woodsman and wrestler when he began contributing to the Boys' Magazine during my editorship. George always wrote his manuscripts in pencil, and almost without a punctuation mark, but what he said made enough sense to justify the time spent in editing his articles. Study his flat-topped letters,

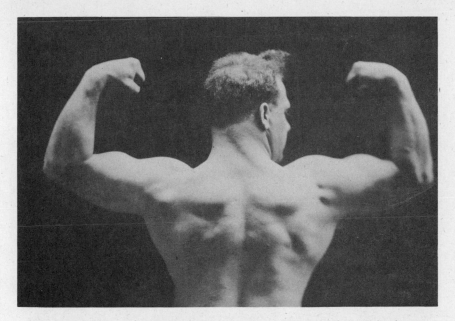

PLATE 61. George F. Jowett, Canadian woodsman, wrestler and physical culture instructor who became world-famous.

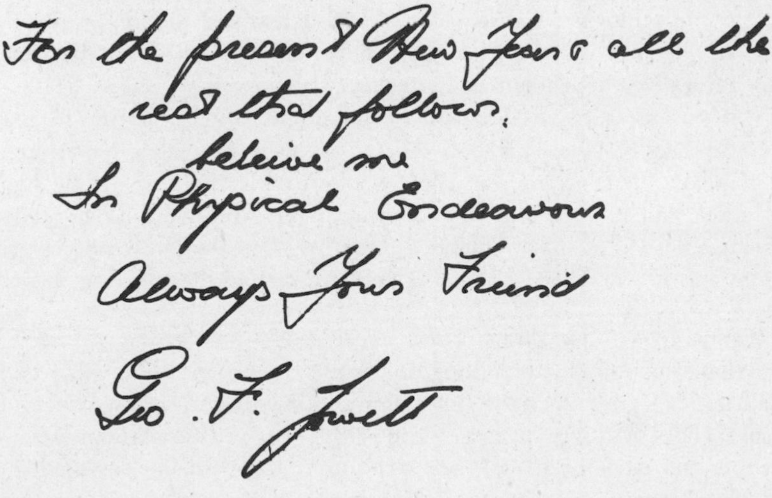

For the present New Years & all the rest that follows.

beleive me

In Physical Endeavour

Always Yours Friend

Geo. F. Jowett

PLATE 62. In this handwriting of George F. Jowett you see the signs of a vigorous and independent thinker.

not just the "m's" and "n's" but even the "s" is broad and rounded. His d-stems did not have any height to them at all, and I never knew a man who cared less what others thought of him. Every word he wrote, however, was part of a picture just as if he had been building a house. Every theory fitted into place. Futhermore, he wrote enthusiastic copy, so that the boys who read his articles on how to build up muscle and health felt like going out and doing something about it. He was thrifty, never wasted a cent that I knew of, and was friendly, kindly and sympathetic. His emotional slant shows this, but it does not reveal generosity. Instead, George was careful, not a spender, nor a waster.

● **SELF RELIANCE ILLUSTRATED**

There is another point which you can easily find for yourself. He set his goal a long way ahead. Instead of being satisfied with his accomplishments in Canada, he looked ahead at that which body building could do for him in the future. The United States looked like a big field with thousands of young men who would be interested in building strong and muscular bodies, so he came over from Canada, found a sponsor, and prepared a course that was for a long time offered by one of the great home study schools in this country, and then set up in business for himself. There is one other trait in this handwriting that you may well make part of your understanding of grapho analysis. The word "Canada" is carefully underscored, although not shown in this plate. This means self reliance and you will learn a great-deal more about it in the next chapter.

Summing him up, George Jowett had a habit of thinking slowly, carefully; he was not wasteful, he was independent in all of his thinking and quite naturally independent in his actions because he acted as he thought. He was enthusiastic, with a sufficient amount of enthusiasm so that he inspired others to follow his lead. His t-bars were not weak, but strong. He had a clearly defined goal, and knew where he was going. If he had not been interested in body building, he might have been a builder of houses, or bridges, or might have chosen anyone of several other trades and professions and he would have gone far because he had the thinking habits that lead to success.

● **MANY-SIDED TALENTS**

Whenever you do something for someone you naturally like to have credit, and an analysis made for Siegmund Klein more than twenty years ago must have had a great deal to do with plans in life. At any rate, when he wrote the story of his life for a popular magazine he devoted a considerable amount of space to telling his readers how much his analysis influenced him, and gave him courage to succeed.

Siegmund Klein's writing reveals far more than ordinary talent in several fields of the arts, but he elected to devote all of his talent to artistry in body building, until his studio in New York became one of the most famous in America. You will often find men and women with more than one talent, who will center all their efforts on one line. Others who are highly talented scatter their energies, trying to make a success in each field. They rarely accomplish their ambitions, because the days are not long enough. The vari-talented individual rarely has the time to cultivate all of the possibilities that they have naturally, but jumping from one thing to another they fail to bring any one to full fruition.

As you become more and more familiar with the principles in this book you will be able to do more and more examining of handwriting. Friends, and strangers will ask you to look at their handwritings, and tell them what you find. Do it. Do it carefully and do it truthfully. You never know when you will be helping a man like Klein find himself, never know when you will be giving him the encouragement he needs to push forward and achieve success.

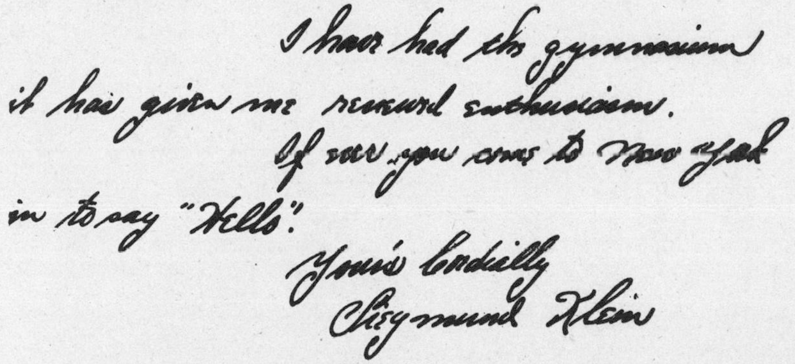
I have had the gymnasium
it has given me renewed enthusiasm.
If ever you come to New York
in to say "Hello".
Yours Cordially
Siegmund Klein

PLATE 63. One of America's most famous body-builders, Sigmund Klein, gives grapho analysis credit for much of his success.

On the other hand, here is a word of warning. You will sometimes feel that you should say just nice things to your friend or the stranger who asks you to analyze a handwriting. Tell the truth as you find it. When you do this, pointing out temper, or super-sensitiveness or lack of faith in one-self, you will be doing the writer a favor. If you dodge the truth, you will not get credit for telling the truth, on points where you are accurate.

Take next specimen for example is plate 64. This is the writing of a one-time famous circus star. He was magnificently built, but he was muscle, not brain. Muscle and emotional reaction. He had showmanship, because he was warmhearted and expressive enough to appreciate applause, but he gave everything he had to his body. Very much like the swimming star whose handwriting you have examined, he was interested in just one thing:

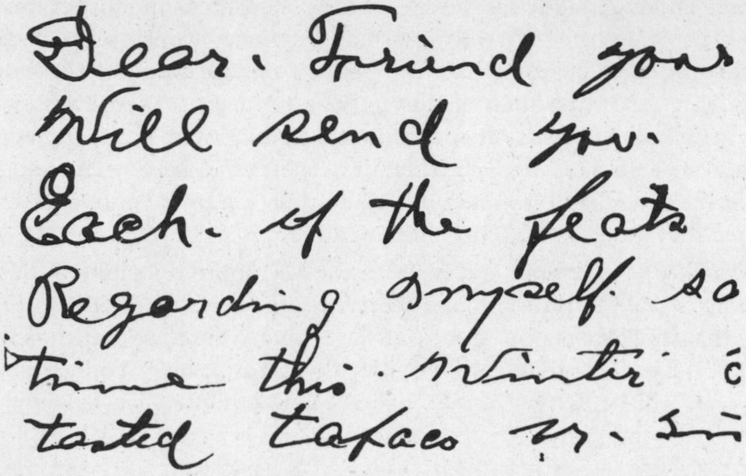

Dear. Friend you
Will send you.
Each. of the feats
Regarding myself so
time this winter c
tasted tafaco y. in

PLATE 64. A successful "strong man" whose handwriting shows him to be a non-thinker.

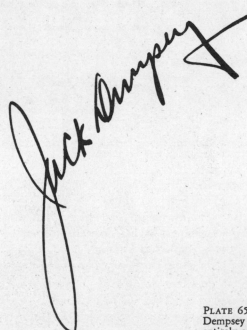

PLATE 65. While this Jack Dempsey signature is not entirely adequate for analysis it does show the writer to be decisive and mentally alert.

his body strength and his ability to demonstrate it for public approval. He was not even thrifty, so that he would not have voluntarily saved money for his old age. His strength, his ability to swing men around in the air while they held onto his long hair, was his life. Study, reading, culture or any other interest was not shown in his writing, and it was not shown in his life. He loved the applause of the crowds. He ate, slept, and put on his strong man act, and did it over and over, day after day. He has no other interest.

Finally we come to the signature of one of the greatest of the world's fighters.

If you have been a Dempsey fan, or if any one in your family has talked about Jack as a great sportsman, this signature may give you an interesting slant on the man. The inverted "v's" are prominent. There is no "e". Further, the base "v's" are prominent. Jack was an explorer, a man who found out, and analyzed what he learned. His final on the "k" shows great decisiveness. But the "p" does not show physical-mindedness or a deep inner desire for physical activity. Instead, there is initiative in the finish of the letter, but the lower part is not a loop at all. Jack Dempsey might have been a merchant, a business man—and that is exactly what he has always been.

Jack Dempsey's writing does not show a love of fighting as a sport, but as a business, approached the same as any other business. He had the

PLATE 66. After Clevio Massimo finished his musical act he returned and, stripped to trunks, put on a good muscular show. See his handwriting in plate 68.

determination to carry thru, the persistence to complete any undertaking, and the decision to come to a point of action, and then go ahead. His wide open "a" reveals frankness, and the signature as a whole is that of a man with a remarkable mind for learning and using what he learned.

In the days when every vaudeville billing had a strong man posing or performance act, one of the most clever was the remarkable show put on by Clevio Massimo. It was far more than a strong man act. It was art, pure and simple. In a full dress suit Massimo came out on the stage with his violin. He was the possessor of far more than average technique. As you study his handwriting you can see how precisely he brings his finish stroke on each letter down to the line. Give particular attention to how he brings his "m's" and "n's" right down to the line, and how he spaces his letter structures. His music in itself was worth a place on the show bill, and then

PLATE 67. Clevio Massimo as a strong man, after putting away his violin.

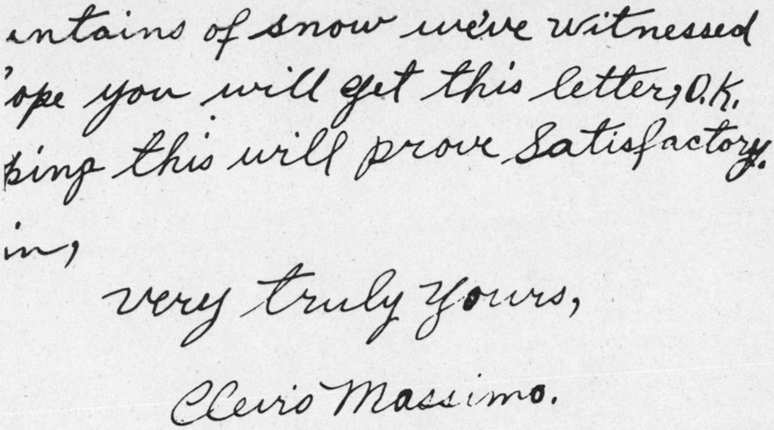

intains of snow we've witnessed

'ope you will get this letter, O.K.

bing this will prove Satisfactory.

in,

very truly Yours,

Clevio Massimo.

PLATE 68. Both music and flair for physical activity is shown in this handwriting of Clevio Massimo.

he would leave the stage and return stripped to trunks. His muscular show drew loud applause, and the combination of music and muscle made him one of the greatest artists of the vaudeville stage.

In this specimen there are only two "p's" but they both show the distinct flair for physical activity that influenced his younger days. At the time this plate was written he was a member of the police force in an eastern city—a job where physical activity is still important, and where his love of music may easily help him to reach and help those young men who find life's problems so very difficult. This handwriting of a man long past his early show days is a picture of the man when he was viewed by hundreds of thousands of ardent fans. His music is still in his handwriting. His love of physical activity is still plain, completing in his written page the story told in his photographs made a long time ago.

When Alan Stephan won the Mr. America title he had two powerful assets in dealing with the public. He had a marvelous build coupled with the fact that he was handsome, but his handwriting shows he had something much more important. He had human appeal. His emotional slant reveals that he was warm-hearted, friendly, and along with these his upper loops show a highly developed sense of philosophy. He put it this way in the specimen of writing he sent me for analysis:

"There is an old saying 'A healthy peasant is better than a sick king.' It is an old saying, but it is a true one. Few people in this competitive old world of ours can make a success of themselves if they must fight the obstacle of poor health.

PLATE 69. From Alan Stephan's handwriting you would expect to find him firm and friendly—just as he actually is.

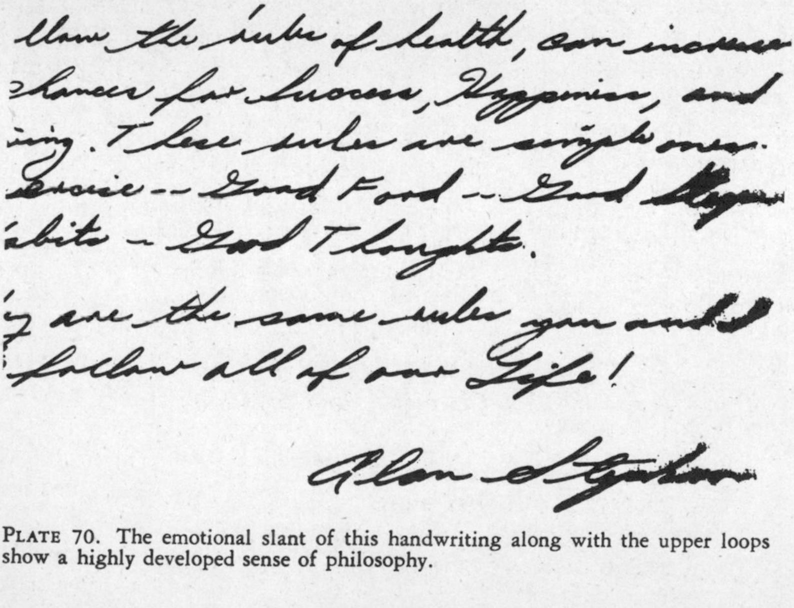

llow the rules of health, can increase
chances for Success, Happiness, and
ing. These rules are simple ones.
ercise -- Good Food -- Good Sleep
abits -- Good Thoughts.

y are the same rules you and I
follow all of our Life!

Alan Stephan

PLATE 70. The emotional slant of this handwriting along with the upper loops show a highly developed sense of philosophy.

"Some people are given a better physique or a stronger vitality by inheritance—others have to work for them. But all of us, if we follow the rules of health, can increase our own chances for Success, Happiness, and Better Living. These rules are simple ones: Good Exercise; good food; good sleep; good habits; good thoughts.

"They are the same rules you and I want to follow all of our Life."

EXAMINATION FOR CHAPTER 6
(Correct answers for this examination will be found in the back of the book.)

In this chapter you have had some very important principles to use, not only in measuring friends, but in determining the ability of an employee. Grapho analysis is usable. It is not merely a pastime like reading cards, but a science that will produce the same results in the hands of an analyst in Australia, South Africa, Canada or the United States. An analyst does not guess because these principles have been tested and proved so many times that you can depend on them.

The more you learn and use them the more certain you will be that you can depend on what you find from a handwriting by using these rules that are based on the structure of each individual letter. Letters rarely look alike but you do not need to find letters that look alike in order to analyze a handwriting and get results. For instance, in this chapter you learned about writing clogged with mud, or heavily loaded with ink. You discovered that such writing, regardless of whether it had sharp or rolling curves for "m's" and "n's" or closed or open "a's" and "o's". The letter that is muddy is not important. It is the accumulated ink that registers the sexy character.

You are not being asked to apply these rules blindly. They are being used all over the world. The writing may be in French, Italian, or English. The language does not matter. The color of the ink has nothing to do with strokes. The color of the paper has no bearing on your findings. It may be blue, green, pink or purple; the color does not matter. It is the strokes within the writing that are important.

EXAMINATION
1 . . *Does Specimen "J" in Chapter 4 show sensuality?*
     Yes_____   No_____

2 . . *Check your reason or reasons below.*
       a. SLANTS FAR TO THE RIGHT.
       b. CIRCLE LETTERS ARE CLOGGED WITH INK.
       c. EDGES OF MANY OF THE STROKES ARE FUZZY.

3 . . *Does the small "p" in Specimen "M" in Chapter 5 show initiative?*

        Yes_____   No_____

4 . . *Check the important part of the letter "p" that shows physical mindedness.*

        a. Long lower retraced stem.

        b. Lower portion of the letter is looped.

        c. The up-stroke moves sharply to the right instead of retracing or creating a loop.

5 . . *If the lower loop is very large, what will be the effect on physical activity?*

        a. Greater.   b. Less.

6 . . *Of the following statements, which are most beneficial to an accountant?*

        a. Large writing.

        b. Pride.

        c. Writing with many inverted "v's".

        d. Writing with many v-bases.

        e. Writing that is crowded or cramped.

        f. Many letters such as "m" and "n" made with rounded top.

7 . . *What does a short-stemmed "d" mean?*

        a. Pride.

        b. Care about details.

        c. Independence.

        d. Sensuality.

CHAPTER **7**

Your Handwriting can Change You

AN AMAZING DISCOVERY ABOUT CREATING A NEW PERSONALITY. HOW BILL CHANGED. WHAT GRAPHO ANALYSIS SAYS ABOUT THE AUTHOR.

"GRAPHO analysts tell us about our weak points but no one tells us how to correct them. If we can change our writing will it change us? Will we be able to overcome our weak points if we change our writing?"

Thousands of men and women in all walks of life have asked me, and asked other professional grapho analysts, this question. Twenty-five years ago it seemed like an impossible order, but it was worthy of consideration, exploration and experimentation. Would it be possible, I asked myself, to work in reverse, changing first the writing with the hope of changing the writer's character? Now the answer can be given very surely with a certainty that you can change your character if you follow certain rules. At the same time there is need for a word of warning.

Do not try to change your entire writing with any idea of changing your character traits all at once. It takes time to build a character. You began in your crib, and you have been creating your personality which is, after all, your character ever since. If you suddenly change your writing, making sharp pointed inverted "v's" for your "m's" and "n's", and start crossing your t-bars with heavy speeding strokes, and start making heavy down strokes on your "g's", "y's", and "j's", all at one time in order to speed up your thinking ability, strengthen your purpose and build enthusiasm, and also become more determined you may easily be headed for a psychiatric ward. It takes months of careful guidance under the super-

117

vision of a professional grapho analyst to make any great number of changes and they must be made slowly.

● CHANGING HANDWRITING WILL CHANGE PERSONALITY

However, there is one trait that you can build for yourself without running into any serious danger. If you are one of those shy, hesitating individuals who lacks self-reliance, you can build your own self-reliance, with reasonable safety. Before we go into how to do it, let me give you two incidents out of life. The first is out of my own life, and it was important in the research necessary to establish the fact that changing handwriting will change the individual.

Even after World War I, I was not a pusher. Actually most people who knew me probably THOUGHT I was afraid. Many years later I met a lady who knew me before World War I and she asked me what I did, and I tried to explain it to her. "Well, you may be telling the truth," she said, "but as I remember you, if you'd been a frog I'd never have bet on your making the water."

However that may be, after World War I a job was offered to me where I had to be responsible for considerable sums of money. This was a new experience. We went to the bank, and the teller gave me the signature card to sign. To this day I remember how I hesitated. Up to this time I had been very proud of my penmanship, and had followed the cue of my favorite handwriting teacher who was rated as one of the world's best. Charlie Ransom, author of the Ransomerian system of handwriting,

PLATE 71. Signature of M. N. Bunker at the time he greatly admired the showman-founder of the Ransomerian system of handwriting.

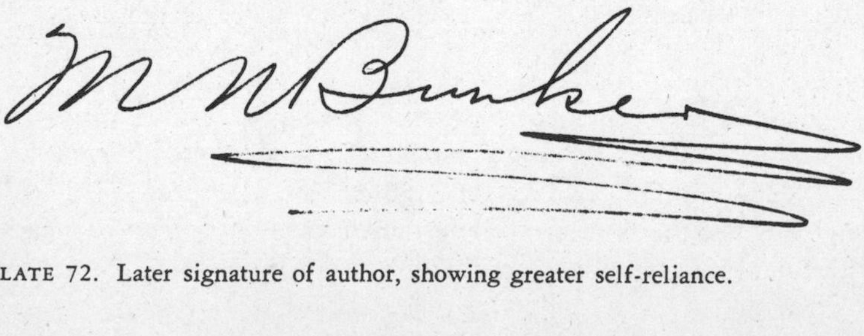

PLATE 72. Later signature of author, showing greater self-reliance.

always made two swinging circles about the last three letters of the Ransom, and I had developed the habit of writing my own name in the same way, similar to plate 71. These flourishes incidentally mean showmanship, and I was making them because I admired Ransom, who was certainly a showman. He had won the world's first prize for a set of penmanship lessons, and he used that as the basis for building the greatest school of penmanship long before World War I.

That day at the teller's window I knew subconsciously that I was going to discard those flourishes. Then I created a new signature that was to be my trade mark for more than twenty years. As I completed my name, I held the pen steady for a couple of seconds, and then wrote the heavy underscores that you find in plate 72. I had made a discovery, but did not realize it until many years after.

No matter how much of a fearful, hide-behind-the-door individual you are, you can add underscores to your signature, and you will get results in increased self-reliance. Before you undertake to make the change, however, let me tell you of just how it works in actual life.

At the time of World War II a man whom I shall call Bill, because that was not his name, was fortunate enough to gain an amusement concession near a huge army camp. When the war was over, if wars are ever over, he suddenly found himself with a hundred thousand dollars after income tax. As far as Bill was concerned, one hundred thousand dollars was riches. He had at one time more money than he had ever dreamed of having, and because he felt good about it, others soon knew about it.

When you get rich you will find that the man with money always has friends, and will also always have chances to double his money if he will just advance some to finance a man who has an idea but no cash. Bill found he had friends, and they had opportunities for him to invest in their various enterprises and double his money while he slept. Bill was rich, and he remembered the days when he had needed financing so he became a financier without any brakes. Ten thousand here, and five thousand there. He was suddenly a partner in a dozen enterprises, none of which zoomed quite as quickly as their promoters had dreamed they would. So Bill followed through and advanced a little here and more there until the day this incident occurred.

Bill was really a great chap to know. Gracious, friendly, a good conversationalist, and the kind that is usually described as big hearted. He would drop into the office, and sit and tell me how his interests would soon be paying huge profits. Finally one day he urged me to ride along while he went to the city on business.

● *$100,000 GONE*

His car was perking along perfectly when we left home, but half way to our destination, something went out. Repair men had to give service, and the check Bill wrote was around fifty dollars. He did it readily, and we went on, checked in at the hotel, with rooms connected by a short hall. That hall is important, because after I had washed up I went down that hall to Bill's open door. He was at the desk writing, and looked up with the whitest face a man could have. "I guess God sent you," he said. "Do you know I was just sitting here writing Kitty a note, and if you hadn't come in they would have picked me up off the sidewalk in another ten minutes."

Bill had written a check without funds in the bank. He had invested his hundred thousand, and none of the investments had paid off. He was disappointed, his faith in himself gone. From the joy and thrill of being a millionaire he was broke and he could not take it.

It was not a time for pretty speeches, and he kept repeating that he could not go ahead. He was whipped. He was broke. He had made his hundred thousand by a lucky chance. He suddenly realized it, and was convinced that he had no chance to ever have a second lucky break.

"All right, Bill," I said, "you'll not be any broker in two weeks, and I'll wager that you can build enough self-reliance in two weeks that you will never again consider suicide."

Bill nodded. He would make a try at whatever I suggested.

His note to Kitty gave me the information about him that I needed. His t-bars were as light as they could be. His "Bill" was nothing much but an apology. He had made his money merely by having been fortunate enough to tie up with a man who had self-reliance, and who knew what he wanted. Bill had not actually made his hundred thousand. He had merely shared in the pot because he was honest, and his partner had trusted him to count the incoming money, and keep the operation moving smoothly. Bill was not a financier, and he would never have been one if he had not been honest, and willing to work. Even then he had taken the mouse's share of the profits from the entertainment venture.

Here is what I told him to do. You can do it. You can do it and get results.

Take an ordinary scratch pad and a soft lead pencil that will not cut through the paper when you press hard in writing.

Then write this sentence crossing the t-bars heavily, as you make the "t", or as you complete the word in which the "t" is in the body of the word. After you have completed the sentence, sign your name just as you ordinarily do, and make two, three or more heavy cross-bars under the signature. You have an illustration of the principle as I gave it to Bill Bradley.

Repeat this exercise thirty times each night, just before you go to sleep. Do not skip one night, and then try to make up for it the next. "Do it every night," I told Bill. He promised he would.

A week later he dropped into the office and reported. "You know it made me sick at my stomach about the third night," he said, "I had to get up and get a drink of ice water. One or two nights I had to take an aspirin. It was doing something to me, but I've stuck to it now for ten days, and it is doing something to me."

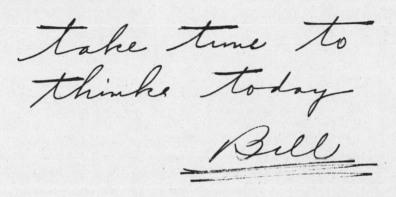

PLATE 73. A tested exercise for building up your self-esteem.

Bill was correct. He attempted too much of a change at one time. He was trying to build two traits of character, and one was enough. However, he did not suffer seriously, and he is a success today. No more suicide in the picture, no more feeling that he is a failure. However, a graduate grapho analyst would take the program slowly, adjusting the changes to fit the individual writer's needs. My experience with Bill was under the pressure of realizing that something had to be done.

If you believe that all of this is just a phantasy, and that changing handwriting will change the writer, discuss with any competent psychiatrist, and he will explain the principle. He may say that you might find it difficult to get results, but when you have tried it, and found that it is effective, you will have proved the truth of the principle for yourself.

Indeed, you will be using the same principle that I wrote into the first textbooks I ever prepared: I pass it on to you. Do not believe a principle just because you see it in print. A great many false theories find their way into type. Take every grapho analysis rule, learn it, use it, test, and prove it. Then it will not matter what becomes of this book. You will know.

● **MAKE HASTE SLOWLY**

After you have tested this principle in connection with building self-reliance you may be tempted to undertake other changes in your hand-writing. You may succeed, but I caution you to move slowly. When it comes to actually changing your character, making genuine changes, you must be careful I learned in my early days of testing that these changes must be attempted and made slowly. If, for instance, you were to attempt to increase your thinking speed and comprehension, at the same time strengthening your will power, and possibly attempting to overcome stubbornness, you might easily run into trouble. In my thirty years of experience I have found it easy to do a great deal of damage to your think-ing processes unless you attempt changes slowly, and know enough about grapho analysis to select and use changes that will not create complications.

You are safe, however, in practicing the underscore. You are certain to benefit and there are no contrary forces to worry about. Go ahead and use the simple rule that you have here. It may give you courage to get a better job, or to meet an emergency. It worked for Bill. It can work for you. It had produced for me, before I realized what I had done, when I changed that signature so many years ago.

You may have one question here that has been asked by so many thousands of men and women on coming in contact with grapho analysis for the first time. They have wanted to know, "Will my handwriting change if I change?"

● **YOUR HANDWRITING CHANGES AS YOUR CHARACTER CHANGES**

Your writing *will* change as you change. I risk the danger of talking too much about myself when I show you some of my own signature changes as they have occurred over a period of at least half a century. In plate 71, you have the signature that I lost that day when I signed the card in the bank. Plate 72 is the change I made. You may find the fact that I made that change not only when signing checks, but that it became part of my life and my permanent signature from that day, interesting. There was no slight inclination to turn back to the flourished first signature.

This signature remained a part of my thinking and writing habits for more than thirty years. During at least twenty of these years it was my lot to take the abuse, and criticism that falls to every pioneer. In the early days of grapho analysis skeptics who saw the accuracy of an analysis took refuge in their criticisms in telling me and those they met that grapho analysis was not a subject based on scientific principles, but some mystic power that I had found within myself, that it was akin to fortune telling, card reading, and soothsaying generally.

PLATE 74. This is the way signature of M. N. Bunker changed after the realization that what people thought about him was unimportant.

Some figured out to their own satisfaction that I had developed some unique bit of magic and that the whole thing was a bit of conjuring. In my research it was only natural that those who were above reproach should condemn the associates that were necessary to know people. Criminals do not fill out questionnaires in order to give you details about themselves and how they think. Therefore, it was necessary to know criminals, become their trusted confidante in order to understand how they thought, and how those thoughts were translated into pen strokes and combinations of strokes.

● SEX AND HANDWRITING

When I began my explorations into handwriting as it reflected sex desires and appetites, it was necessary to know prostitutes, rapists, homosexuals. Oh, there were all sorts and kinds of men who trusted me, and with whom it was necessary to mingle on a free and easy basis.

There were many nights I slept in the room with a sex criminal, many times without daring to trust my eyes to more than close. All of this because if I were to understand the individual it was necessary to know him as he was.

This led to criticism, sometimes abuse that to a sensitive man became a burden—and in those days I was sensitive. Finally, the realization that what people thought about me and my research was unimportant. It was the job I did that counted. The day this fact was driven home on my subconscious mind, my signature changed, and plate 74 took the place of the underscored signature. The "k" in the body of my signature developed a huge hump or upper hump, which in time I was to find revealed complete indifference to criticism.

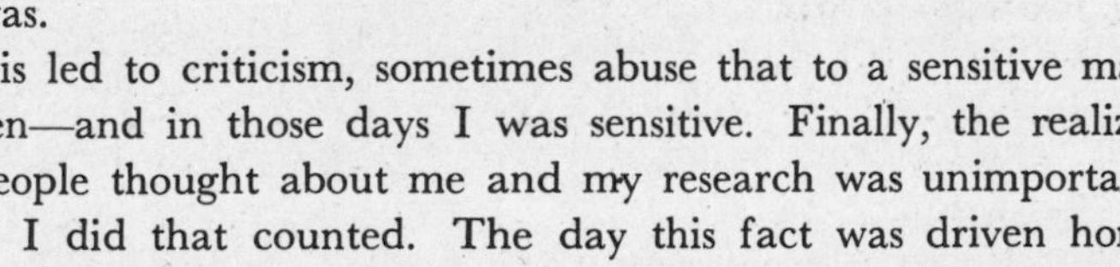

PLATE 75. A later signature of the author, M. N. Bunker. The message your mind sends through your nervous system controls your handwriting.

It is said that every man has deep-rooted desires, things he wants to do and which seem impossible of achievement; possessions that seem as unattainable as a trip to the moon. All my life I have traveled by railroad train, bus, automobile, and finally by plane. It has been nothing to sleep one night in New York, the next in Montgomery, Alabama, or New Orleans, and riding all night to be in Seattle the next day. It has been necessary if I were to know people, and get the answers to what their writing told about them. Many a day has rolled into a second without sleep. Through all of this one desire has held on with a grip that nothing could shake. I wanted a home, a place to call my own. As this desire grew, another signature developed. This is plate 75.

It is entirely possible that my signature will change again. It is just as possible, if my life had been a placid one, filled with getting up in the morning, going to the office, keeping books or typing letters all day long, my signature might not have changed. But it has, and changing it has reflected the changes in my pattern of thinking. I know this. So if your writing changes, do not worry about it. Your mind is merely sending a different set of messages through your nervous system to the part of your body that controls the writing instrument. It is not necessarily your fingers. In a later chapter you will learn that the writing of those who hold the pen staff with their teeth and lips, or between the stubs of arms can also be analyzed as effectively as though they held the pen or pencil between the fingers.

For a long time serious medical men have recognized that changes in mental condition show in the writing of the patient. Scores, possibly hundreds of grapho analysts have found this is true. Indeed, many grapho analysts without medical training have worked effectively with law enforcement officers, and medical specialists in giving them the facts revealed about a writer, by his writing.

When this is true, it is only natural that the whole rule may be worked in reverse. It seems impossible to the layman, but it has been, and is being done. You will find this is true when you use the principle of building self-reliance.

This trait is not going to give you a good personality. It was my privilege over a period of many years to watch the progress of two young people who learned of this principle, and used it effectively. They were both completely self-interested. This is a condition where a man can gain self-reliance to his own detriment. At any rate, these two fellows were as selfish a pair as have come up in my years of experiment. However, they both followed the underscore principle, and it ruined them.

One was deceitful, narrow in his views. When he added self-reliance it gave him confidence that he could profit by even small time thievery, padding bills, because he had the confidence that he could get away with it. His handwriting did not show a brilliant mind, and for a long period of time he was watched as he betrayed the confidence of an associate who trusted him. Then, without warning the self-confident young man who had used his self-confidence to bolster his life of narrow views, misrepresentation, even fraud, found himself out in the cold without a single chance. That was self-confidence built on a sandy foundation.

The other one of the two had much the same experience. He built self-confidence, with an even more selfish, stingier attitude, and though he was not thrown out he would have been if he had not had the common sense to get out just before the ax fell. Therefore check your own motives. Consult a grapho analyst if you will, but do not try to build self-confidence unless you have a character that will justify it. Otherwise your newly developed trait may drive you into a corner where you will suffer not because of grapho analysis, or the fact that you have gained self-confidence, but because your general character structure was one that would not carry such confidence.

The chap who has the self-confidence to think that he can scheme and work to steal, and betray and ruin gets the rewards of those characteristics, and because he is self-confident about it, multiplies his results from the other traits—and they are rarely good.

EXAMINATION FOR CHAPTER 7

If you have used the principle explained in this chapter you have gained. It is possible that you may be self-reliant, not afraid. If this is the case, you are fortunate. A majority of people are afraid. They may not have the slightest idea what they fear, but they are afraid. Cornered, they will admit it.

The principle in this chapter is easily tested and produces results. Just a few weeks ago Jimmie who has always run away from school, a job or anything else in life he found difficult, was given the simple exercise. At first he forgot every other night and then tried to make up for lost time by doing the exercise twice as many times in order to make both his maximum and minimum as instructed.

When he discovered that such slip-shod methods did not work, he settled down and stuck to his exercise every night. That was less than six weeks ago and he is doing better on his job. He is not nearly as ready to quit or give up in the face of emergencies.

You have no test for this chapter, but instead, are asked to try the test of self reliance. Prove for yourself the difference in thirty days. But remember, every night you must do the exercise, not once in a while. Like Jimmy you will soon see the reasons for regularity and will benefit from it.

CHAPTER 8

Handwriting Reveals
the Famous

*FAMOUS PRESIDENTS AND THEIR WIVES:
HERBERT HOOVER, GROVER CLEVELAND,
WILLIAM HOWARD TAFT, THEODORE AND
FRANKLIN ROOSEVELT, JAMES A. GARFIELD.
MRS. THEODORE ROOSEVELT, FRANCES
CLEVELAND, MRS. HERBERT HOOVER, BESS
TRUMAN, MAMIE DOUD EISENHOWER. OTHERS,
INCLUDING EDWIN BOOTH, WENDELL PHIL-
LIPS, BEATRICE HARRADEN, THE AUTHOR OF
"CURFEW SHALL NOT RING TONIGHT", FON-
TAINE FOX AND TOONERVILLE TROLLEY;
OTIS SKINNER, EMILE COUE, REV. CHARLES
COUGHLIN, WHITTAKER CHAMBERS, AND
ANDREW CARNEGIE.*

You live every day of your life as part of the greatest show in all history. You wake up and listen to long political speeches on your radio; you hear the neighbors quarreling in the next apartment one minute, and making up the next. You listen to evangelists who make every effort known to public speakers to stir your emotions, and you listen to and watch the latest TV star.

All of these and countless other actors touch your life each day, but you know only what you see and hear. Your whole understanding of them might be changed if you could only see how they think, what is back of their various emotional appeals. Then you would know them, and could value or devaluate them according to the true man or woman who is back of the decorative curtain.

You can have this knowledge. You CAN. You have already had numerous keys which will be worthless unless you use them. You have learned to determine the emotional nature of a writer—and as you go through life you will find many speakers who seem to be highly emotional, who stir your own feelings, who are merely putting on a show, and are deep within themselves cool, calculating.

● **GRAPHO ANALYSIS HELPS YOU REALLY UNDERSTAND PEOPLE**

When you know, you will not need to worry about what someone says about someone else. It may be someone in the public eye, or it may be one neighbor talking about another. With grapho analysis you will know, and knowing you will be safe in drawing your own conclusions, and making your own plans. You will be protected against phony sales appeals, regardless of whether they are religious, political, or a matter of offering you a chance in a lifetime to buy something that really has no value to you—but which the sales promoter is glossing over with appeals, while underneath he is planning to take you.

It will not be necessary for you to distrust someone because his hair is curly, or believe that the woman across the back fence is a thief just because she was in your living room a few minutes before your purse disappeared from the coffee table. If you have her handwriting you will know positively whether she can be a thief. All day long you will have protection, and much more important each day will be filled with a new appreciation of the people with whom you come in contact, regardless of whether that contact is over radio, your telephone, in your own kitchen or office.

In exactly the same way you can know your ancestors, and the people, men and women, who have made history, in music, art, literature, politics. You can check back and understand the people who are gone, and who

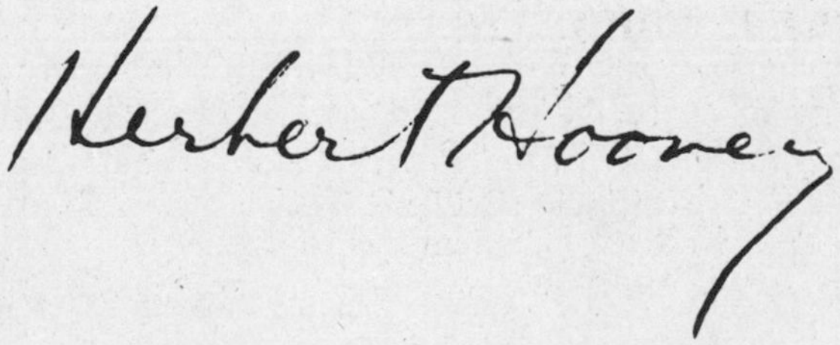

PLATE 76. Herbert Hoover. Notice the well-rounded o's and e's, showing broadmindedness.

PLATE 77. Grover Cleveland. Analysis of his signature bears out what history knows of his nature. For example, short d-stems show his independence.

by their activities have, in some way or another affected your daily living today. Grapho analysis makes all of this possible, and the more you learn, and the more you use what you learn, the more quickly you can read an old letter found in your attic, and know the personality of the writer, or examine a history book with the signature of some famous man or woman and know something about the writer as he lived, affected the lives of others, even down to the present time.

Here, for instance, is the signature of Herbert Hoover, the man who bore the brunt of the blame for the depression of the 30's. This signature gives a very interesting picture of the man, not merely as the chief executive of the United States government, but the man. The tall plain capitals show a man without fear, but one who would not cross the street to attract attention. The well-rounded "o's" show amazing breadth of view in regard to other people and their rights. Although Mr. Hoover is known to all Americans as a member of the Quaker faith, he would certainly never be prejudiced in regard to other people's religions or politics. This is verified by the two well-rounded "e's", the first one in the last half of the "Herbert", and the second in the "Hoover". However, one of the "e's" is closed, showing that he was capable of having a closed mind on matters of a personal nature. When you take the three "e's" you have the major evidence in favor of broadmindedness. He was something of a dreamer, and very much a creator. You have already learned the value of the flat top "r's", and well rounded "n's", and Herbert Hoover had the flat topped "r's" of an engineer. He was a simple, quiet man, confident rather than weak, and economists who are untinged by political prejudices admit today that Hoover had nothing to do with the depression. No more than you or I, and as an engineer he lacked the ability to do the dramatic thing to take the minds of the people off their financial problems.

Well before Hoover there was Grover Cleveland, with wide open "o's" and the open "d", who was perfectly frank, and had the ability to stir emotions in others because he was personally a highly responsive emotional man. His short-stemmed "d" registered his complete indifference to what others might think of what he did or said, while the very short points on the "n" reveal that he was not a student. Instead he formed surface opinions, based on surface knowledge, and with such knowledge possessed the emotional appeal to sell his ideas to others.

PLATE 78. Compact signature of William Howard Taft shows his conservatism.

William Howard Taft was a man who expected to rule. The slant of the final stroke in the capital "t", and the last stroke in his signature both show a desire to tell others what to do. His compact writing revealed his conservatism. He was not a man to throw away a dollar, while the initial hook that occurs in the capital "W" shows a strong desire to possess. The small "m" reveals an eager desire for knowledge, which, of course, was verified by his appointment to the Supreme Court, where he was for years the Chief Justice.

Two Roosevelts served as President, and though Franklin D. held the office for three full terms and was elected for a fourth, he did not have much more of an appeal to the voters than his distant cousin Theodore had in his day. The only difference was that Theodore followed the precedent of only two terms for a President of the United States, and Franklin D. broke the precedent. Both men loved to talk. Their neighbors could have easily classed them as "mouthy"; both were highly emotional in their appeal to the public, but here the difference began to show.

Theodore was more of a waster than Franklin D., whose handwriting showed his very genuine absence of generosity or freedom in regard to

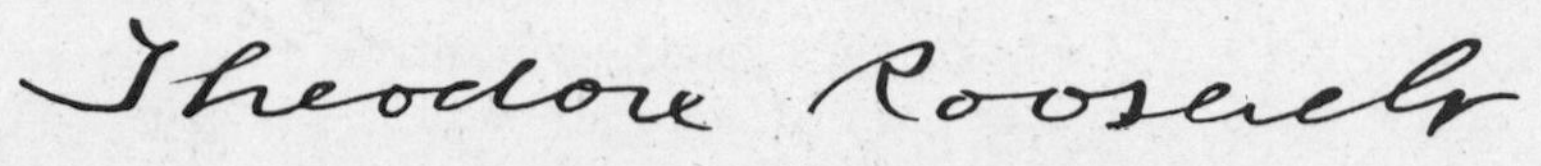

PLATE 79. This signature of Theodore Roosevelt would indicate that the writer of it was talkative and emotional.

spending. Critics of Franklin D. have pointed out that though he spent money lavishly in government operation, he was not spending his own money. His signature shows conclusively that those critics were right. Franklin D. Roosevelt was not a generous man. He was a dreamer, with a vast amount of personal pride that at times reached the point of near-vanity. On the other hand, Theodore did not give a continental whether people liked what he did or not. That short "d" in "Theodore" shows his complete indifference to convention or customs.

Franklin D. possessed one trait that his biographers have missed almost completely. Commentators, politicians, historians since his death have all commented on his unusual ability to catch and follow public opinion long before others sensed it. This was natural. Examine the letter Roosevelt sent me in 1939 (chapter II, plate 10) when I made his grapho analysis. At that time I told him his single greatest trait of character was his psychic sense, or the ability to feel what people were thinking before they were conscious of their own thoughts or desires. This made him a master politician, not super intelligent, because his handwriting does not reveal it.

He was a weak-willed, actually purposeless individual except as his psychic sense caught the drift of feeling, and then he was determined in carrying out a project.

Where Theodore did not care whether his actions caught the public fancy, Franklin D. loved the limelight, and did everything possible to focus that light on himself. In this he was peculiarly selfish, but contrary to the insistence of many of his critics, this writing does not show he was stubborn. He was opinionated, and there was another reason he would not admit defeat. He was exceedingly self-conscious and all history shows that the self-conscious individual, having taken a stand, will not admit that he is wrong. Franklin D. Roosevelt was exceedingly self-conscious—just as the small child, speaking his first piece in the second grade may be self-conscious, and afraid of what people may think or say.

Incidentally, although it is past history now, Franklin D. wrote me saying that my findings that his self-consciousness would make him un-yielding, and his psychic sense would guide him, was correct.

PLATE 80. James A. Garfield. The small d indicates independence and other signs point out that he was a good organizer.

Two presidents who were the subjects of assassins' bullets—James A. Garfield and William McKinley—are next analyzed. Garfields signature (plate 80) shows a man capable of organization with the same independence that is revealed in the Theodore Roosevelt small "d". Garfield, however, was not the talker that either of the Roosevelts were, instead was more likely to keep his own council in many things. We know this from the fact that the capital A is wide open, but the small one is closed, although not tied. Garfield was an organizer, a trait that was not true of either of the Roosevelts.

He was not a particularly brilliant man. The point on the "r" is nothing more than a tiny hump, and the small "i" is very short. However, Garfield stood up well in comparison to William McKinley (plate 81), whose "n" and "m" were almost shapeless, indicating a man who merely gathered surface knowledge. The two men had another trait in common. Although Garfield had organization ability he did not have any interest in details, and this was even more clearly shown in the William McKinley signature where not one of the three "i's" is dotted.

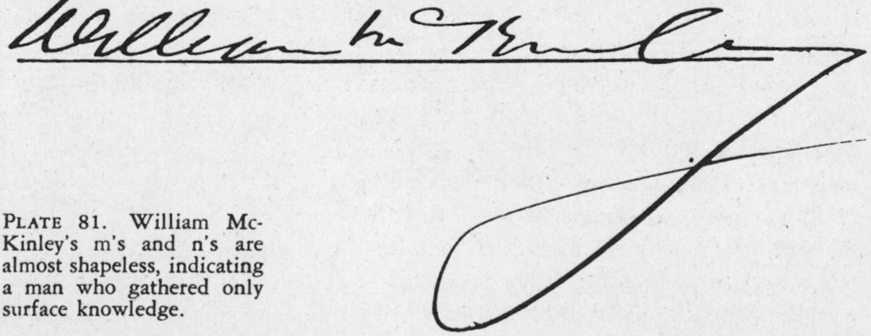

PLATE 81. William Mc-Kinley's m's and n's are almost shapeless, indicating a man who gathered only surface knowledge.

Summing up this evidence as it was written by each man about himself, there is nothing to identify an unusually strong character, or man of unusual ability so that the old joke about the average American looking forward to the time when his son may be president is not to be discouraged. Indeed, the average president has been just an average man, and as as leader of the United States has been just as subject to mistakes as any man in a lesser plane of influence. With the exception of William Howard Taft and Herbert Hoover, all of these men were strongly responsive to emotional appeals, and so capable of appealing through their own emotions to the emotions of the great mass of voters.

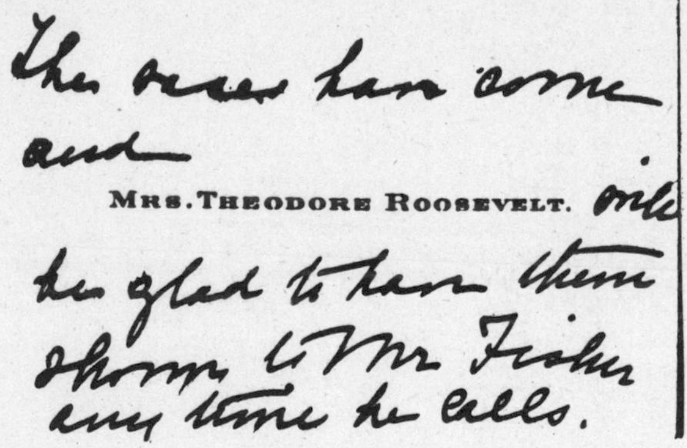
The roses have come and
MRS. THEODORE ROOSEVELT.
will be glad to have them shown to Mr Fisher any time he calls.

PLATE 82. Mrs. Theodore Roosevelt. Sharp pointed t's and wedge-shaped m's and n's indicate brilliance.

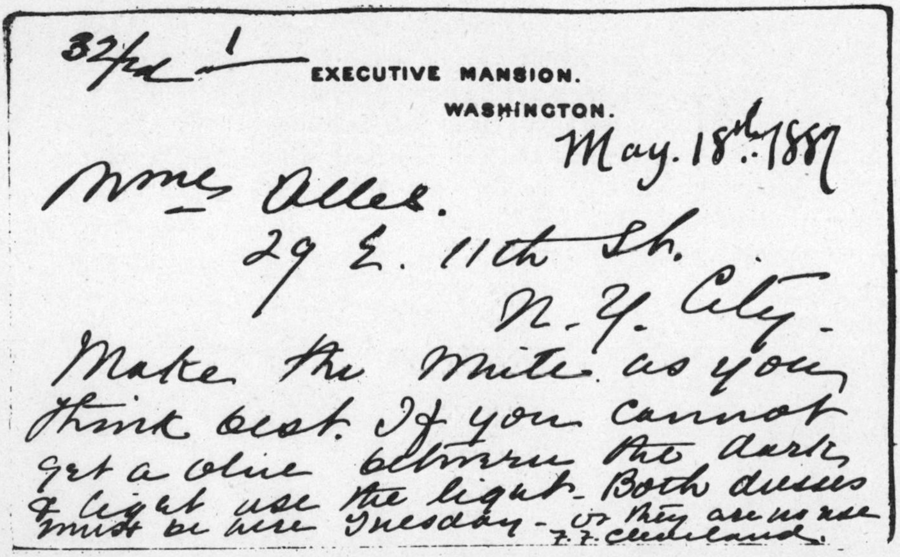
32/ed 1
EXECUTIVE MANSION.
WASHINGTON.
May. 18th 1887
Mme Allee.
29 E. 11th St.
N. Y. City.
Make the suite as you think best. If you cannot get a blue between the dark & light use the light - Both dresses must be here Tuesday - or they are no use
F. F. Cleveland.

PLATE 83. The handwriting of Mrs. Grover Cleveland indicates that she had a better mind than that of her husband.

Their wives, too, are interesting not merely because they were wives of presidents of the country, but because, as every wife is well aware, the wife has an influence on her husband and what he does. Mrs. Theodore Roosevelt was a brilliant woman shown by her sharp pointed "t's" and wedge shaped "m's" and "n's". She was decisive, and just as independent as her husband.

Frances Cleveland possessed more of a learning mind than her husband, although his grasp of surface ideas was much quicker than that of his wife. It was Mrs. Garfield, though, who had concentration as indicated by the very small handwriting. She could give her entire attention to one thing at a time, and this little specimen of her writing shows that she was very frank in all of her dealings with family, friends and even strangers.

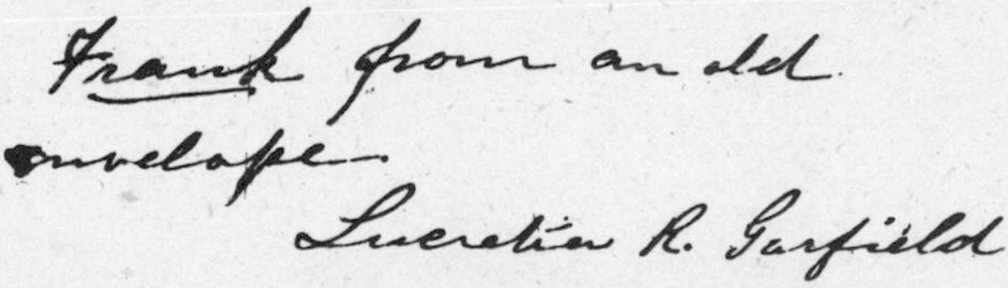

PLATE 84. Mrs. James A. Garfield's small handwriting indicates concentration.

You will find it interesting to compare the Hoover handwritings. This specimen is part of an autograph, and reveals Mrs. Hoover's high emotional response, friendliness, warmth and brilliant mind. Study the m-points which reveal her exploratory thinking, and the down-stroke showing determination.

PLATE 85. Lou Henry Hoover (Mrs. Herbert Hoover) reveals exploratory thinking in her m-points and determination in her downstrokes.

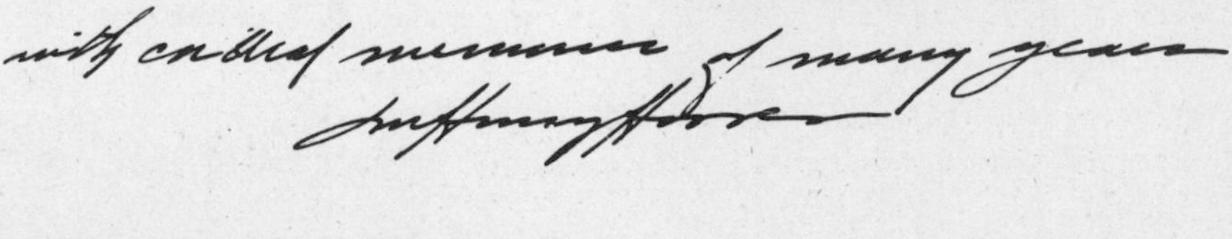

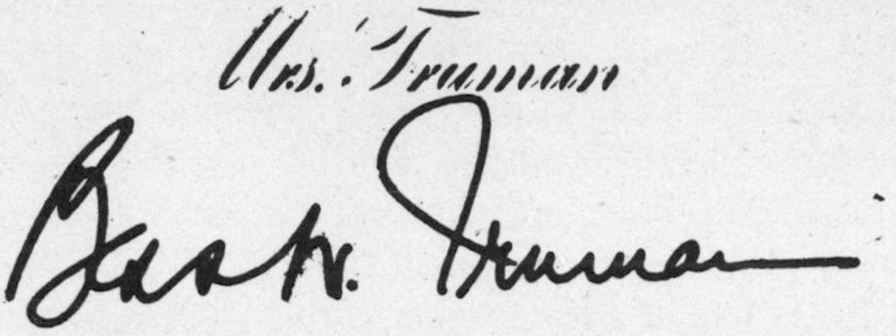

Mrs. Truman

Bess W. Truman

PLATE 86. Interesting signature of Mrs. Harry S. Truman.

Both Bess Truman and Mamie Doud Eisenhower make an excellent showing as wives of men in the chief office open to Americans. Both show keen, exploring minds, a genuine eagerness to learn, that has fitted them for the tremendous work that is part of the job of being a President's wife.

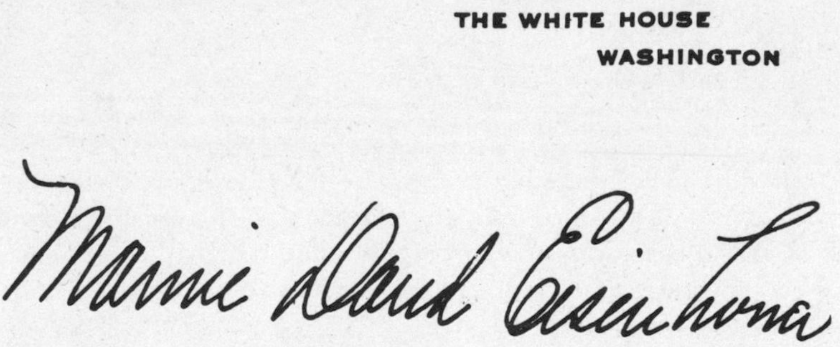

THE WHITE HOUSE
WASHINGTON

Mamie Daud Eisenhower

PLATE 87. Mrs. Dwight D. Eisenhower shows a sense of humor in her handwriting as given in this signature. (Thorough analysis is not possible from a signature only.)

Mrs. Eisenhower's signature shows a stronger sense of humor. Certainly there are few places in American life where such a trait is as valuable as it is to the First Lady of the land.

Presidents and their wives are, of course, only a small part of our American life. There have been bankers, doctors, business men, each of whom has had a terrific impact on the country as a whole. Each is worthy of your study because after all each has had some influence on your life and the world in which you live.

One of the early financial wizards in America was Clinton B. Fisk, who, according to this page, plate 88, was both a brilliant and a selfish man.

There are no generous strokes in this entire page, and the points indicating keen comprehension are long and sharp.

Also he was an irritable individual, as well as a sarcastic one. The irritability shows in the arrow-like i-dots, the sarcasm is the knife blade-like t-crossings, but there is something highly significant about these cross-bars.

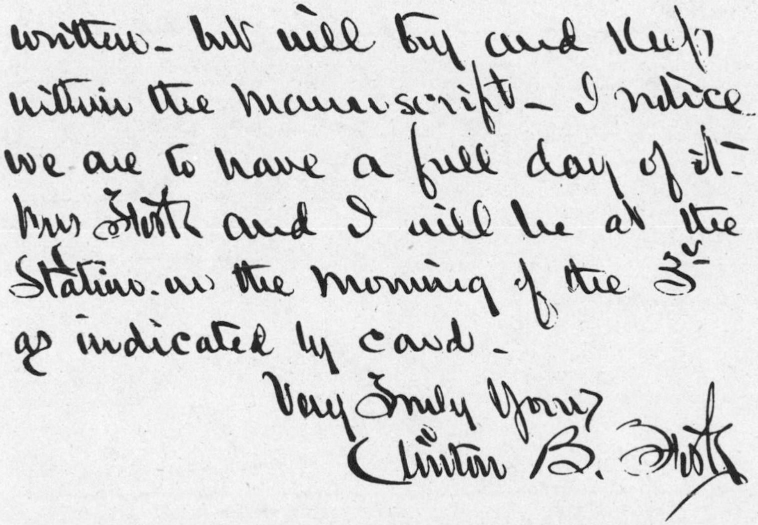
written — but will try and keep within the manuscript — I notice we are to have a full day of it. Mrs Fisk and I will be at the Station on the morning of the 3rd as indicated by card —

Very Truly Yours
Clinton B. Fisk

PLATE 88. Financial wizard, Clinton B. Fisk, shows not one generous stroke in this holograph. Notice the arrow-like i dots.

Quite a good many of them are made like inverted basins. Clinton B. Fisk was attempting to control his sarcasm, and so he bent his t-bars time and again, just as you might attempt to bend a steel bar. However, the Fisk writing does not show any real purpose in the t-bars. They are light, so that you know, as you examine the writing, that he was not a purposeful man; rather he was selfish, brilliant, irritable, and naturally sarcastic, but had made an effort, possibly only half-heartedly, to control the latter trait.

One of the greatest of early American actors was Edwin Booth, brother of Lincoln's assassin. As you examine his writing you will immediately recognize the strong emotional response the man had for emotional situations —a natural quality for a man who was to portray highly emotional scenes back of the footlights. The writing does not reveal a brilliant scholar, except under pressure. Compare the sharp points of the "n" in "Edwin" with the rest of the specimen. The signature "n" shows remarkable comprehension, but it is the only place you will find it in this page note. This is significant.

Men who handle a tremendous amount of mental work frequently reach the point where they skim over ordinary everyday activities, and do not exercise their great mental capacities. However, when you find such writing, and other lines of the same writing, or a signature that is as greatly different as in this case you know that the writer is merely skimming the surface, and is actually exceedingly brilliant. It is a striking fact that the brilliant individual will show that brilliance in any handwriting that he

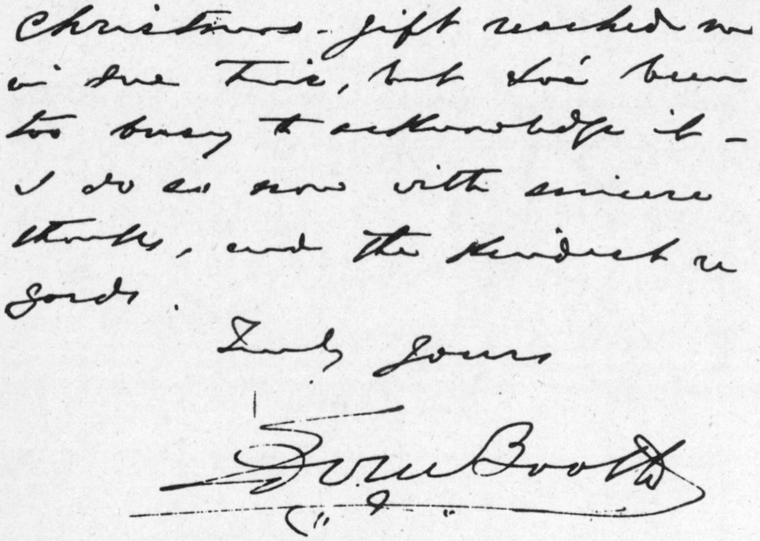

Christmas-gift reached me in due time, but I've been too busy to acknowledge it — I do so now with sincere thanks, and the kindest regards.

Truly Yours

Edwin Booth

PLATE 89. Actor Edwin Booth, brother of Lincoln's assassin, shows a contradictory handwriting—but it can be explained.

completes. He may show that he skims the surface but there is something in his mental make-up that rejects letting such a picture of himself go out to the public, and he will reveal his true mental ability somewhere in a page or even in a few lines. Edwin Booth did it, and though the writing seems contradictory it is not. It represented the two sides of the man's nature: One to hurry, give little if any attention to matters he considered uninformative, and then draw on the vast reserves of his mental ability when he needed to do so.

This specimen is included here to show you that you should in fairness to the writing you will attempt to analyze have enough evidence to draw an honest conclusion. For a great many years men and women who had read a book of some kind on handwriting analysis would set themselves up to analyze handwriting from a line or a signature. It cannot be done accurately. For instance, if you had only the Edwin Booth signature you would see the truth about the man's ability, but you would not have the complete story, i.e., that there were many times that, though brilliant, he was entirely indifferent, actually did not take the trouble to use his mind on matters that he considered unimportant.

Wendell Phillips was an impassioned orator a hundred years ago. He was—but why discuss the man's past? You have his character shown in this five-line specimen, along with his signature. He, like Edwin Booth, was capable of feeling and showing how he felt—and so capable of stirring and swaying the feelings of others. He was capable of mild enthusiasm. The reason we know that his enthusiasm was not strong is because the long t-bars are very light. He could feel enthusiasm, but he had to depend on his emotional appeal to stir his listeners.

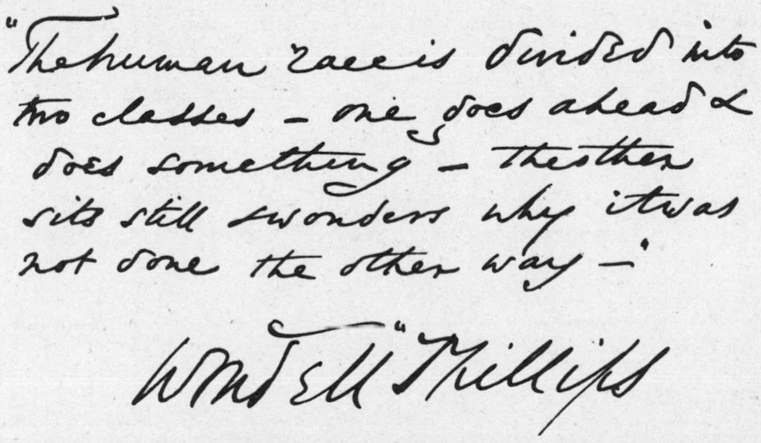
"The human race is divided into two classes — one goes ahead & does something — the other sits still & wonders why it was not done the other way —"

Wendell Phillips

PLATE 90. Wendell Phillips, famous abolitionist, had long t-bars but as they were very light his enthusiasm was not strong.

He lacked imagination, but he had a consistently eager mind when it came to learning. As he learned he had the ability to take what he learned and turn it into a message that was based on his capacity to stir the feelings of others. He has three "e's" made like the Greek "e", showing minor, but not a dominant interest in culture. Combine this quality, however, with the frequent breaks between letters in words, and we know that it was easy for him to appreciate, and possibly write music or verse. If you check the man's history you will find that his speeches, and his life reflected both of these traits, so that living now you can look back and understand the man AS HE WAS while he was living, and making his part of history.

● "SHIPS THAT PASS IN THE NIGHT"

When I was in the grades, many years ago, our country school had a library of possibly a hundred volumes which I read and re-read. "Vanity Fair", and the poems of Robert Burns, and many others, but one volume stood out in my memory, and though the book is long out of print, you may find it in an occasional library. If you do, read "Ships that Pass in the Night", by Beatrice Harraden. It was a psychological novel, written long before psychological novels were thought about, and long after reaching adulthood I offered rare book dealers $25 to get me a copy. The offer did not bring results, but one day browsing in a Chicago book shop I found a copy for forty cents, thereby saving twenty-four dollars and sixty cents.

Why did that story make such a lasting impression on my memory? Let us see what the handwriting of the author says about her. First of all, you will recognize the remarkable concentration. This intensifies every

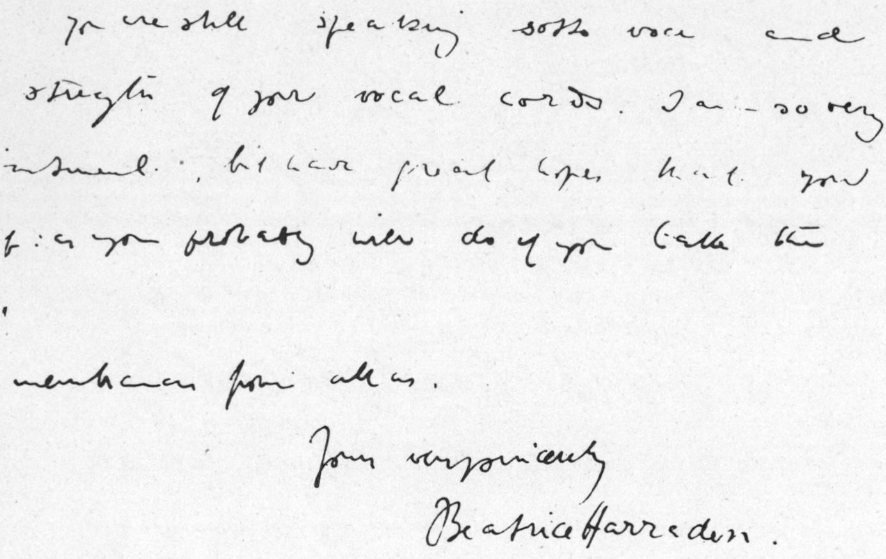

PLATE 91. This handwriting of Beatrice Harraden, author, is revealing in many ways. For one thing, it shows almost complete absence of emotionalism.

other trait shown, just as if you were using a high powered magnifying glass. Much of the writing is without formation, the habit of many who do a vast amount of writing that is necessary but unimportant. Here and there you will find a large but never completed lower loop—an imagination never put to its full use. A high percentage of her small "g's" are made like badly formed figure 8's, a sure sign of literary adaptability. Such writers frequently succeed without any seeming reserve of ability, because of the talent they have for weaving word patterns. There are numerous tiny ticks or dashes that may not reproduce well in this plate, but which reveal a consistent state of irritation. Not vigorous, not apparent to others, but still annoying like a bug that gets under your collar on a spring day.

Some of the "d's" are looped, showing sensitiveness, and of course the concentration increases the sensitiveness, but even the most liberal interpretation of the looped "d's" will not give Beatrice Harraden more than a mildly sensitive nature. There is one trait that you have all the way through this writing that explains the quiet calm of her story.

There is an almost complete absence of emotionalism. The book left a cool, quiet, soothing effect. It told a story. It did not have any message, it was not an appeal to feeling, but rather a story well told. That must

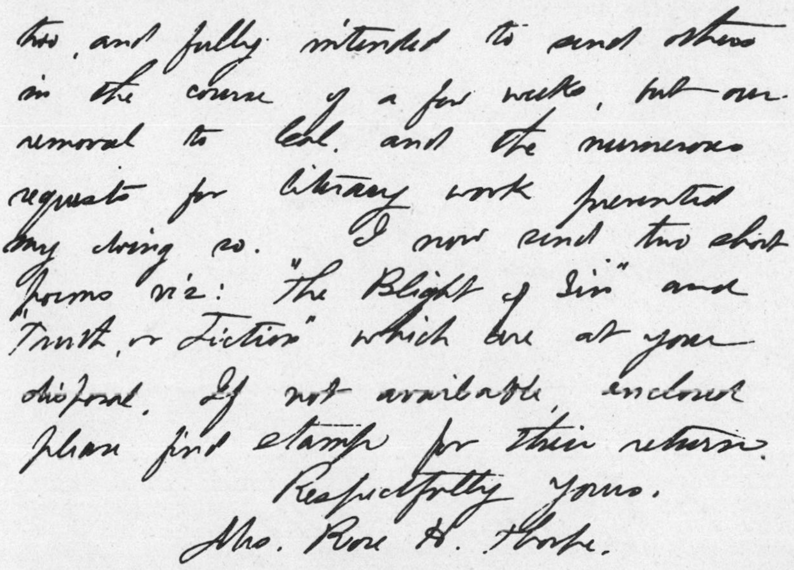
two, and fully intended to send others
in the course of a few weeks, but our
removal to Cal. and the numerous
requests for literary work prevented
my doing so. I now send two short
poems viz: "The Blight of Sin" and
"Truth, or Fiction" which are at your
disposal. If not available, enclosed
please find stamps for their return.
Respectfully Yours.
Mrs. Rose H. Thorpe.

PLATE 92. Rose H. Thrope in her d's and t's, especially, shows many interesting traits. She wrote "Curfew Shall Not Ring Tonight."

have been the reason that book made such an impression on the boy of twelve who read it, re-read it and remembered it all through the years. This may be a free endorsement, for a book you may find entirely too late, but if after a hard and distressing day or week, or longer period in life, if you can locate "Ships that Pass in the Night", it may give you relaxation that you will not find in any book published in the last half century.

Another writer of the long ago who made a name for herself in every home in the land was Rose H. Thorpe. Her name is not well remembered. But her "Curfew Shall Not Ring Tonight" was a favorite on public school closing days when Johnny or Mary stood before the room filled with parents and loudly spoke a piece—and that piece was the ballad that Rose H. Thorpe wrote while still a school girl. It was published in 1870 and from a Detroit paper that used it the verses went all over America.

The slant shows emotional response, and appeal. The letter structures are close together but are evenly spaced, showing rhythm. Your attention is called particularly to the way in which most of the "t's" and "d's" are made. There is an upstroke, and then a downstroke that is well separated from the upstroke. When the two strokes are made as they are in this

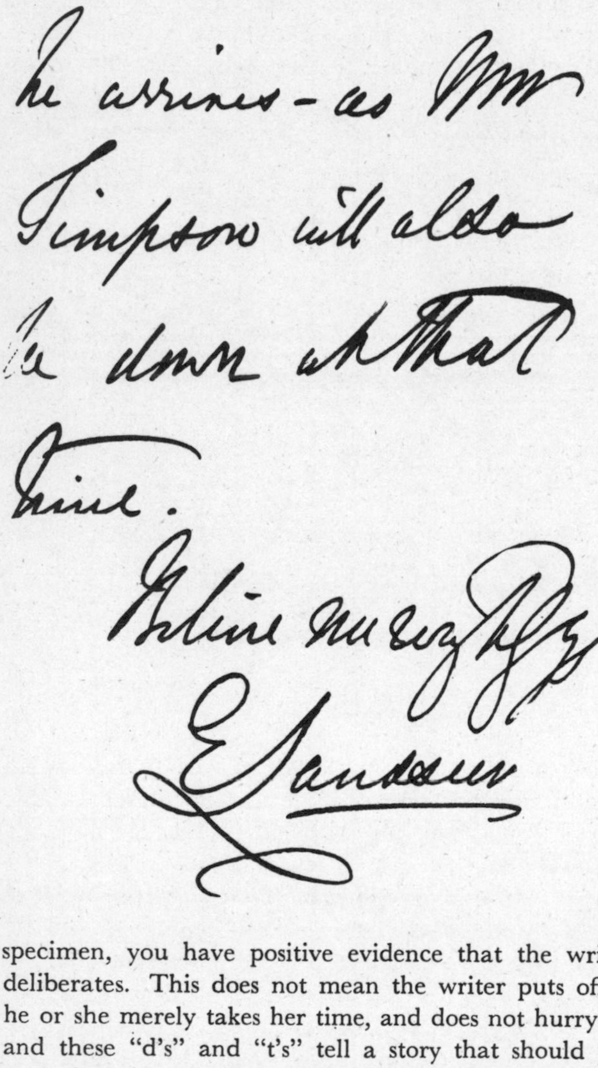

PLATE 93. Handwriting of Landseer, the great artist, which gives you a remarkable illustration of one dominant character trait.

specimen, you have positive evidence that the writer will not hurry; he deliberates. This does not mean the writer puts off doing things; instead, he or she merely takes her time, and does not hurry. The slant, the rhythm and these "d's" and "t's" tell a story that should provide a basis for you ,to find many other interesting traits in the author's writing.

You may be interested in comparing the writing of Ella Wheeler Wilcox (chapter 2, plate 5), and Mrs. Thorpe. Ella Wilcox was the most

popular romantic versifier in the early days of the 20th Century. She was
read and admired all over the Western Hemisphere and in Europe. She
was extremely impulsive, a woman who hurried all the time, who had a
brilliant mind, but never took time to relax. Mrs. Wilcox wrote me while
on shipboard bound for Germany. "I deserve no credit for my success. I
write because I must. All her life my mother wanted to write verse. Instead
she had the hard work of a Wisconsin housewife, with a family. She
worked, and I write because she wanted to do so. People say that I am
writing something that helps them, that makes life happier for them, but
it is my mother who deserves the credit. I do not."

● PRACTICE REGULARLY TO GAIN SKILL

You may find this specimen interesting, just to work it out for yourself, and get your own analyses. After all, you have had a great many
principles explained to you and there is nothing in this writing that you
cannot handle. You can determine how much of a learner Mrs. Wilcox
was; you can tell whether she was sarcastic or domineering—and if so,
when. You can determine for yourself whether she was a frank, or independent woman, and finally you settle for yourself whether her emotions
were deep or short-lived. Do these things for yourself, and you will gain
confidence in the rules you have studied.

Your next two specimens provide the work of two great artists, each
famous in his own field. The first specimen is the writing of Landseer, the
great artist, whose writing gives you a most remarkable illustration of one
particular character trait. Study those cross-bars for the "t's"; long, sweeping, the first exceedingly heavy, showing great force of will. The second
lighter, but each is made with a long bow-like stroke, which is proof of
great conscious self-control. A professional analyst could take this page of
writing and tell you exactly what the great artist was controlling, but the
point of real value to you is that these two strokes illustrate in an effective
way how self-control is shown in cross-bars for the "t".

The second specimen is from my collection secured from one of the
great autograph dealers who have been locating specimens of rare handwriting for me during the many years that grapho analysis has been developing. The comic strip artist, Fontaine Fox is gone. James Montgomery
Flagg, who made this drawing of Fox has been forgotten by all except our
oldsters, but the Fox handwriting still endures a permanent picture of the
man, and how he thought and worked.

Give attention to the cross-bars of the "t's". There are just two, and
they reveal much that would have been important to anyone working with
the great cartoonist. In case they did not understand the trait of character
expressed by these two t-bars, they might have run into trouble. Fontaine

PLATE 94. Three words and a signature tell you much about Fontaine Fox who made friends of millions of readers who followed his "Toonerville Trolley" cartoons.

Fox wanted what he wanted when he wanted it. Both t-bars are written well up on the stem, one of them almost at the top of the stem.

The man was working toward a goal. He was not exactly a dreamer according to the evidence in the last t-bar, but he was not a chap who sold himself short on what he could do. As a result, he knew that he going some place, and the weight of the t-bar is strong enough to show that he had a very clear picture of where he was going. When he wanted help he wanted it. Anyone working with him would have been better qualified if he had read Elbert Hubbard's "Message to Garcia" with its terse message to the young worker to get things done, and not stand around asking questions. These two t-bars within themselves give you a picture of an important trait the artist had and which directly affected his associates, and those around him. Get it done. Get it done now.

PLATE 95. Long under-scoring shows self-reliance in the signature of Otis Skinner, great American actor. Tremendous capacity for colorful expression shown in this heavy writing.

He may have been domineering, but he was also broad-minded, as his well-rounded "e's" show. Both of the points on the two "s's" are exploratory, showing an eagerness to learn, which the weight of the strokes in "with" in particular show a strong sense of color. Keep in mind that in using the word "color" the actual meaning is that he had a strong taste for anything that appealed to the senses, colors, tones, odors, even the sense of touch. He would have preferred to touch something with a sensuous reaction to picking up stones, but if the stones were brilliant hued, he might have found them interesting.

The American theater never had a greater name than Otis Skinner. You can find some of the reasons in this brief autograph. Sometimes you can get a great deal from only a few written words. In other cases, because there is not much in the writing, you need a full page or even pages to get a clear picture of the writer's thinking and character.

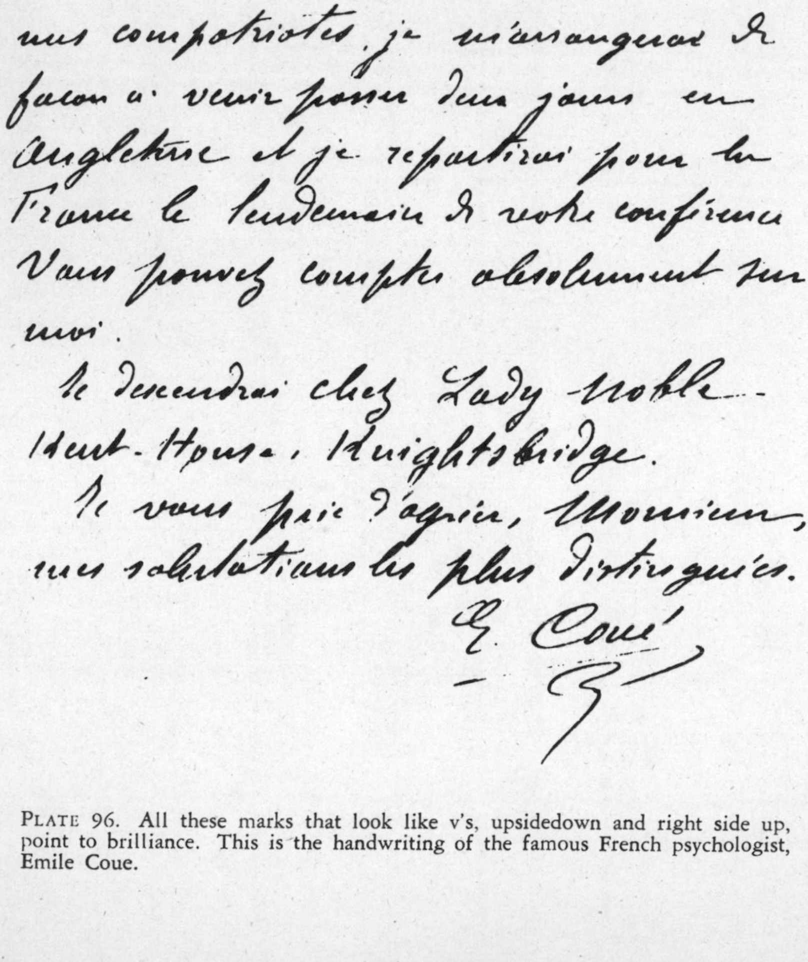
mes compatriotes, je m'arrangerai de
façon à venir passer deux jours en
Angleterre et je repartirai pour la
France le lendemain de votre conférence.
Vous pouvez compter absolument sur
moi.
Je descendrai chez Lady Noble
Kent House, Knightsbridge.
Je vous prie d'agréer, Monsieur,
mes salutations les plus distinguées.
E. Coué

PLATE 96. All these marks that look like v's, upsidedown and right side up, point to brilliance. This is the handwriting of the famous French psychologist, Emile Coue.

Otis Skinner was not afraid. That long underscore shows his self-reliance. It is long, sweeping, and grows heavier at the right of the long stroke. That indicates a man who was not only self-reliant, but forceful, overcoming obstacles. The increasing weight of the stroke has the same value as the long, sweeping t-bar that grows heavier from left to right. There is increase of purpose, or force to overcome obstacles, or objection.

Otis Skinner's comprehension worked like a needle. His i-dots show irritability and his down-strokes reveal determination. Otis Skinner was self-reliant and the things he started he would carry through because of his determination.

Right after World War I the western world was treated to a visit from an eminent French psychologist whose books became household musts in millions of homes. His suggestion "Every day in every way I am getting better and better" was repeated by hundreds of thousands of old and young who believed that the suggestion would set their world right. This French psychologist was Emile Coué, whose handwriting is exceedingly interesting because of his impact on the post war years in America. As you examine it you find that there is a preponderance of sharp upper points, and that the base joinings between strokes are sharp wedges. Actually Coué's writing was largely a matter of "v's", rightside up and upside down. You do not need to read French to know that this man was brilliant, one who would do endless research, who was not a dreamer, but a severe analyst of everything

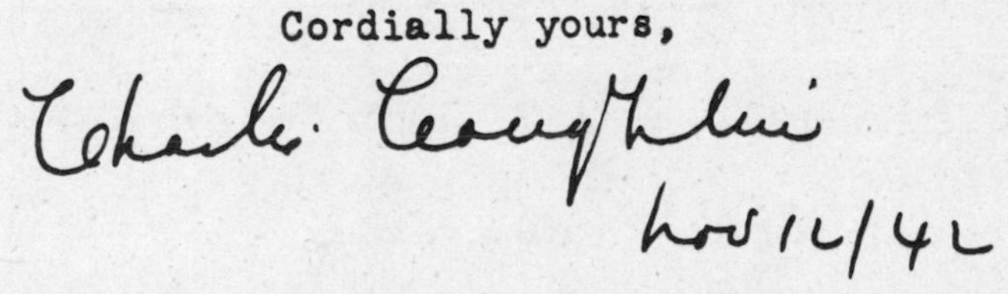

PLATE 97. Handwriting of Father Charles Coughlin, radio priest of the mid-thirties. On the emotional scale this writing measures vertical to slightly back-hand, indicating a cool objectivity.

he learned. Although he was friendly, he was not an emotional extremist, he did not plunge into any project impulsively nor rush headlong into any decision. It is interesting, isn't it, to understand a man whose message you may not be able to read, but whose picture of himself is so clearly defined in his handwriting.

During the depression years of the 30's there was no more vigorous radio speaker than Charles Coughlin, a Catholic priest in a suburb of Detroit. His enemies called him a rabble rouser, his followers swore by him as a great man. Let us see what his own signature reveals about him. First, this writing is vertical, to slightly backhand. Such writers are cool, objective, rather than impassioned. And if they make high emotional appeals it is because their judgment says it will be productive of results.

Such writers look after themselves, especially if there is no evidence of generosity in the writing, and there is none in this signature. The small "a" and "o" are completely closed with ink. The n-points are sharp, but they are exceedingly short. The same sort of point is used for the "r" in "Charles". The closed "e" in the first name is made into a point, but it too is relatively short, considering the height of the writing. All of this evidence shows that Charles Coughlin was a man whose information was gained from the surface rather than from scholarly research, and his messages were studied appeals based on his own best interests. He may have been an advocate of many reforms, but this writing shows a man who was interested in reforms for his own personal interest, not for the good of the world.

After World War II most of the world was in a dither regarding what the Communists would or would not do. Plate 98 is taken from a letter written by a man who acted as a spy, turned reformer, and became one of the most controversial figures in spy history of the 50's. The writing is exceedingly heavy. Much of it is muddy. Almost every circle is closed.

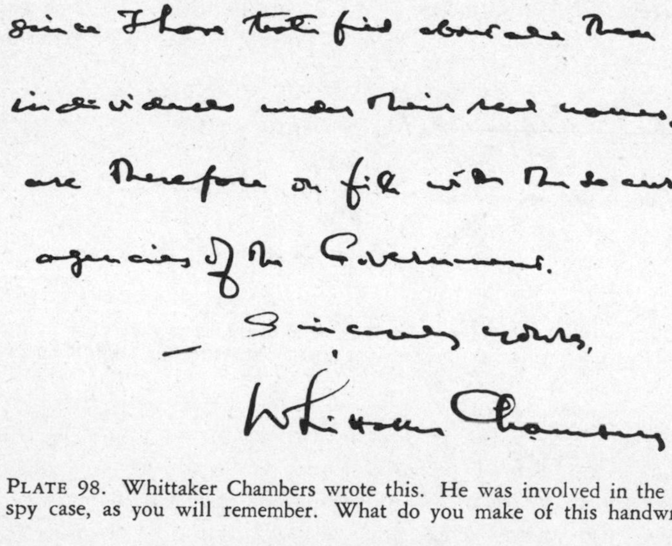

PLATE 98. Whittaker Chambers wrote this. He was involved in the Alger Hiss spy case, as you will remember. What do you make of this handwriting?

There are no upper loops showing a complete lack of philosophy or spiritual outlook. Instead the writing is that of a rank materialist whose appetites are strong. The "d's" and "t's" are short-stemmed, and time and again the "d's" are looped, but the sensitiveness would never have much affect on the writer's conduct. He was too completely indifferent to what others might think and say to be hurt easily. The vertical writing revealed a writer who was ruled by self-interest, who acted only in his own interest. This would be true when he was a spy, and later when he confessed and participated in an effort to reveal what he knew as a spy for Russia.

This is the writing of Whittaker Chambers, one time a member of the staff of TIME, the man involved most deeply in the Alger Hiss case that has made spy history in a land where politicians, ministers, teachers, and business men alike are subject to the strain of worry concerning a possible next World War.

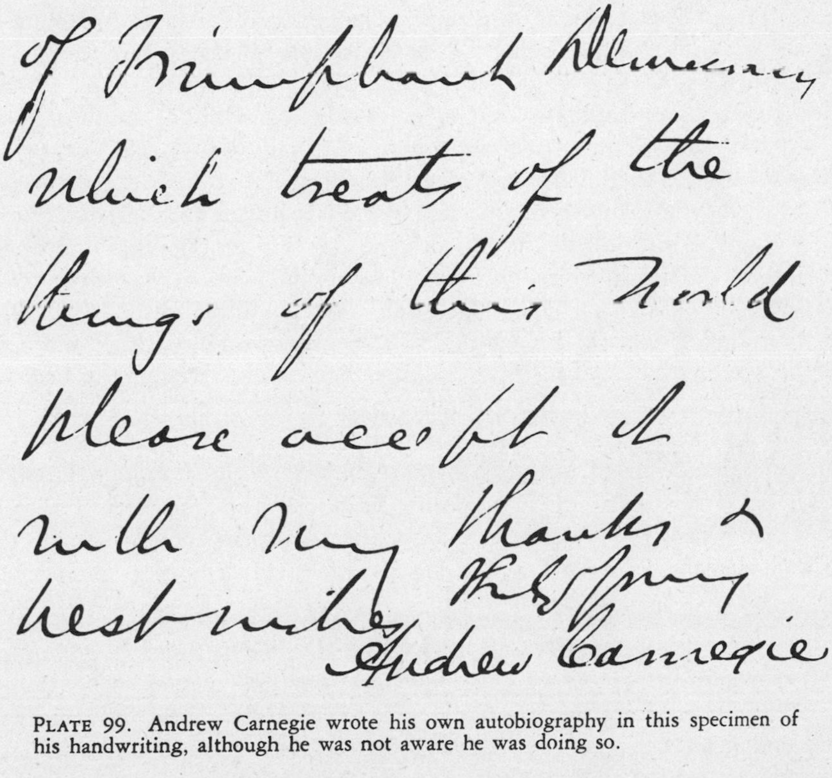

PLATE 99. Andrew Carnegie wrote his own autobiography in this specimen of his handwriting, although he was not aware he was doing so.

You started this chapter with the study of a great engineer, and now you have the handwriting of a man responsible for scores of libraries across the country—a man who was mighty in the steel industry in the early days, a man who was accused of many bad traits by those who hated him, and lauded by those who benefited by their dealings with him. You can make your own discoveries about the man, and know him, not as his own age and generation knew him, but as he was, and as he revealed himself in his writing almost a hundred years ago.

It was the great British dramatist and author, Oscar Wilde, who wrote, "The one duty we owe to history is to rewrite it." You will be redoing history as you get an objective understanding of Carnegie, one of the western world's first great millionaires.

First of all, he is not selfish, nor stingy. He was kindly, but not intensely sympathetic. He was not in any sense stingy, nor selfish, but neither was he generous. His thinking was not that of a great scholar, but a man who skimmed the cream of information, and went ahead. His writing shows a very considerable development of imagination that was never put to active use. He was broad-minded, with a highly developed sense of philosophy or spirituality. He was exceedingly diplomatic, and his tastes were simple. If given the food that he would like he would have chosen plain fare, and his clothing and surroundings would have been in line with his choice of food. His pride was strong, sometimes almost reaching vanity. He was frank, talkative, rather than highly secretive.

He was quick to see an opportunity and take advantage of it, but though he was one of the world's richest men, he was not impatient, domineering, nor sarcastic. His determination, once he started a venture, was very strong, but he was not strong-willed, nor capable of seeing a long distance purpose, and working toward it. Instead he had to see opportunity as it existed, take advantage of it, and push forward rather than being far-sighted in business or social life. In simple language, he was something of an opportunist, who did not hesitate to push forward when opportunity developed.

This is Andrew Carnegie's story of himself, written more than sixty years ago. It is a true picture because he created it as he wrote this note which you have reproduced here. So you see you can actually rewrite the history of men, when you have their own stories of themselves as they put those true pictures into handwriting.

EXAMINATION FOR CHAPTER 8

(Correct answers for this examination will be found in the back of the book.)

In this chapter you have had a great many rules. Some of them you will undoubtedly miss on first reading, yet each is important and will make it easier for you to understand vital facts about any writer.

In preparing these chapters it has been the purpose not only to give you rules, but to present them as they are illustrated by the handwriting of men and women who have made a place in history. This has been done because to merely give you rules would mean very little. You must understand how the rule applies to individuals and the way they live. If the president of a great corporation is sarcastic, it means that he will be less successful in handling a highly sensitive employee. On the other hand, if the employee whose "t's" and "d's" are made with large loops is carrying an unnecessary burden, he will suffer many times without reason.

Your own knowledge of grapho analysis as you gain it will be of little use to you unless you can put it to use. When you get a hand written letter, go over it letter by letter and check it for everything you can find. When you do this you will be surprised many times how much the handwriting has helped you understand the reasons back of the letter. This is true because people act and write as they think and you are gaining a key to understanding how they think. Learn every rule and do not be satisfied with anything less than a perfect score on these questions.

EXAMINATION

1 . . *What does the flat topped "r" indicate in connection with the writers' natural aptitudes?*
    a. LITERARY ABILITY.
    b. CREATIVE ABILITY AS IN ENGINEERING.
    c. ANALYTICAL ABILITY.

2 . . *What would you look for in a handwriting to determine if the writer had "hunches" or a "psychic sense"?*
    a. LARGE WRITING.
    b. SMALL WRITING.
    c. FLAT TOPPED "R'S" AND WELL ROUNDED "M'S" AND "N'S"
    d. CONNECTED WRITING.
    e. FREQUENT BREAKS BETWEEN LETTERS OF A WORD.

3 . . *What letter structure reveals frankness?*
    a. CLOSED "A'S" AND "O'S".
    b. LARGE LOWER LOOPS.
    c. LOOPED "T'S" AND "D'S".
    d. WIDE OPEN-MOUTHED CIRCLE LETTERS.

4 . . *What reveals the ability to concentrate?*
    a. WRITING SLANTED FAR TO THE RIGHT.
    b. LARGE WRITING.
    c. TALL D-STEMS.
    d. SMALL WRITING.

5 . . *What stroke reveals an effort to gain self-control?*
    a. LONG SWEEPING T-BARS.
    b. T-BARS BENT DOWNWARD AT EACH END.
    c. DISH SHAPED T-BARS.
    d. SHORT T-BARS.

6 . . *What does a Greek "e" signify?*
    a. MUSICAL ABILITY.

    b. STUBBORNNESS.

    c. CULTURAL TENDENCIES.

    d. SENSUALITY.

7 . . *Sensitiveness is shown in what letters or letter?*

    a. LARGE LOWER LOOPED "G'S".

    b. LOOPED "D'S" AND "T'S".

    c. RETRACED STROKES FOR "P".

    d. SHARP POINTED "M'S" AND "N'S".

8 . . *How are t-bars that show sarcasm made?*

    a. ARROW-LIKE STROKES, HEAVY AT THE START, THIN AT THE FINISH.

    b. WITH BLUNT, CLUB LIKE ENDS.

    c. LONG, SWEEPING STROKES.

    d. CURVED LIKE A BASIN.

CHAPTER **9**

Are You a Criminal Type?

*A NEW LOOK AT CRIMINALS AND WHAT
MAKES THEM. THE AUTHOR IS SWINDLED;
THE TRAIN ROBBER WHO REPEATED; THE
HOLD-UP MAN WHO LOST HIS HEAD—A
HOTEL REGISTRATION CARD WARNING—THE
CHANGE IN A WOMAN MURDERESS—THE
"NICE" MAN WHO KILLED.*

You have heard the term "criminal type". You may even have used
it, and thought you knew what you were talking about. Actually crimes
in the general sense are not committed by "types" but by people who pass
among their neighbors as good fellows, or swell girls, but who have some
weakness. Then at an opportune time the weakness and the temptation
chance to coincide and they commit a crime that under other conditions
they might never have thought of committing.

Although research in what is now grapho analysis started in 1910, it
was not until fifteen years later that I had a really striking example of such
a coincidence. In 1924 a detective magazine was being published in Chicago. They called on the writers' professional journals for manuscripts, and
the thought occurred to me that what I had been doing in the way of
research might fit into that particular book. The editor agreed. I wrote the
manuscript, and because neither of us expected any terrific response, I
offered to analyze the handwriting of any reader who submitted a specimen.

Inside of a week after the magazine hit the news stands the mail carrier
was carrying huge bundles into the editor's office. The article which had
been intended for a single appearance had sparked a department. The pay-
ment for that first article is not important except in relation to something
that happened shortly after.

My new department had run for possibly two or three months when an automobile struck me and I was in the hospital unable to write a column, or do any analyses. Let me say here that in all my years of contributing to all sorts of magazines, and getting all sorts of checks, editors have been uniformly honest, courteous and considerate. A circumstance over which neither the editor nor myself had any control, had occurred, and the editor was in a jam. Any other editor would have published a box, but not this editor. He continued the department that was cooked up out of books on graphology. He put a new name at the top, and when I wrote him I was back in circulation he ignored the letter.

A long time after when I was in Chicago I stopped by his office, and found a badly flustered editor. When I remarked that he had a new writer who was handling the department differently than I had planned, he grinned a sickly grin, "Yes, you know I found a Paul Bunker out at the University of Chicago and he's doing the column. Sorry you could not continue, but I had to have copy and he gets the mail all right."

His assistants looked at one and the other as much as to say that it was the first they had heard of a Paul Bunker, but there was no use in starting any argument. The editor had found someone who would give him a hand-writing analysis department, made up of analyses, and nothing else. The analyses might have fitted almost anyone, but as far as I was concerned the incident was closed.

● **SIGNS OF EGOTISM AND VANITY**

After the demand for grapho analysis instruction had become so strong that I had established a school, my advertising manager went into Chicago, and paid the publisher of the detective magazine a visit. Then the story of the department came out. It is this story that makes this page of hand-writing (plate 100) so important. It is taken from an autographed copy of a novel the editor of the magazine had written and which I had merely put into my book shelves without opening.

It seems that when the editor of the detective book found himself without a contributor he made up his own column. He made up the analy-ses out of words, padded in a few opening paragraphs, and got away with it. That was seemingly easy, so he kept on writing the column and selling it to his own magazine, and incidentally raised the pay for the copy to $75 a month. Over the years he had collected something like $9,000 for his department which he sold to his own magazine.

When I learned the true story I dug the autographed copy out of my library, and found this autograph. If I had given it any heed earlier the story might have been much different, for this handwriting reveals just why the man pulled the trick that no self-respecting editor would have dared to do.

Earlier you learned that very tall "d's" and "t's" show vanity. You will notice that the "d" in the signature is very tall. Also that the capital letters are all out of proportion to the small letters. These exaggerated capitals show egotism. Finally, as you examine the handwriting you will find initial hooks that show a desire for possession in the final stroke of the capital "B", in the "c" in "compliments", in the way the two small "s's"

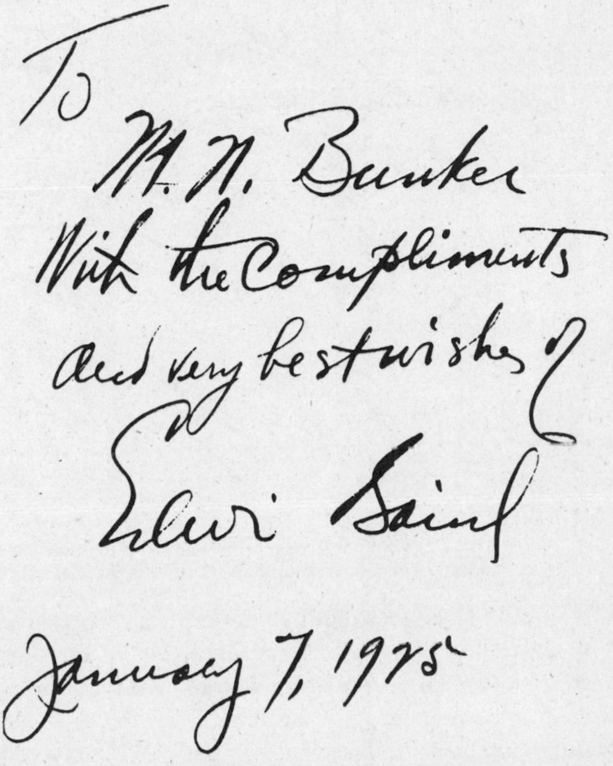

PLATE 100. Notice the beginning hooks which may be called "desire for possession" tendency.

are made in "best wishes". Each of these beginning hooks represents a desire for possession. You have already learned how to find intentional deceit. Put the deceit, the vanity, the desire for possesion, and egotism together and you have the ingredients of a swindler.

Yet to his associates he was probably a nice enough chap. He was not a "criminal type", yet he had an opportunity to swindle, and did it. Years later when I was editor of MODERN PSYCHOLOGIST I asked him to contribute an article telling just how the first magazine article on grapho analysis was ever published. He submitted it, but I did not use it. Instead, it merely went into the files, and though he asked repeatedly for his money.

he was not paid. However, the manuscript stuck to the story he had told me; that he had found a Paul Bunker who had developed the department. Up to his dying day he never learned that the treasurer of the publishing company had provided a complete record of how he had sold the manuscripts to the magazine which he edited, representing to the treasurer's office that he was still paying me, although I was not living in Chicago at the time.

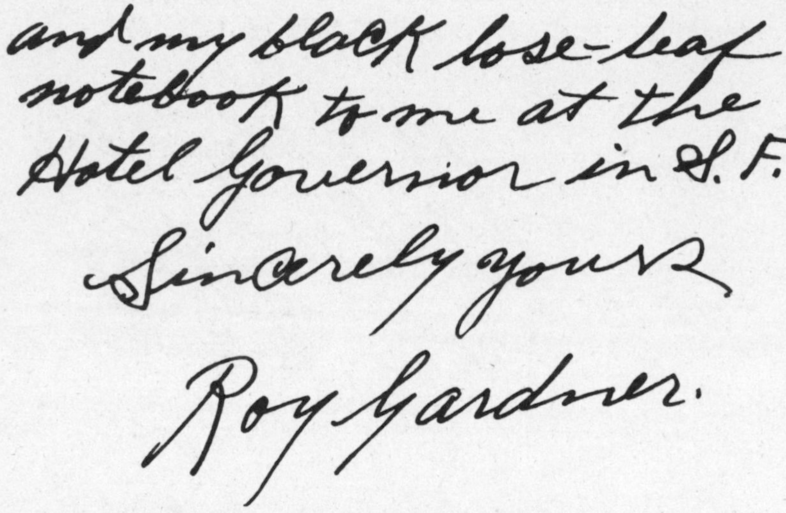

and my black lose-leaf notebook to me at the Hotel Governor in S. F.

Sincerely yours

Roy Gardner.

PLATE 101. Can you tell from this handwriting that the man was a notorious train robber? There are clear indications of dishonesty here.

Plate 101 was written by another man who certainly had plenty on the ball mentally. He might have succeeded in any one of several fields, but instead he made a record as a train robber. He would be caught, convicted and sentenced, then he turned on his personality and began using his natural intelligence. He won sympathy. He saw the "error of his ways", and if given a parole promised he would certainly become a good citizen. He won friends. He would get his parole, and then commit another hold up. He was a "criminal type", lacking intelligence. He shows in his writing exactly why he was a repeater. He was not deceitful, so when he was selling his good intentions to his sponsors he was merely using his natural warmth of personality and may have believed that if he were freed, he would go straight. But with his freedom he resented people, things, and wanted to strike back at society.

● "DESIRE FOR POSSESSION" HOOKS

Roy Gardner did not plan a crime as much as he plunged into it. He would plunge, and get caught, make good resolutions, and after serving time would win a release and repeat because he was ruled by his feelings, not master of them. Part of the reason was a desire for possession. Others had, and he wanted. In this short note there are three clearly defined acquisitive hooks, one at the start of the Capital "S", one in the "c" in the body of "Sincerely", and another starts the "y".

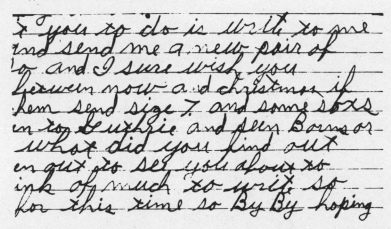

PLATE 102. The crimes of the man who wrote this could haae been avoided if someone had analyzed his handwriting in time. It is all spelled out in this piece of writing.

A professional analyst would find others in the body of some of the words, but three as clearly defined as these, are sufficient to show a strong desire for possession. Roy Gardner wanted to possess and he struck back at society in order to gain his desire. If he had not had such strong resentment, his desire for possession was not strong enough to turn him into a train robber, but the two traits fitted hand in glove to lead him to a life of crime.

A very high percentage of crimes is committed by young and old alike simply because they lack character enough to fight against temptation. Plate 102 is the writing of a man who was married. He had a wife and children, and they were in debt. The writing shows that he lacked the earning ability to bring in a comfortable income. You have already learned enough about grapho analysis to examine this page of writing and know that he may have been frank, but he lacked the ability to learn a great deal.

When faced with an urgent need for money he tried to hold up a dry cleaning shop. The young woman on the cash register resisted. He was not impulsive, but he was frustrated. He had tried to commit a crime. He had failed, so he beat the girl unmercifully and escaped. The girl did not die. He was not a murderer, but just as he had not had the courage and intelligence to face life and its financial problems he lacked the courage to face the results of his criminal attempt—so he committed suicide.

The writing in plate 102 gives a very important warning of the danger of freeing the writer. You do not need to be an expert grapho analyst to check the way in which the "t's" are crossed. Each t-bar is slanted at a sharp angle down from left to right. You have already learned that such a slant made by a strong bar indicates a writer who dominates and when the bar is made like an arrow, it shows domineering. These t-bars vary. Some of them are dominant, others domineering. Both such bars are indicative of a writer who demands, who expects others to comply with his wishes.

PLATES 103 and 104. Guilty of an atrocious sex-murder. Thomas Cochran's signature shows his true nature. Note particularly the muddy handwriting that warns of abnormal sex appetite.

Turn such a man loose without education, and his days will be very rough. Society will not meet his demands. He will not have all of the things he wants, and there will be only one way for him to get them. The criminal way.

This writer grew up on a cotton farm. As a lad he had nothing. His family lived on a hand-to-mouth basis. Poor food, few clothes, and when there was cotton to plant, chop, or pick, the family spent long back-breaking hours in the field. The boy did without things that other boys had. He developed a corroding desire to have, not through reaching or to possess, but through demanding. As a result he was on a criminal road almost before he would have been out of high school.

Sociologists may say he never had a chance. Possibly they are right, but at least you will recognize why he found his way to the penitentiary. Society, the conditions that denied him education, decent food and clothing, and because his family could not earn them from a cotton patch, explain the whys. Not that he was a "criminal type", because under normal conditions there is nothing here to show that he would not have been a "normal" boy.

This young man, Thomas Cochran, is quite presentable in the full page photograph. You might even have invited him into your home, especially if you had a daughter of high school age that you hoped might be a motion picture find. At least others who knew nothing about grapho analysis did just that when he went into one of the major hotels in South Florida, where he introduced himself as a motion picture scout. Mothers courted him, they encouraged their daughters to have dates with him, without knowing that Cochran had given warnings of his true nature in the signature on his hotel registration card. You will find it in plate 104, and have the explanation. First, the handwriting is backhand, which shows self-interest. Second, the last half of the name "Thomas" is not a blot made by accident, but a blot made because of the sex appetites of the writer.

Cochran was convicted of murdering one of his dates that had rejected his advances. His handwriting gave the warning. Muddy handwriting is always sex appetites, sex appetites out of normal proportion to the writer's personality. It is a warning that holds good every time.

Your next specimen in this chapter, plate 105, is the writing of one of the most notable women murderers in the last century. Winnie Ruth Judd lived in Arizona. She had two women friends, who later were accused of being lesbians. Newspaper reporters made much of the whisper that Winnie Ruth had become one of a triangle, and when things got hot, she killed the two women.

After killing them she packed them in a truck, shipped them to the west coast, and an express company employee investigated, discovered the bodies, and tracing the source of the trunk was just about as simple as taking candy away from a baby. Winnie Ruth was accused, arrested, tried and convicted. That is all history, and her writing is included here so that you can examine it. Check it and you will find that the years she spent in prison helped her build a new character. There is one other point you can learn from this specimen. Winnie Ruth had a rather amazing record for escapes. After gaining her freedom she had never made an effort to hide. She merely wanted out of prison.

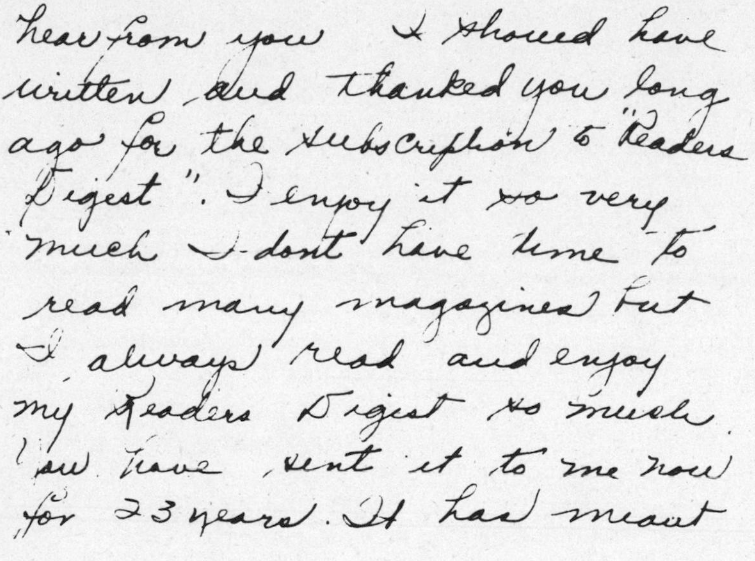
hear from you I should have
written and thanked you long
ago for the subscription to "Readers
Digest". I enjoy it so very
much I dont have time to
read many magazines but
I always read and enjoy
my Readers Digest so much.
You have sent it to me now
for 23 years. It has meant

PLATE 105. Notice these initial strokes—straight and inflexible, indicating resentment. Winnie Ruth Judd, notable woman murderer.

You have the explanation in the initial strokes in these 10 lines of writing. In "should", "written", "and", "subscription", and "so" the first stroke is straight, inflexible. Such initial strokes reveal resentment. Winnie Ruth went along for weeks and months; became bored, resentful. She wanted out of prison and immediately started figuring out how to make her escape. She was not planning to run away. All she wanted was out.

When you find such repeated resentment strokes you may know that the writer is suffering an urgent desire to get away. It may be to get away for a short time from pressing demands of business or professional life. It may be that life has become an impossible bore. The writer may not resent anyone near to him or her. The writer merely resents conditions.

You will find such instances coming up in your own field of acquaintance. I know of one that broke up a happy home because one member was so imposed upon that he became beaten down, trod upon by those who demanded his services. A member of the family knew grapho analysis and felt that she was being resented, and rejected. Home life went from bad to worse, and finally went on the rocks, not because there was any natural lack of understanding, but because the one member was so imposed upon by friends and clients that she developed a constant alertness against imposition. Breaking up the home did not change matters; the home was gone, but it did drive the professional member of the team to take drastic steps to shed the imposition. Then the writing changed. The resentment strokes disappeared—but too late.

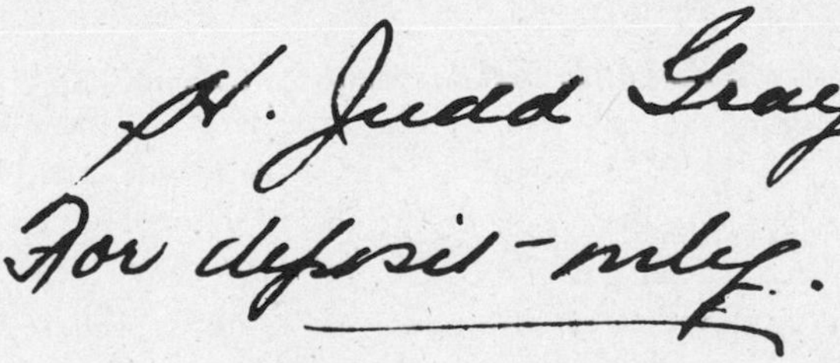

PLATE 106. There is evidence of sex desire shown in this handwriting of H. Judd Gray, murderer.

If you have someone whose writing shows these straight strokes, starting at the base line of the writing, and slanted up straight to the start of the body of the letter, do not look for something to find fault about in them. Help the resentful person who is imposed upon to free himself from the imposition. You can do it, and the strokes will disappear.

H. Judd Gray killed his sweetheart's husband. Judd Gray had a good job, he was respected, but he became enamoured of another man's wife. They became so much in love that reason or right had no part in the picture of their lives. She whispered to him. He listened. His handwriting, however, does not reveal a man who would plan a crime. The only evidence in his writing, is shown by the sex desire in this signature. It is not exceedingly strong. Judd Gray was not a sex maniac in any sense of the word. He merely became involved in an affair similar to affairs carried on by countless other married men with married women. Certainly Gray was "sexy" but only mildly so. He would not have gone out to rape and kill merely for the love of sexual satisfaction, yet he did not hesitate to hammer a man to death.

The husband was an obstruction to Judd Gray's desire, but Judd was not grasping. If he had been, the woman with whom he was having the affair would not get enough money from her husband's death to make cash or jewels a natural or strong temptation. Judd Gray committed murder because he yielded to just one temptation, and he gave up his life because he impulsively did something that he had no natural inclination to do.

Yet in all of these specimens there is a key to the weakness that led to the crime. The Cochran signature showed his over-sexed nature. Gregory Sullivan's writing showed his lack of ability to earn money, to handle wisely what he did earn, and the probability that he would go into debt over his head. It shows that he would yield to temptation because he lacked the character to not do so. Judd Gray's signature shows great independence, but it also shows dignity in his independence, yet he killed a man.

EXAMINATION FOR CHAPTER 9

You will not have any specific questions on this chapter because each point has been so completely illustrated and explained that you cannot miss any of the principles explained.

You can spend several evenings studying these specimens, not only for their value as covered in this chapter, but because they illustrate other character traits and strokes which you have already studied.

One thing has been driven home to me by resident and home students. They read a lesson, or a book, get half clear ideas and then start trying to use principles that they have not studied sufficiently to understand. This is one reason that so many of the illustrations in this book are large. Each gives you an illustration not only of a principle, but of many principles and you cannot have a better plan than to jot down various traits as you recognize them during your study of each individual plate. When you do this, you will be amazed at how much you discover about the individual.

If, on the other hand, these principles were divided up into sections, with one for example, showing "Laziness" and another, "Ambition" you would miss completely the application of the principle to life.

In the first place, no man has a right to set down a list of traits and say "these are the traits that portray an ambitious man." Those traits in themselves may be valuable, but the same writer may have other traits that completely or almost completely nullify the valuable ones. The human character is not made like a sausage, the same ingredients in each one. It is the influence of one trait on another that determines the final value. This is called evaluation, which is as vitally important to your use of grapho analysis as air is to your lungs. Therefore, do not merely examine a handwriting and say, "This writer is a dreamer" because even a dreamer who concentrates has an excellent chance in making his dreams come true.

In the same way, you cannot say "This writer is a criminal type", because as in the case of Roy Gardner, he may have some of the finest mental qualities, but one little quirk can turn all of his good points sour. Then he is a criminal, not because of a majority of "criminal" tendencies, but because of one or two traits that ruined the value of the good ones.

CHAPTER 10

There's Hope for the Handicapped

THE PARALYZED ARTIST; HAROLD WILKE AND WHAT HE LEARNED; THE TEXAS BUSINESS WOMAN; THE ARMLESS BILLY RICHARD, A MUSICIAN. BESSIE BLOUNT WHO WANTED TO HELP.

WHEREVER there is a functioning mind there may be writing, and no matter how it is written it will reveal the writer's mental habits. For example, for many years a Canadian named Andrew A. Gawley traveled with Ripley's "Believe It Or Not" shows. This was the first of many studies I have made of handless people who write with steel limbs. Since World War II there have been hundreds of veterans who have been equipped with steel hands and who write just as they did before losing their arms or hands.

In this chapter, however, you have an entirely different approach to the problem of what a handicapped person's writing will reveal about him. In each case the history has been checked, and the points covered here which you will be able to recognize from rules you have already learned, have been found to be true.

In an early chapter you learned that heavier than ordinary writing showed a strong sense of color, as well as deep emotions. There are a great many heavy strokes in the following specimen written by a young lady who had been paralyzed by polio for eleven years. Her writing as you can see, shows a highly sensitive writer. There are a great many broad-topped "m's" and "n's" and the small "r's" are flat-topped. There is imagination in the lower loops, and a highly developed spiritual sense shown in the upper loops.

161

Combine all of these traits and it is easy to understand that Aileen Lattin, the writer, has been a successful artist for many years. Her writing, even though she has no use of her hands and arms, still shows her natural talent. She began using a long brush, holding it between her teeth, and slowly, steadily mastered the technique of painting. She uses a similar device to write, and certainly her writing is clearly legible. I have never seen one of her paintings, but you will know from her writing that she has an excellent sense of color, appreciation of lines, and that her work will be imaginative.

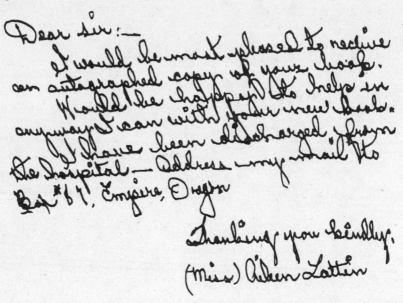

PLATE 107. Aileen Lattin has no use of her hands and arms but is a successful artist. This handwriting tells you that her work is imaginative.

There is poise, secrecy, enthusiasm and determination, in plate 108, which is the writing of Harold Wickes. He wrote me "I write with the toes of my left foot, with the paper on the floor, when I sit; or I write sitting on my desk, also.

"When I was nine months old, so goes the tale, I grasped a pencil between the toes of my right foot, transferred it to the left and started the hieroglyphics. It seems I had little difficulty learning how to write."

You will find sensitiveness shown in Harold's "d's" but not his "t's", which are, more often than not, made as straight or retraced strokes. Time and again he ties his strokes showing his persistence, which to a man with full use of his arms seems to be an important character trait.

In addition to learning writing, Harold Wickes became a complete master of dressing himself, and performing ordinary daily functions without difficulty. He learned even to tie his necktie, although some of the problems of dressing called for unusual physical dexterity. However, the size of the writing in this plate shows that when he was learning to do anything, even as a child he centered his full efforts on it.

Most surely young men of Harold's age, and young women in their early twenties can get a vast amount of encouragement from his accomplishments, and those of Thelma May (plate 109), a Texas girl, who operates her own business, drives her own car, and writes with the pen staff held between her teeth. Her emotional slant shows a friendly and warm-hearted nature that responds readily to emotional situations. In a full page of her writing you will find evidence of some self-consciousness, a highly developed philosophical nature, and considerable diplomacy. At the time this specimen was written she had just completed a very difficult selling contest in which she had proved to be the winner by a nice margin. She did not win because

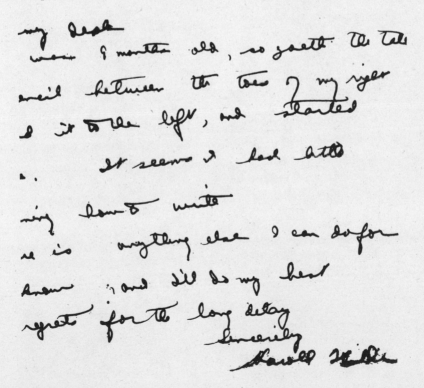

PLATE 108. Harold Wickes' "handwriting" done with the toes of his left foot. Shows same character traits as conventional handwriting.

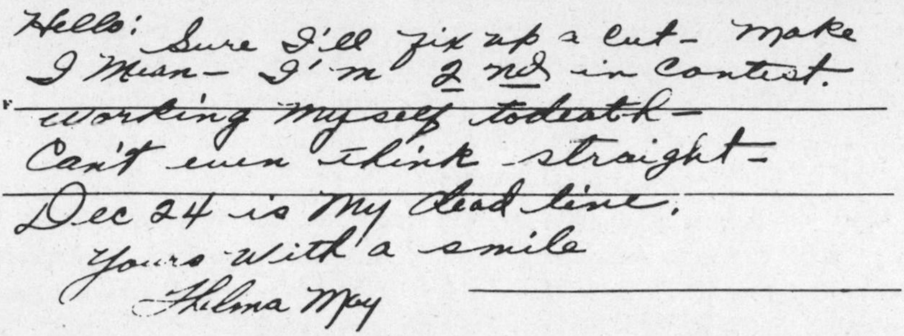

Hello: Sure I'll fix up a lot - make I Mean - I'm 2 nd in Contest. working myself todeath - Can't even think straight - Dec 24 is My dead line: Yours with a smile Thelma May

PLATE 109. "Handwriting" written by Thelma May with pen held between her teeth portrays her personality traits clearly.

PLATE 110. Billy Richard, born without arms, reveals traits through writing done with toes.

she did not have arms, but because she worked. She worked because she would not admit defeat.

It is interesting to look back at hundreds of thousands of handwriting specimens that have gone across my desk during the years, among them scores written by physically handicapped men and women, boys and girls. Almost every handicapped writer has shown persistence, the spirit that will not admit defeat, whereas this is one trait that is not common even among men and women with all of their physical powers. They are the ones who admit defeat, and cry quits, when the going gets rough. Not the handicapped folks who fight through and win.

Thelma May is more sensitive than Wilke, but neither lets the sensitiveness hurt him too badly if we are to take the evidence here, and this is final. What people may think has nothing to do with it. These two handwriting pictures are correct. They tell the truth.

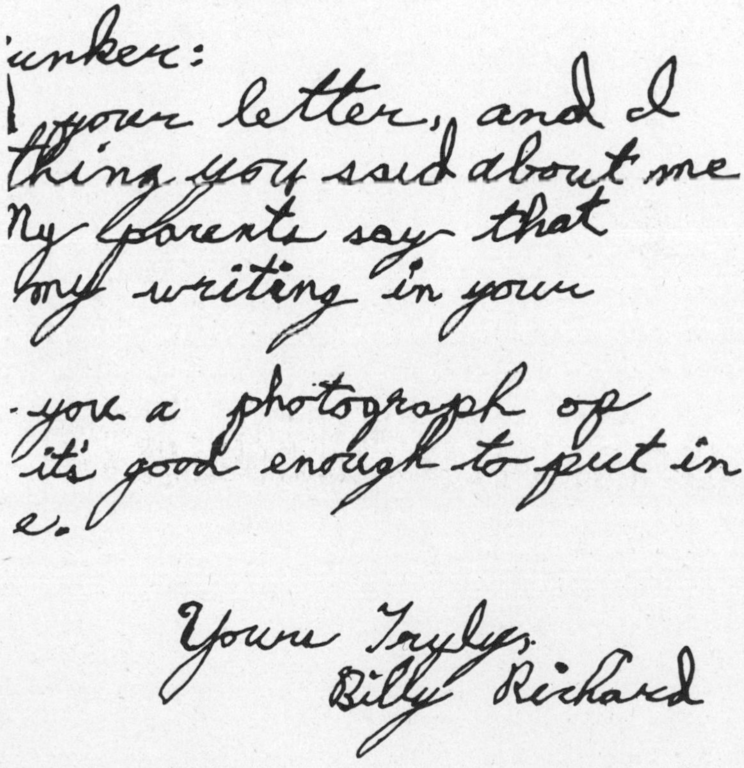
unker:
your letter, and I
thing you said about me
My parents say that
my writing in your

you a photograph of
it's good enough to put in
e.

Yours Truly,
Billy Richard

PLATE 111. Carefully dotted i's and flat r-tops say the same things when written with toes as when written with the hand. Billy Richard's holograph.

One of the most interesting cases of a physically handicapped lad I've ever seen was Billy Richard. He sent me his pen writing, for an analysis and his note included here tells the story. As you can see, he is very sensitive, but Billy was only eight when he wrote this letter. You will find his long lower loops interesting, showing as they do love of travel, change, and variety. His r-tops are flat revealing exceptional engineering and creative talent. You might expect a boy without arms to feel that he has not had a square deal out of life, but there is no resentment in Billy Richard's writing. As you examine the plate you will find a great deal of pride, while his "i's" are carefully dotted showing close attention to details.

You will find plate 112 very unlike the others, because it is from a different writer who thinks differently, acts like himself, not like others who may or may not be handicapped. This writing shows first of all concentration, the habit of centering his efforts on one thing at a time. When he

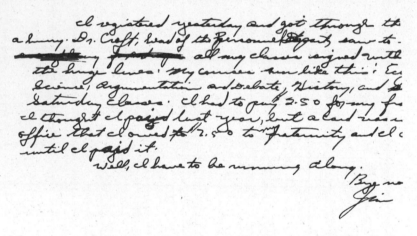

PLATE 112. A university pre-law student reveals a lot about himself in his d's, t's, a's, o's. Grapho analysis enables you to understand this young man without even meeting him. It is not necessary to know whether or not this student is handicapped.

wrote this he was a second year pre-law student in Kentucky University, and doing very well. His "d's" and "t's" show pride, and though he is generous he is not extravagant. There are many wide open "a's" and "o's" showing that he is capable of talking easily, frankly. But there are other circles that are closed so that in the sum, he will be still or secretive when he should not talk, and will talk readily when conversation is in order.

In several sentences of writing there are a good many long cross-bars for his "t's", and some are written high on the stem, and others low. This shows by evaluation that he builds a good many long distance plans, or sets a goal a long way ahead, but that when it comes down to everyday life he is very much inclined to take one step at a time. This is important.

A writer who has a long distance goal, a place in life, he hopes to originally fill, or purpose that he believes he can finally accomplish is really a very rich individual. At the same time if he has this ability, and is also capable of looking at short range purposes, he will work out the goal that is most easily achieved, and then go on from there. If his purposes in life were all short range, if he continually sold himself short on himself, he would lack the powerful force that a long distance goal gives an individual. So if some of your own t-bars are lower down on the stem, and others are at or near the top, do not become discouraged. You are far better off than if all of your t-bars are low. If they are low you should do something about it—very quickly. Do not be satisfied with merely shooting at a short range goal in life. Set it ahead. Work toward it, and your t-bars will climb slowly and steadily upward.

In a letter Ellis Phillips writes, "My fingers are paralyzed, and I cannot grip a pencil to write. However, I manage to hold a pencil between my thumbs and first fingers." As a result you have a clear picture of his thinking in this specimen. He possesses remarkable creative ability as shown by his "r's". His pride is highly developed, but as all of his lower letters are high, he does not show vanity, but pride. His "e's" arc well rounded, registering a broad-minded or generous outlook in regard to others, while his down strokes are strong, or heavy. At the time he wrote this specimen

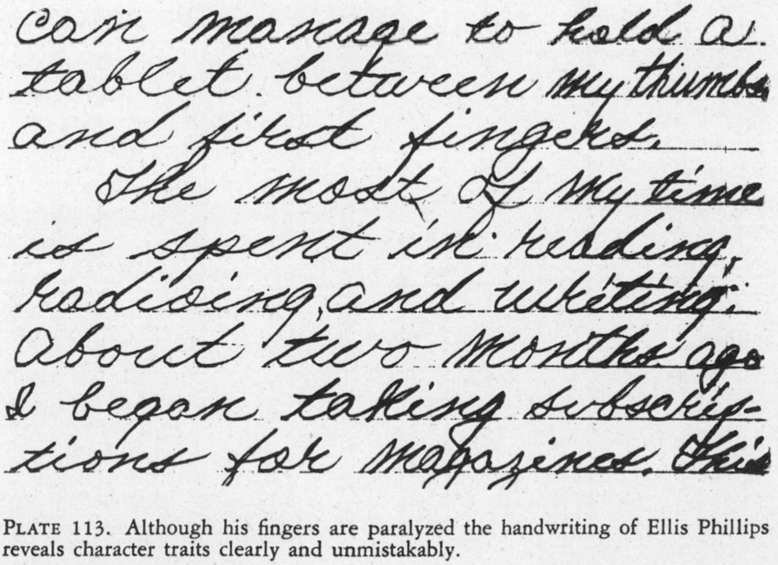

PLATE 113. Although his fingers are paralyzed the handwriting of Ellis Phillips reveals character traits clearly and unmistakably.

(plate 113) he had just started his own business, and was doing well. He does a vast amount of writing, and reading, and you will not be surprised at the latter because his "m's" and "n's" are all made like upside down "v's". Ellis Phillips does not merely read, instead he reads to get the answers, to find out, to learn.

Your final specimen for study is not the work of a handicapped writer. Instead it is the writing of Bessie Blount, who has developed the ability to write with the instrument held between her toes, and also between her teeth. Bessie Blount did not need to acquire this skill, but she did it to prove a point to her parents who had lost their arms, legs, and were otherwise handicapped. Miss Blount writes equally well with either hand, or with the writing instrument held between her toes as shown by her three signatures.

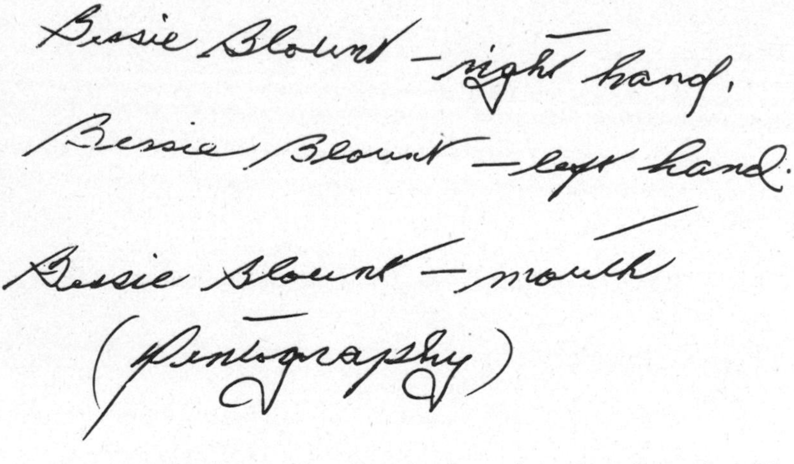

PLATE 114. Bessie Blount, although not handicapped, has learned to write holding her pen between her teeth and also between her toes. The story her "handwriting" tells is the same no matter how she chooses to do it.

Bessie is an exceedingly generous person, ready to give time or effort to help others. Her finals are long, illustrating the rule about generosity shown much earlier in this book. Thousands of handicapped men and women have heard and witnessed her lectures and demonstrations, and she is a competent grapho analyst who can not only inspire the man without arms to write, but as he acquires skill, she can determine how he thinks, and so help him overcome weaknesses.

As you study these specimens, using the rules you have learned, you may ask yourself if they do not provide something of importance to you. If you are fully equipped with arms, and legs and hands you certainly can gain inspiration from the accomplishments of these writers who have had every excuse for not learning to write. Billy Richard is an accomplished musician. Thelma May and Ellis Phillips each own a business and make it pay. Jim Lyons was attending college, planning to be a lawyer.

Each of them may be handicapped physically but not mentally, and because their minds are active they adapt their bodily equipment to meet the demands of their minds. Bessie Blount is a natural giver, one who simply had to share with others, and inspired by this inner desire, she saw an opportunity. She learnèd to do the very things that she wanted her patients to do. So she learned to use her toes so she can not only write but sew with them. She learned to put a pencil or fountain pen between her teeth, and write with it. She learned to write rapidly and easily with either hand. She did all these things in order to help others who have lost arms and legs, and whom she felt would be encouraged by what she did, not merely by what she told them to do. Undoubtedly scores, possibly hundreds of men and women who have lost an arm or both arms, have found in Bessie's demonstrations new hope.

She did it not, as she says, "because I had a college education, because I haven't. I had to dig what learning I have, but these folks needed help, and just telling the man who had lost a right arm, that he could learn to dress himself, or write, or do a lot of other things with his left, was not enough. I did it, he could see that he could do it."

Bessie shows by her long finals that what she has said is just the way she thinks. She wants to help. She wants to give and this is her way of giving.

EXAMINATION FOR CHAPTER 10
(Correct answers for this examination will be found in the back of the book.)

Review is necessary. You cannot master grapho analysis, indeed, cannot even gain a passable working knowledge of it from the first reading. Every grapho analyst has reviewed. There is no other way. There is just too much to learn, not only about the science itself, but about human nature. Each individual is entirely an individual—no two like. You many find two writings that look alike on first examination, but when you carefully check each stroke you will find that there are differences that frequently affect the conduct of each individual in a very pronounced way.

Because review is necessary, your questions on this chapter are review questions more than based on what you have learned here. This chapter was included to give you proof that handwriting, even when written by some odd means, still reveals the mental forces back of the strokes.

There is one point which should be emphasized in this connection. The truths revealed by handwriting are not judicial, and you have no right to judge others. All you analyze handwriting for is to get the truth. Just as in the case of the handicapped writers in this chapter, each individual regardless of age, is affected by surroundings and conditions. To say that one of these handicapped writers is extravagantly generous for example, is to state a fact and not criticize. Summed up, my advice to you over a lifetime of research and analyzing handwriting is simply this: Do not criticize or condemn. Get the truth, and stop right there.

ne pays for one's birth with one's life...
p - high up to the dizziest peak.
e more the grand rise of the sun.

SPECIMEN N

EXAMINATION

1 . . *Does the above specimen reveal a man who will approach projects and problems in life cooly and without emotional tantrums?*
    YES_____   No_____

2 . . *Does this writing show a deeply emotional nature, or one that has a severe experience and forgets about it in a few weeks?*
    a. DEEPLY EMOTIONAL.   b. FORGETS ABOUT IT.

3 . . *Does this writer possess concentration?*
    YES_____   No_____

4 . . *Is his determination strong?*
    YES_____   No_____

5 . . *Does he sell himself short on his own abilities?*
    YES_____   No_____

6 . . *Is there temper in this writing?*
    YES_____   No_____

7 . . *Is he positive in making decisions?*
    YES_____   No_____

8 . . *Would he prefer rich foods and fine fabrics for his clothing?*
    YES_____   No_____

9 . . *Does he have a keen, inquiring mind?*
    YES_____   No_____

10 . . *Is he satisfied with surface knowledge?*
    YES_____   No_____

11 . . *Is he a keen analyst?*
    YES_____   No_____

12 . . *Is he agressive?*
      YES_____   No_____

13 . . *Is there any enthusiasm shown?*
      YES_____   No_____

14 . . *Does he show executive ability?*
      YES_____   No_____

15 . . *Is there any extravagance shown?*
      YES_____   No_____

16 . . *Are any of the circles muddy?*
      YES_____   No_____

17 . . *Does this reveal anything about his taste for foods, odors and tones as in music?*
      YES_____   No_____

18 . . *Is there anything to indicate that he likes to attract attention?*
      YES_____   No_____

CHAPTER 11

Are Beautiful Penmen Good?

*TAMBLYN, WHOSE WRITING TOLD HISTORY;
RANSOM'S GENEROSITY; BEDINGER'S SENSI-
TIVE INDEPENDENCE AND SELF RELIANCE;
THE OKLAHOMA BANKER; TWO GREAT PRO-
FESSIONALS WERE NOT ALIKE; THE PROFES-
SIONAL EGOTIST.*

In the early days of grapho analysis one of the most interesting arguments against it was based on the idea that when a youngster learned muscular movement in school his handwriting pattern was set for life. School children learned to make their ovals and push and pull exercises in order to earn a Palmer Proficiency Certificate, or a Zaner & Bloser certificate of penmanship skill, and a great many people believed that those school days settled the matter. It did not. The handwriting of the best professionals proved it. You can see it for yourself when you examine the plates in this chapter.

The first is the handwriting of F. W. Tamblyn, a man whose advertising was carried for years in various magazines. F. W. Tamblyn began teaching penmanship by mail early in the century. He began his school while he was teaching for the old Brown's Business College in Kansas City, but as his student body grew, he established the Tamblyn School of Penmanship. Plate 115 is a reproduction of a copybook specimen from his textbook, that was provided home study customers as well as to pupils in schools where the Tamblyn system of penmanship was taught. Study this carefully, especially the way in which the "n's" and "m's" are retraced. Next, compare the Tamblyn plate with the larger specimen of the writing of Platt R. Spencer (plate 116), one of the first experts in America. Where the Tamblyn writing retraces the "m's" and "n's", the Spencer writing divides at the base line, making a clear though narrow "v" between the sections of the letters. This is just one difference, and it is important.

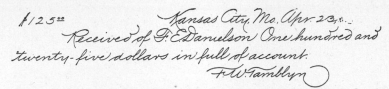

$125⁰⁰ Kansas City, Mo. Apr. 23,...
Received of F. E. Danielson One hundred and
twenty-five dollars in full of account.
F. W. Tamblyn

PLATE 115. Handwriting of professional penman F. W. Tamblyn who learned to appreciate grapho analysis.

It was inevitable that Tamblyn and I should meet, but we were never close friends. In the first place, I had studied handwriting with Charles Ransom and Tamblyn told me once that Ransom had not told him the truth, all of which is another story.

Tamblyn did not believe in grapho analysis. He would smile and say nothing when the subject was brought up even indirectly in our visits, until one day it seemed to me that his Doubting Thomas attitude had gone far enough. Up to that time I had never voluntarily examined his handwriting. You will find, as I have, that after you have been using the principles in this book until they are familiar to you, you will be able to read pages upon pages of writing without looking for the grapho analysis values except when you want to know about the writer's character and personality.

When Tamblyn handed me the specimen which he wrote at his desk, it was clear why he had been skeptical about analyzing handwriting. His well-rounded "m" and "n" curves, even the well-rounded first part of his "s's", all showed that he had to take time to think out a decision. As we covered the various points, including his lack of enthusiasm in the short cross-bars of the "t's", his strong sense of spiritual and philosophical matters revealed by his upper loops, his face relaxed, and he settled back in his chair.

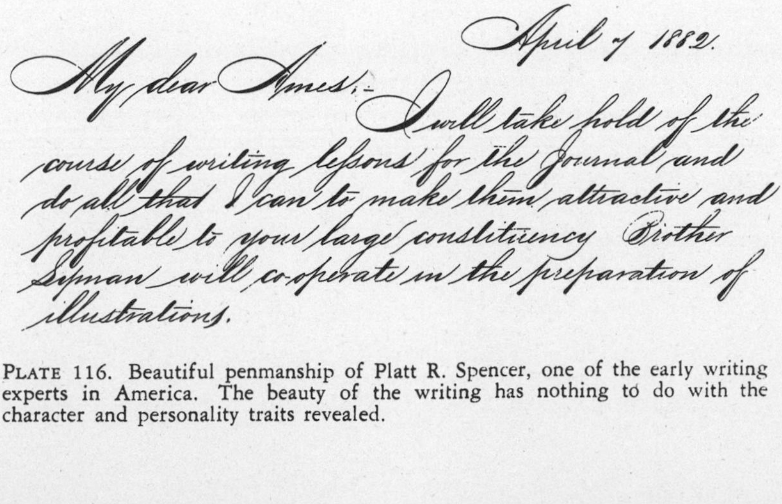

April 7 1882.
My dear Ames:—I will take hold of the
course of writing lessons for the Journal, and
do all that I can to make them attractive and
profitable to your large constituency Brother
Lyman will co-operate in the preparation of
illustrations.

PLATE 116. Beautiful penmanship of Platt R. Spencer, one of the early writing experts in America. The beauty of the writing has nothing to do with the character and personality traits revealed.

Finally, I came to his conservatism shown by the broad curves of his three letters. Then he chuckled. "You mean I'm just plain tight", he said. There was just one answer to make, "you are ultra conservative". After that Tamblyn was satisfied that grapho analysis was not a racket, and on one or two occasions before he retired he called on me to make examinations of employees in his school. Indeed one young man who was a skillful penman was let out because of certain traits shown in his professional penmanship.

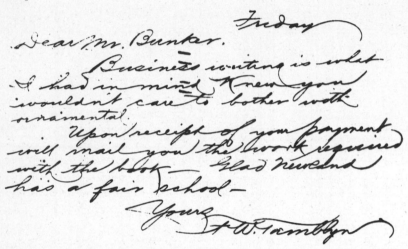

PLATE 117. After 20 years the writer's personality had changed and it showed up, inevitably, in his handwriting.

Plate 115 of the Tamblyn writing was prepared in 1923, but men change. As they change their handwriting changes too. In 1943 I looked over my own handwriting certificates, diplomas from great schools, and then at my own almost legible printing. Suddenly I knew I wanted a Tamblyn certificate. Also, I wanted to see if I could practice and bring back the old smooth flowing lines of my earlier penmanship teaching days. I practiced several hours, and it seemed that it might be possible, so I wrote Mr. Tamblyn. Plate 117 is his reply. He was still conservative, but the man who had been "tight" had disappeared, and in his place you will find a great many very generous final strokes in this card.

As you change, no matter how legible or illegible your original handwriting, you will find that your handwriting changes just as much. This is only natural. You think differently in order to change your character, and when you think differently you write differently.

Tamblyn's writing was plain rather than oranmental, whereas Ransom's

PLATE 118. Author's name written with flourishes by penman C. W. Ransom.

was much looser with strokes well spread one from another. Where Tamblyn made modest flourishes, Ransom made showy ones. There was no reason for the two men to be close friends, either professionally or otherwise because they were so much different that their interests could never meet.

Compare the writing of Bedinger with either of the others and you will find a distinctly different stage of letter formation, and an equally different personality.

Mr. Bedinger's large looped "d's" shows his sensitiveness, while the cross-bar for his "t's" showed great enthusiasm. Bedinger was like Ransom in that he was generous and willing to spend time or money easily. You will find one other interesting trait in his signature. His self-reliance.

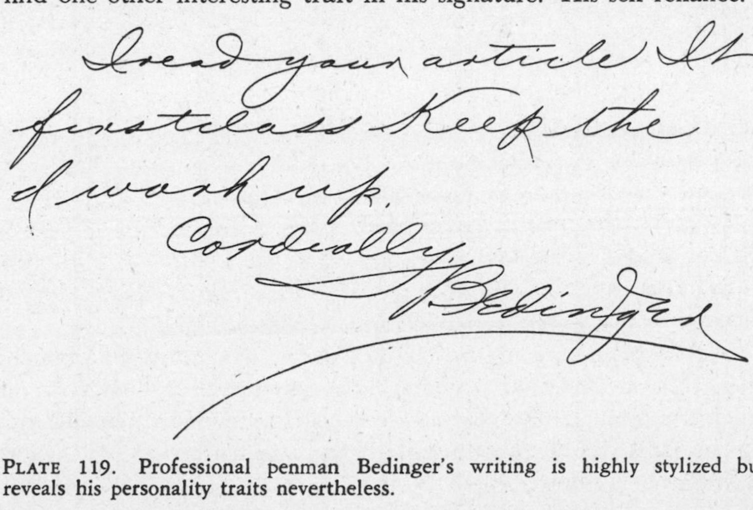

PLATE 119. Professional penman Bedinger's writing is highly stylized but reveals his personality traits nevertheless.

Young D. E. Carter who was teaching penmanship in a business school when he was fifteen went on to be an Oklahoma banker. His handwriting remained fluent but it was different. Where Tamblyn, who had been a teacher, retraced his "m's" and "n's" because he was thrifty, Carter made a marked separation, and also his writing was very much smaller, showing concentration. Also, like Ransom, rather than his teacher, he put long finals on his words, revealing the same willingness to give to others—to share with them that started my research into why I put such finals on my own words, an investigation that led to the principles of grapho analysis.

PLATE 120. Penmanship teacher D. E. Carter went on to become a banker. Read his handwriting to know why.

For a half century there were two principal publishers of penmanship manuals—Zaner & Bloser, and the A. N. Palmer Company. Both systems were widely used, literally millions of school children worked on the exercises that were prepared to guide their penmanship habits. There were striking similarities between the writing of the two authors. For example, each made long cross-bars for his "t's", indicating that at least some of their success was rooted in contagious enthusiasm about their work. Zaner's writing was smaller than that of A. N. Palmer, and a careful comparison will give you many minor differences. The point is that there were differences, and these differences identified the two individual personalities that directed much of the penmanship skill that affected the last two or three generations.

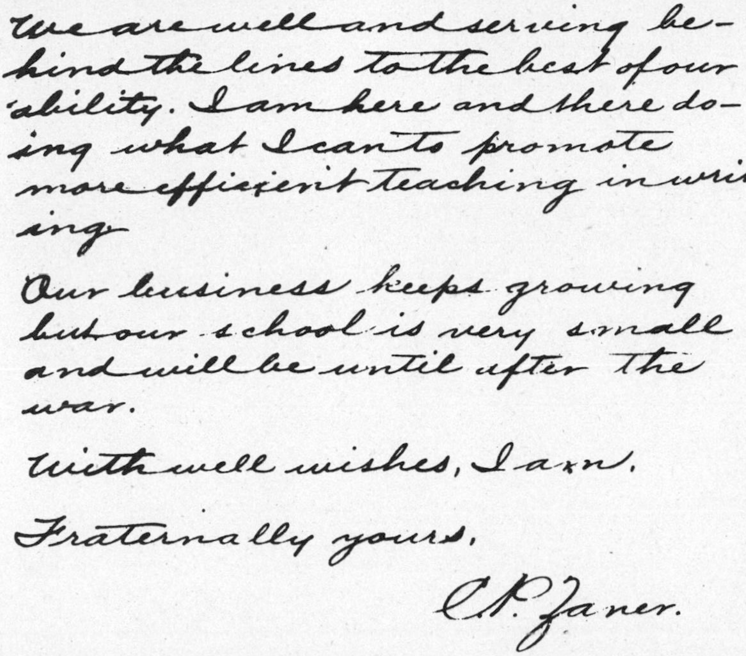

We are well and serving behind the lines to the best of our ability. I am here and there doing what I can to promote more efficient teaching in writing

Our business keeps growing but our school is very small and will be until after the war.

With well wishes, I am,

Fraternally yours,

C. P. Zaner.

PLATE 121. The handwriting of one of the founders of Zaner & Bloser Publishing Company whose exercise books guided the penmanship habits of millions of school children back a few years ago.

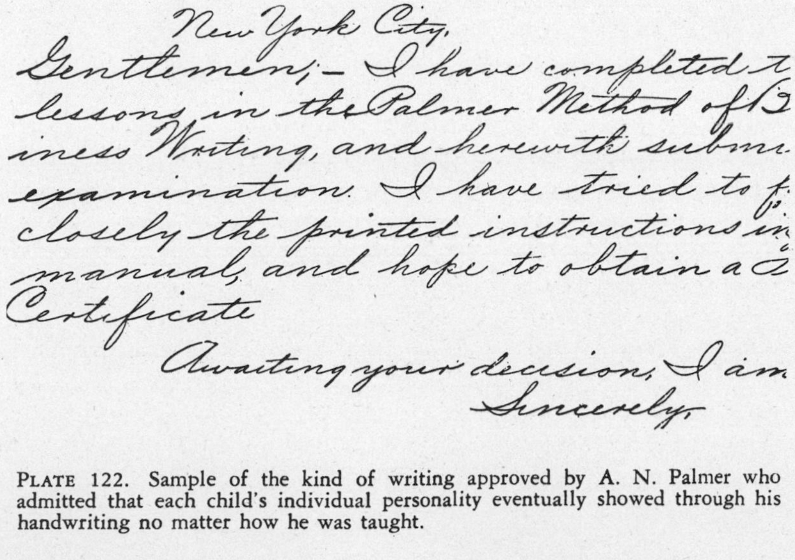

New York City,

Gentlemen;— I have completed t lessons in the Palmer Method of B iness Writing, and herewith submi. examination. I have tried to f closely the printed instructions in manual, and hope to obtain a C Certificate

Awaiting your decision; I am

Sincerely,

PLATE 122. Sample of the kind of writing approved by A. N. Palmer who admitted that each child's individual personality eventually showed through his handwriting no matter how he was taught.

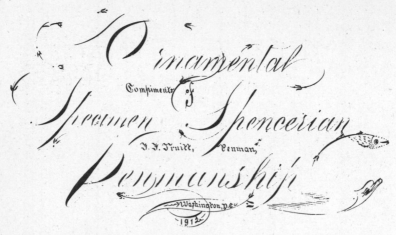

PLATE 123. The rococo writing style of F. F. Truitt who called himself "the world's best penman." Some of the gaudiness has been lost in reducing the size of this plate to fit this page.

There is one very important point in relation to their penmanship, however, that you should recognize. They were professional penmen, and made their living by adhering to what they taught, but their students, the boys and girls in grade and common school, and high school who used their manuals did not become proficient penmen. Further, even though the youngsters gained a certain amount of formation skill from their practice, they did not become good penmen. Not one in ten thousand stuck by what he had practiced in school. Indeed, this was so true that the director of the A. N. Palmer Company once told me that they did not expect the children to do so. "We try to help them cultivate a legible style of execution, but after they are out of school, they begin to show their individual personalities, and their writing becomes the picture of the individual writer."

Even the best penmen revealed their differences from the normal or common letter formations. Take this plate written by F. F. Truitt, a penmanship writer who was quite famous for a time. Indeed, Mr. Truitt proclaimed himself the "world best penman" and you can see why he did it. This plate is filled with decoration, too much decoration, in fact. Such a display in the handwriting of a professional penman or any other writer, legible or otherwise, is always a certain sign of the show-off, the ostentatious person. You will find their homes or personal possessions chosen for display, and to attract attention. Truitt was a long way from being the world's best penmanship teacher or artist. But he simply had to claim it because he was built that way, and the feelings he had were expressed in the over-dressing of his handwriting.

PLATE 124. During those days when ornate penmanship was the envy of every school boy, Madarasz, whose handwriting appears in this plate, was at the pinnacle of his fame. Notice the snap of his shading. He was equally famous as a teacher and his books of reproduced specimens are now in demand as collectors' items.

You will find a number of other plates in this chapter, merely as expressions of the personalities and the difference in personality that identified one from another. Great penmanship is almost a matter of history. Here and there you will find someone who still does magnificent flourished birds, and writes an ornate or decorative hand in his own particular style, so that these plates will provide you with not only comparison material in order to apply your principles of grapho analysis, but represent a choice collection of some of the work of the great penmen who influenced our fathers and mothers and their fathers and mothers before them. They are worth study for they are some of the strongest proof any skeptic can have of the truth that skill does not lessen the individuality of the writing.

S. M. Blue

C. E. Doner

PLATE 126. Each of these signatures is the work of a great penman of the early part of this century. The writing of each man identifies him just as surely as his fingerprints indentify him.

C. C. Lister

EXAMINATION FOR CHAPTER 11

(Correct answers for this examination will be found in the back of the book.)

In this chapter you have had striking proof that no matter how much a man may try to follow the path laid down by another, it is not possible. Most of the fine penmanship developed during the early part of the 20th Century stemmed from the influence of two men: Zaner and Palmer, yet they did not write alike, and none of their followers wrote like either their teachers or one another.

It is true that many of them gained an easy flowing hand, and ease of execution, but those who were conservative placed their letters close together and those who were less thrifty, spaced them further apart. They made small loops instead of large loops, or straight strokes where, according to the copybook, there should have been a loop.

Further, as you gain experience, as you come up against the rough and tumble of daily life, you will develop traits that will change your handwriting. So radically will your handwriting change in some cases, that a casual observer would say that your older writing could not have been executed by you. In exactly the same way, handwriting that showed strong character traits may not necessarily continue to do so. Some terrific emotional upheavel occurs in the life of some persons so that they become weaker rather than stronger.

Handwriting will show a change that is taking place before the actions of the writer show that change. Because this is true, a thorough knowledge of the rules may sometimes help you save a life. Not in the sense of keeping a man or woman from committing suicide, because there are no "death strokes" in a writing any more than there are strokes that show the writer will become rich. Such ideas are groundless, but when you see danger signs you can make suggestions that will help the writer overcome traits that for him might be disastrous.

EXAMINATION

1 . . *Does muscular movement penmanship materially change the permanent writing habits of the individual?*

   Yes_____   No_____

2 . . *In the Tamblyn writing, what showed conservatism?*

   a. Rounded "m's" and "n's"

   b. Carefully retraced downstrokes of "m's" and "n's"

3 . . *What character traits were prominent in the writing of Bedinger and Ransom?*

   a. Thrift

   b. Friendly emotional response

   c. Generosity

   d. Showmanship

4 . . *What traits of character are shown in Carter's writing that gave him natural ability to keep records and become an active business man?*

   a. Generosity

   b. Showmanship

   c. Concentration

   d. Friendliness

5 . . *What trait did you find in one or more of these specimens that showed a desire to attract attention or showmanship?*

   a. Forward slant

   b. Large writing

   c. Flourished writing

   d. Compact writing

6 . . *Check the names of the penmen whose writing showed the greatest desire for showmanship or to attract attention.*

   a. Tamblyn   b. Spencer   c. Ransom   d. Truitt

   e. Carter   f. Bedinger   g. Zaner   h. Palmer

CHAPTER **12**

Are Homosexuals Criminals?

HANDWRITING REVEALS STARTLING TRUTHS ABOUT AN AGE OLD PRACTICE. ARE HOMO-SEXUALS SICK, OR CRIMINALS? CASE HISTO-RIES STUDIED FROM HANDWRITING. OSCAR WILDE AND LORD ALFRED DOUGLAS; JERRY AND HIS CAREER; LARRY, WHO "TOOK" HIS LOVERS.

A very famous woman medical doctor, with years of teaching in a famous medical college has this to say about sex when she was asked this question: "Why is it that there can never be a discussion of sex with an impersonal slant?" Her comment which follows is the finest brief concept of sex relationships I have ever heard from a speaker's platform:

"With love the sex act is a sacrament. Without love, it is as exhilarating as spitting and gives relief in the same fashion."

Sex is everywhere. You and I would not be here if it were not for it. Handwriting reveals sex appetites and desires the same at it reveals whether the writer is a potential thief, or a domineering, acid-tongued individual. It is this fact that caused me to answer a question badly a good many years ago. In a class in Hollywood, attended by people from all walks in life, including a priest who had traveled some 3,000 miles to take the week's work, some one in the audience put up a hand. "Can you tell from hand-writing if a man or woman is a deviate?"

● **THE HOMOSEXUAL AND HANDWRITING**

What the questioner meant was whether handwriting revealed homosexuality. My answer was a positive "yes" rather than an evasion of the question. After that in various schools held from coast to coast it invariably happened that some man or woman, or several of them would come up after a class closed, hand me a slip of paper, and in a strictly hush-hush tone ask "Is he?" or Is she?" If I assumed ignorance they stammered and stuttered and ended up by saying "you know what I mean." Certainly I knew what they meant, but as sex is rather primary to life it did not seem to me to be necessary to whisper the question, nor the answer.

However, I should have made my answer to the first question more complete. Handwriting shows homosexuality in some cases and in some it does not. If the writer is conscious that he or she is a homosexual, and is concerned about it, it will show in the handwriting. But if the writer recognizes the situation, and is not bothered by it, or is not worried by what others think, it will not show. It is the mental attitude that shows, not the actual practice of homosexuality.

There are, for instance, thousands of men and women whose handwriting shows latent sexuality that is classified as "abnormal" who are lost,

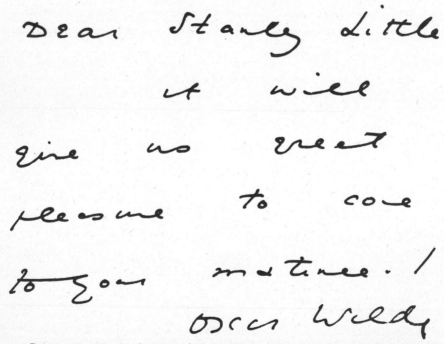

PLATE 127. The handwriting of Oscar Wilde, who served time in prison for homosexual activity, shows no sign of any unusual sex interest. It is the fear or feeling of guilt that reveals itself in handwriting, not the homosexuality.

wandering through life. In such cases the handwriting will show the existence of homosexual desires, even though the writer does not recognize that he or she is one of a minority. On the other hand, you have as your first illustration in this chapter the handwriting of Oscar Wilde (plate 127), who served time in a British prison for homosexual activities, and there is nothing in his writing to show any unusual sex interest. Oscar Wilde was a homo-

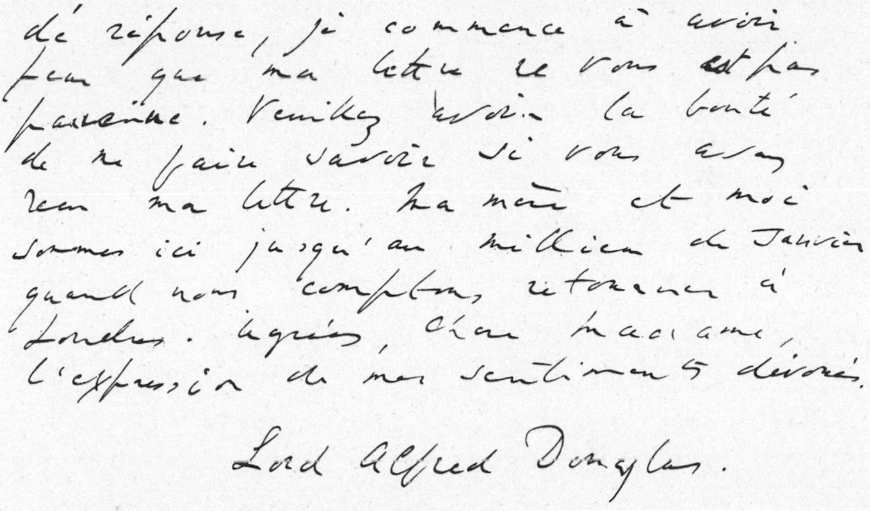
de réponse, je commence à avoir peur que ma lettre ne vous est pas parvenue. Veuillez avoir la bonté de me faire savoir si vous avez reçu ma lettre. Ma mère et moi sommes ici jusqu'au milieu de Janvier quand nous comptons retourner à Londres. Agréez, chère madame, l'expression de mes sentiments dévoués.

Lord Alfred Douglas.

PLATE 128. Lord Alfred Douglas was a homosexual with a subconscious feeling of guilt which showed up in his handwriting.

sexual. It did not bother him. It was not a burden to him. He accepted the fact, and let it go at that.

Lord Alfred Douglas was a homosexual with a subconscious feeling of guilt, and it is the fear or guilt feeling in his mind that created the evidence in his writing (plate 128). However, there is one indication that shows a possibility of the existence of homosexuality. When lower loops are made as square circles, very small, the writer may be married, and have a half dozen children, but the basic inclination was present, and has never been aroused.

There is one truth that handwriting reveals not only about sex in general but about homosexuality. Sex crimes are committed by over-sexed, or under-sexed individuals, but they are not committed by homosexuals because they are homosexuals. They are committed because the writer was basically a criminal, and also a homosexual. There is one other truth that I have proved since the first sex research in grapho analysis was started in 1919. Up to that time no attention to sex appetites had been given my research. Then a fan who had read one of my books and whom I was considering making an assistant on a magazine I was editing at the time, told me he was a homosexual, though he used a different word. Actually he was a little tramp sexually. However, in our conversations I learned enough about him to determine that if sex variants showed their differences in handwriting I would find it. The simple rule illustrated above is the only single rule that applies, and it is an indication only.

● DIGGING OUT A SECRET

However, a professional grapho analyst, using evaluation, can make the discovery. In this regard, a case that developed prior to World War II illustrates the truth of this. Our organization was short of help. Particularly

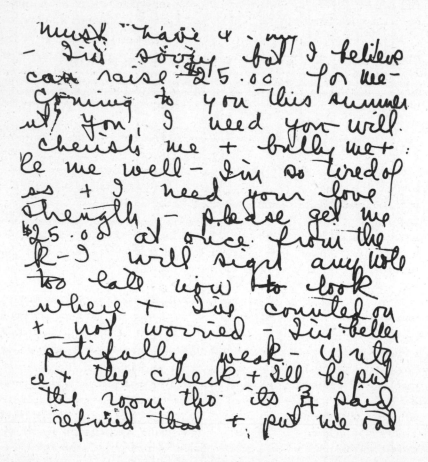

PLATE 129. These ill-shaped and almost formless letters are an accurate measure of the writer's mental ability.

short of young men as office boys, and to operate office machinery. We advertised extensively, and one day a young fellow fairly danced into the office. He had traveled some five hundred miles to get a job, and he fully intended to be hired. However, we did not need him. "Come down and let me buy you a Coke," he said. As we sat across the drug store table, he grinned and said, "You know I think you have a tremendous racket, but if you make money, it is all right with me—and I want a job."

It may have been bait. At least it worked. As a result he followed my suggestion and wrote a half dozen lines and handed it across to me. After you have become thoroughly familiar with the principles of grapho analysis your mind sorts out evidence very rapidly. The professional evaluates a full page in a few minutes even though it may take several hours to work out a complete survey of the findings and be sure of absolute accuracy.

He nodded as I pointed out certain characteristics, agreeing without reservation. Then I added "your writing shows you are a homosexual." He blew his top. He was not a homosexual, and he was insulted. However, when I pointed out that if he had agreed with all of the other traits that had been identified he must fit into the category where his handwriting showed he belonged.

Several weeks later we put him on as office boy. Within three months he had married a girl in the filing department, but they did not live happily "everafter". Instead, they existed, and she clung to him in spite of the fact that he would leave her for weeks without funds, and would return and tell her just anything he thought she might believe. Before too long he quit, and it was not until years later that I heard my named called. He was standing back of me in a hotel lobby. "Come on upstairs," he said, "I've a confession to make—one that you will be glad to hear because it shows that grapho analysis is correct."

● *GRAPHO ANALYSIS SUBSTANTIATED*

He had bummed around over the country. He had been in veterans' hospitals and in public institutions. He had been kept by two different doctors, and had left each of them on the spur of the moment. Finally, while he was in a great western hospital the doctor hand contacted a state hospital in the young fellow's home state and they had transferred him there for psychiatric treatment. It took the psychiatrist several months before he found that the fellow was a homosexual. The patient had never admitted to himself while he was being kept that he was anything but a normal young man in a tight spot financially, and making use of sex to satisfy not his own desires but as a means of making a livelihood.

It may seem strange but there are many such actual cases. Jerry was one of them. His family was completely without morals. His father and two brothers, though normal sexually were criminals, and his sisters were prostitutes. Therefore, when he ran away from school and the two dismal rooms where the family lived, he knew that men wanted small boys and young men. He put himself in a spot where he could be approached, and became accustomed to homosexual activities, but with nothing but great disgust for his customers who he made a point of "rolling", just as his sisters did with theirs.

You will recognize as you examine this plate of Jerry's writing that his mental ability, his capacity to learn was very low. He had never completed the sixth grade, and then only because he had stayed in the room

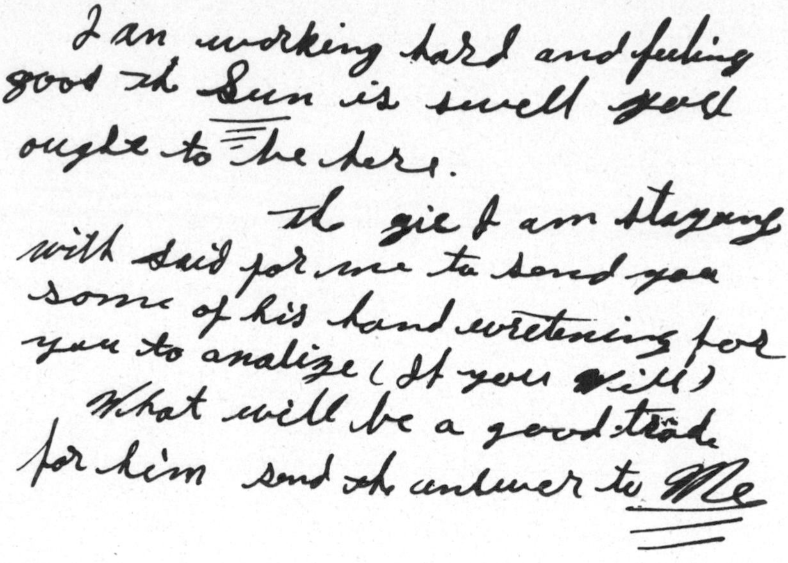
I am working hard and feeling good the Sun is swell you ought to be here.
The gie I am staying with said for me to send you some of his hand writening for you to analize (If you will) What will be a good trade for him send the answer to Me

PLATE 130. Criminal tendencies show up in this handwriting, but no homosexuality.

long enough that his teacher had to do something with him so she sent him on to the next grade. These ill-shaped letters, actually almost formless, were a perfect register of his mental ability. He knew the criminal underworld, but he did not participate in it except to steal anything and everything he saw that he momentarily wanted. He always gave what he stole to someone or merely left it in a hotel room when he moved on to another city. The last time I saw Jerry he was married and had a string of girls, a young man entirely without morals, but never a homosexual.

Larry was a homosexual. He was also a criminal, because he had only one object. To avoid work. He was disgusting in appearance, brilliant enough to have made a great scholar, and he had money enough available to have gained a broad education, and added something to the good in the world. But he was completely selfish and physically lazy. He did not want to study even though he was capable of making top grades, so he did not work. He was a homosexual, but he was not a criminal because he was a homosexual.

He had the criminal tendencies but handwriting did not reveal any signs of homosexuality. He accepted his situation casually, indifferently, and blackmailed men who fell for his offer of sex. He would have found some other avenue of blackmailing if he had not been able to use sex as an excuse. Every waking hour, and probably many of his sleeping ones when his subconscious mind was functioning, he devoted to schemes for getting something for nothing, or without working. He broke up homes, wrecked his lovers financially and physically and went on his merry way, because right down in the depths of his nature he was a born crook.

● **HOMOSEXUALITY AND CRIME**

Since 1919 I have known and studied literally hundreds upon hundreds of sex cases from murderers who had knotted a kerchief around the neck of a mistress to a street corner fairy. When they have found how completely their handwritings revealed their innermost thoughts, they have almost uniformly been as frank as in confessional. Possibly part of this was due to amazement which resulted from the accuracy of their analyses. Possibly part of it was a deep desire to confide in someone. At any rate, throughout the years homosexuals have confided in me with confidence that I would not betray their trust.

Records of cases have been kept in locked files, and even at the risk of losing my life, I have kept in touch with and studied them. During these years there have been scores of major crimes reported in the press, and in a great number the accused has been charged with being a homosexual— and in some cases the stories were true. However, long and expensive investigation has proved conclusively that the crime was not committed because the accused was a homosexual, but that he was a homosexual AND a criminal.

There is one marked exception. Homosexuals are both male and female and both sexes have committed crimes, usually murder, when they were married and the inability to cope with married life caused an emotional explosion. Time and again a man has killed his wife, and he could not tell the reason. His handwriting would, however, reveal that he had attempted a pattern of life for which he had not natural inclination or even possibility of adjustment. Eventually the situation became unbearable, and he escaped by doing the obvious. Destroying the cause of his misery.

There is one other point that should be faced in dealing with homosexuality and what handwriting says about the condition. Older homosexuals do not lead younger girls and boys into homosexuality. Not in one case in a thousand. Checking handwriting after handwriting one fact has stood out clearly. It is not uncommon for an older homosexual to introduce a young person into homsexuality, but the handwriting of the younger one showed the tendencies toward homosexuality long before.

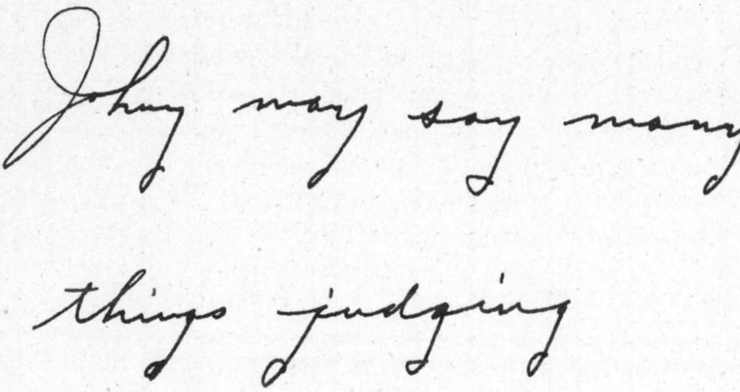

PLATE 131. This writing specimen illustrates the signs that indicate (but do not prove) homosexuality. Notice particularly the tiny squared loops and the ends of the downstrokes in g, y, and j.

This ends the correction to the statement I made so many years ago. Handwriting does reveal a homosexual nature but only under certain conditions. All homosexuals do reveal the homosexuality in their handwriting when the handwriting is in the hands of a professional analyst. It does not show to the layman, except by the repeated presence of the small to tiny squared loop at the ends of down strokes in "g", "y", and "j". This is an indicating sign, not conclusive proof, and when you find it, do not rush off madly and assert that So-and-So is a homosexual for, if you do, you may easily get yourself embroiled in legal difficulties out of which it may be costly to escape.

Some of the greatest men and women in history have been homosexuals. Indeed, the Wolfenden Report issued in Great Britain makes one finding that is important in understanding this variant from what is usually classified as "normal". The report says, "In some who work with notable success in occupations which call for service to others, there are those in whom a latent homosexuality provides the motivation for activities of the greatest value to society." Grapho analysis can help you help others.

EXAMINATION FOR CHAPTER 12

Sex is the basis of continuing life. Animals have it and man, because he is animal, is primarily sexual or possessed of sex desires.

It is also one of the most misundertood subjects, possibly, with which man has to cope. Children grow up and learn from other children because the parents very often lack sufficient knowledge of sex.

In this chapter you have studied the handwriting of a large number of people, including citizens of the United States, Canada, and elsewhere in the world. Homosexuality was encouraged under the Hitler regime in Germany, while many other parts of the world handle it as a criminal offense, something of which to be ashamed. Many reformers have a blind but honest belief that homosexuals are actually criminals. This is as far from the truth as it can possibly be. Some of our greatest musicians, artists, engineers, even some of our greatest athletes have lived out their lives as homosexuals.

The research back of this chapter has proved conclusively that a man's handwriting need not show homosexual tendencies or actual practice. And you have learned when the homosexual is most likely to reveal this quirk.

You should be able to answer each of the following examination questions correctly.

EXAMINATION

1 . . *What is the most prominent evidence of strong sex desires?*
    a. VERTICAL WRITING
    b. WRITING SLANTED FAR TO THE RIGHT
    c. WRITING WITH CIRCLES CLOSED WITH INK AND MUDDY EDGES ON LINES
    d. VERY HEAVY WRITING, WITHOUT MUD
    e. BACKHAND WRITING

2 . . *Which combination of traits represents the most signs of dangerous sex explosions?*
    a. HEAVY, MUDDY WRITING CRAMPEL
    b. MUDDY WRITING WITH STRONG PURPOSE AND DETERMINATION
    c. SECRECY, MUDDY WRITING AND LETTERS CRAMPED TOGETHER
    d. SECRECY, HEAVY BUT CLEAN WRITING, AND LETTERS CRAMPED TOGETHER

3 . . *In addition to sex desires, what does clean, heavy writing indicate?*
    a. LAZINESS
    b. LOVE FOR COLORS, ODORS, TONES, LUXURIOUS SURROUNDINGS.
    c. DEEP EMOTIONS, EXPRESSED OR UNEXPRESSED, DEPENDING ON SLANT OR LACK OF IT.

4 . . *Would the combination of heavy muddy domineering and compressed writing be dangerous?*
    YES_____ No_____

CHAPTER **13**

You Can Know People

SOMERSET MAUGHAM, CORDELL HULL, HON.
FRANCES P. BOLTON, MAXWELL PARRISH,
CARRIE NATION, DOROTHY DIX, STRICKLAND
GILLILAN, HORACE GREELEY, SIR ARTHUR
CONAN DOYLE, JULIA WARD HOWE, VICTOR
HERBERT, VIDOCQ, CHARLES SPURGEON, DR.
MARCUS BACH, EDGAR WALLACE.

GRAPHO analysis has given me one reward that cannot be measured in dollars and cents, or for that matter, in any other way I can describe. It has given me the ability to know people. All kinds of people. There have been famous religious leaders like Stephen S. Wise, the great Jewish Rabbi, and Hal Wallis, the famous motion picture producer. Great artists, some of the world's great poets, and singers, motion picture stars, and some that society describes as "rats". There has been a lot of good in many of them, but none of them has been quite as good or nearly as bad as the public gave them credit for being. Not necessarily the public, but very often their close associates, even their families.

● *KNOWING PEOPLE THROUGH THEIR HANDWRITING*

Many of these people I have never met, although very often we have and because I knew the individual from handwriting, we managed to find a mutual meeting on interests. There is one of the greatest of the old time motion picture stars still playing in Hollywood. We have never met, although we have tried hard enough, but I know her and she knows that I do, for this is what she had to say about the analysis of her handwriting.

"Grapho analysis revealed me to myself as I never thought it would. It even uncovered traits of character that I knew subconsciously that I had, and when faced with them had to admit."

192

In this connection I am reminded of the first time I met Charlie Ransom, whose ornate handwriting you studied in an earlier chapter (plate 118). Ransom was tall, and I was short. He put out his hand, looked down at me, and said, "From the letters you write I figured you were as big as I am." Charlie merely read what I had written, and in 1911 I did not know enough about handwriting and what it reveals to have any idea whatever about him. Years later when we were to work on questioned documents together, that little incident would come to mind, and I would smile, but I never mentioned it. However, in those later days I knew

PLATE 132. W. Somerset Maugham, one of the greatest word painters of the 20th century. See plate 133 for his handwriting.

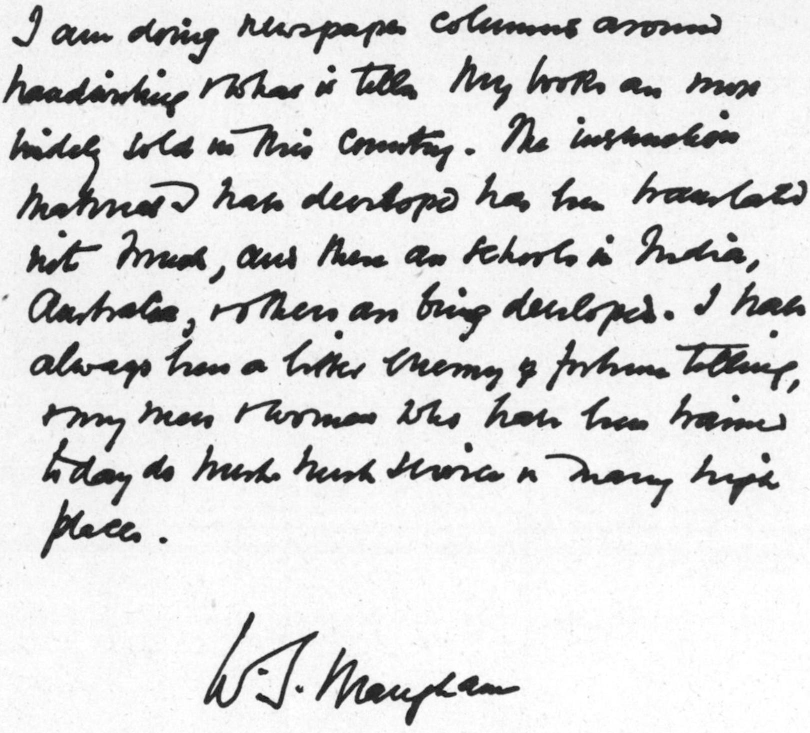

[Handwritten letter reproduced, signed W. S. Maugham]

PLATE 133. The letter "g" made something like a figure 8 shows a literary tendency. Also discernible is W. Somerset Maugham's love of color.

Charlie better than he ever knew me even though he studied some grapho analysis.

When "The Moon and Six Pence" by Somerset Maugham appeared, it was sent to me by the publishers for review. It was a great book, and I said so, but it was not until years later when Maugham sent me his handwriting that I understood his appeal to that vast audience that love his stories for their word tones, as well as for their message. Study this plate and you will find the figure 8 "g's" that show literary tendencies, but the greatest thing in the whole page is his love of color. So, though he did not become famous as a painter with oils, he won a vast following thru the pictures he painted in words that reached ten thousand times as great an audience as if he had been a Raphael.

You will have the same experience very likely with your own favorite author. Somewhere along the way you will get his or her handwriting, and you will understand the individual back of the written words. That will

make both the writer and the book much nearer to you—because you too
will know the author. This is true whether your favorite author is alive or
"out of print", physically as well as in the book market. There was, for
instance, Augusta J. Evans Wilson, whose St. Elmo was a popular parlor
stand title right alongside the Bible and a mail order catalog fifty years ago.
Looking back it is possible to take this stately bit of her writing, and understand the dignity, even the stiff formality of her greatest seller. And it

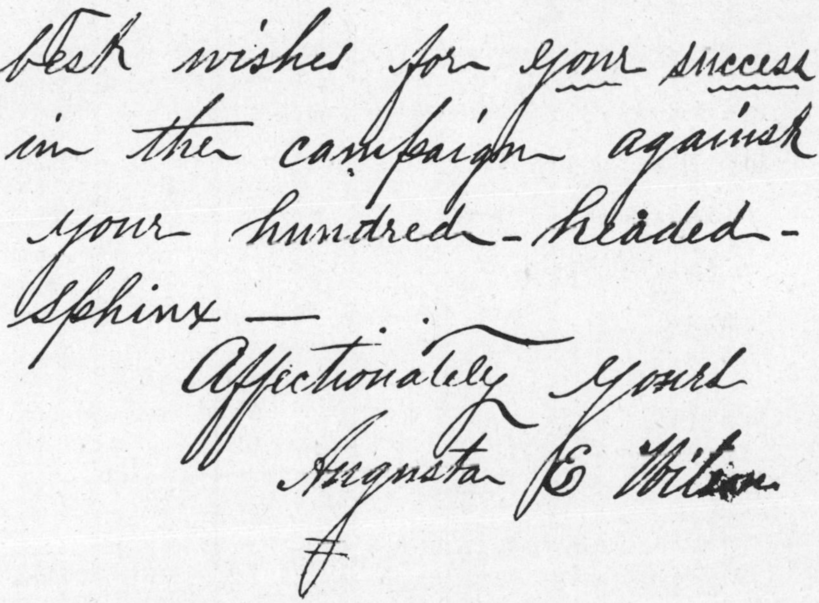

*Best wishes for your success
in the campaign against
your hundred-headed-
Sphinx—
Affectionately yours
Augusta E Wilson*

PLATE 134. Although you may never have heard of Augusta J. Evans, the
author, this specimen of handwriting will reveal things to you that even the
readers of her well known books never knew about her.

is just as easy to take the signature of Edgar Rice Burroughs, author of
the Tarzan Tales, and understand how he stuck to his belief in Tarzan of
the Apes, even though he walked the streets of Chicago with holes in the
soles of his shoes, doing his best to peddle the book. He had determination.
He had written a book, and he was going to sell it, which he did, opening
up a brand new market for a long string of titles.

A good many years ago one of the major political parties engaged
me to prepare analyses of some of the most popular United States Senators.
They were each famous, but the analyses were never published. The reason
was very simple. Some of them were not quite what they seemed to be
to their devoted followers. When I turned the analyses in to the man who

had given me the assignment, he asked me "what did you find in Senator So-and-So's writing?" My answer, "I would not believe him on a stack of Bibles a block high," brought a grin. "At least your grapho analysis is truthful. I have known the fellow for years, have watched him win election after election, and personally I wouldn't believe him on any stack of Bibles."

On the other hand, when Herbert Hoover sent me his writing in the dark depression days when even his own party was giving him milk and water support, I knew the man was honest, he was a builder, and he would have built if political opposition had not tied his hands. He was not a diplomat, and he did not know how to meet political chicanery except by straightforward talk, and the thinking an engineer would give to a major project.

Scores of men and women who have been trained have written me in election years that "we are fighting a man on our own side, solely because he is not qualified to handle the problems he will meet." These grapho analysts knew their candidates, and they were better off for knowing, even though they may have helped to defeat him. It is quite a number of years now since an analyst brought me the handwriting of a man who was a candidate for office in a middle western state. At the time I did not know of his candidacy, but that would not have made any difference. The analysis told the truth. That truth, circulated in proper places, closed the door to his election just as certainly as if he had been dropped in a cavern in the midst of the Rocky Mountains where there was no escape.

● SELECTING A DOCTOR THROUGH GRAPHO ANALYSIS

There have been times when grapho analysis has given me a personal protection that could not be measured in dollars and cents. My doctor told me that I needed an operation for a mastoid. Ordinarily many of those afflicted fear the operation, although competent surgery has made it far less dangerous than in years gone by. I called a specialist whose handwriting I had analyzed. "Who", I asked him, "would you have operate if it were a member of your own family?"

"Call St. Louis, get Dr. Robert Votaw. He knows such conditions like he knows his a, b, c's. Don't write him, for he is probably too busy to reply. Call him." We made an appointment in St. Louis and I went there without knowing whether the doctor would perform the operation. But during that first interview I spotted a note pad on his desk. When he left the room I analyzed the handwriting, and a few days later when they rolled me into the operating room I was not worried. The surgeon would do his best. He will probably want to wring my neck for including this incident because doctors are very ethical about advertising, but this is not advertising, and does show how grapho analysis affects my own decisions. Not always. I have kept people around me for years after analyzing their handwriting, letting time prove the accuracy of what that writing had revealed. This has applied to both men and women, without regard to age, and as a pioneer it has meant financial loss, personal emotional agony, but always in the end grapho analysis has proved to be correct, and because this is true, the experiences I have had need not be repeated in your case. You have protection when you use the science that began to be developed back in 1910 when I set out to find why I put long finals on my words.

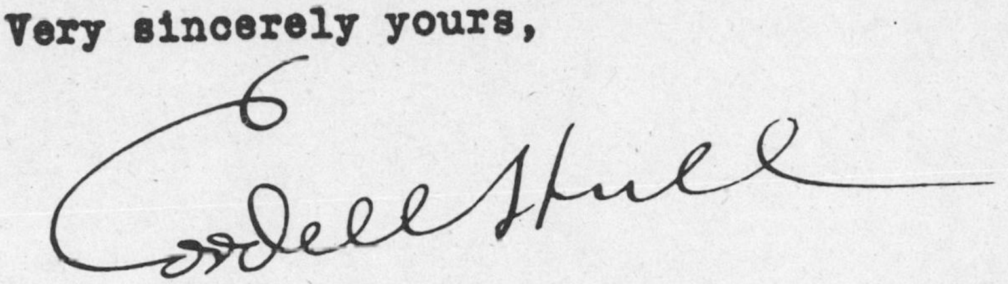

Very sincerely yours,

Cordell Hull

PLATE 135. Former Secretary of State Cordell Hull. His "e" is well rounded, showing his broad-mindedness.

All of this is far apart, however, from the people I have known who are or have been in the limelight. The public names have been prominent, and many of the writers have been well worth knowing. Take the handwriting of Cordell Hull, for example. He was, first of all, a Senator for many years, then he was Secretary of State at a time when conditions were very serious. He was criticized, condemned and praised, but let us see what his signature says about him as a man. First of all, there is a huge loop in the small "t" (not illustrated here) showing supersensitiveness, which would have been a disastrous trait if it were not that his writing ranged from vertical to backhand. The lack of slant, the up and downness of it, shows his ability to take criticism and even abuse without too strong a reaction. To be sure he may have felt the sting of criticism. That was natural, but his poise gave him the ability to meet it without an emotional upset. His single "e" is well rounded, showing his broad-mindedness, the realization that other people's ways could be good. He was very frank, and equally generous.

Another longtime stateswoman, Frances P. Bolton, sent me only three lines of her writing which showed her remarkable comprehension, her ability to keep things to herself. Note in particular the way in which she makes the "a" in the word "made". It is a complete circle, and when you find this you have a writer who can close up like a clam, keep a poker face, and talk with you all day without revealing an important secret. When

Mrs. Bolton got her analysis she wrote me, "It is a long while since I have had anything as thorough as this, and I am very appreciative of the care with which it was done." Her report had run several pages, although there were only a few lines of writing from which to work, but when you know grapho analysis you can get a great deal from even a few strokes of the pen.

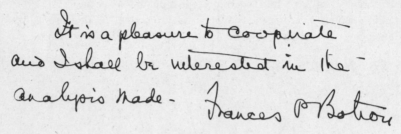

PLATE 136. Writing of Congressman Frances P. Bolton. Note in particular the way in which she makes the "a" in the word "made." This indicates ability to keep a pokerface. Mrs. Bolton congratulated the author on the thorough analysis he made of her handwriting.

Mrs. Bolton then asked me to do something she considered unusual, but which was not. "Would you let me know whether it would be possible for you to do a rather unusual thing in the way of analyzing handwriting? I have in mind diagnostic use of it—three or four, or even five different samples of the same individual's writing with a view to a very constructive helpfulness to that particular individual." My memory fails me, but it was probably done, because that is one phase of grapho analysis that has been responsible for the growth of the science of grapho analysis. Every student who has ever been trained has been advised over and over again to get the job done. Overwork may compel delay, but get it done.

PLATE 137. This autograph of artist Maxfield Parrish proves that he simply had to be an artist. For one thing, the heavy writing registers color.

If you appreciate art you will find this autograph by Maxwell Parrish interesting and certainly it proves that he simply had to be an artist. You have heavy writing registering color. The flat-topped "r's" show high development of creative talent. His short d-stem reveals that he would think and act for himself. Finally the most prominent trait shown in this signature is his remarkable sense of line values, or the effect of lines. His capital "M" is ornate, but not ostentatious. His capital "P" is unique, but the flourish is graceful, while the stem of the "P" is equally so.

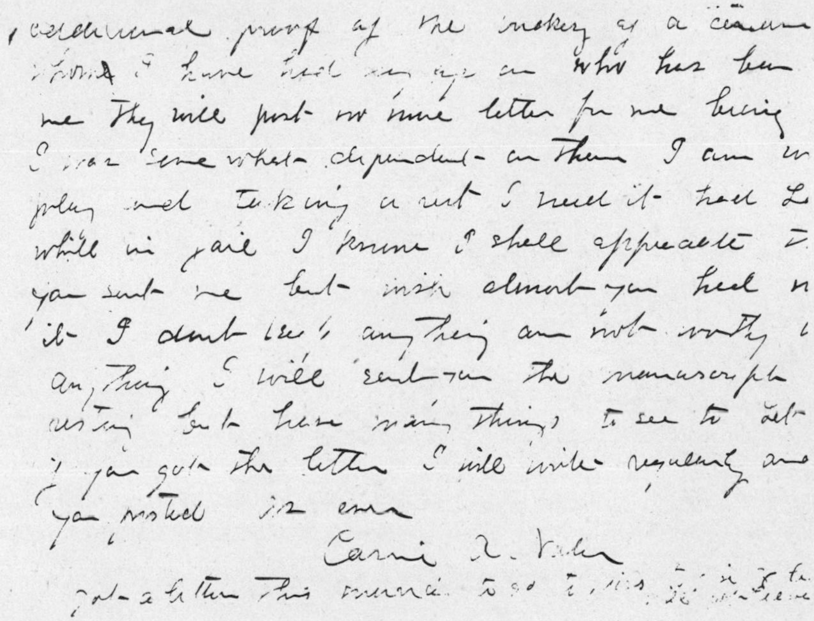

PLATE 138. Carrie Nation's open a's and o's are most revealing. Notice the t-bars ahead of the stem, indicating temper, and the straight down strokes on her y's denoting lack of imagination.

In the early 20th century days two unique women came onto the scene at about the same time. One of them hit the front pages of newspapers from coast to coast with huge black headlines, a blazing trail of destruction and reform, that was to affect a new approach to a situation which she considered outrageous. That was the dumpy, direct, and storming Carrie Nation of "hatchet" fame who was feared by bartenders and liquor men all over the country. The other was the woman who, just starting became America's most read and most famous newspaper woman, a quiet, unassuming, but brilliant woman, Dorothy Dix. Carrie's handwriting intrigued me and provided a new light on the woman who gained such an army of followers among church people and was so reviled and hated by the liquor interests.

You will be interested in the number of times she made her t-bars ahead of the stem. As you will recognize, this showed her temper. She was not a brilliant woman, but she did like to talk, as her open-mouthed "a's" and "o's" show. She was not, however, highly impulsive. Instead, she

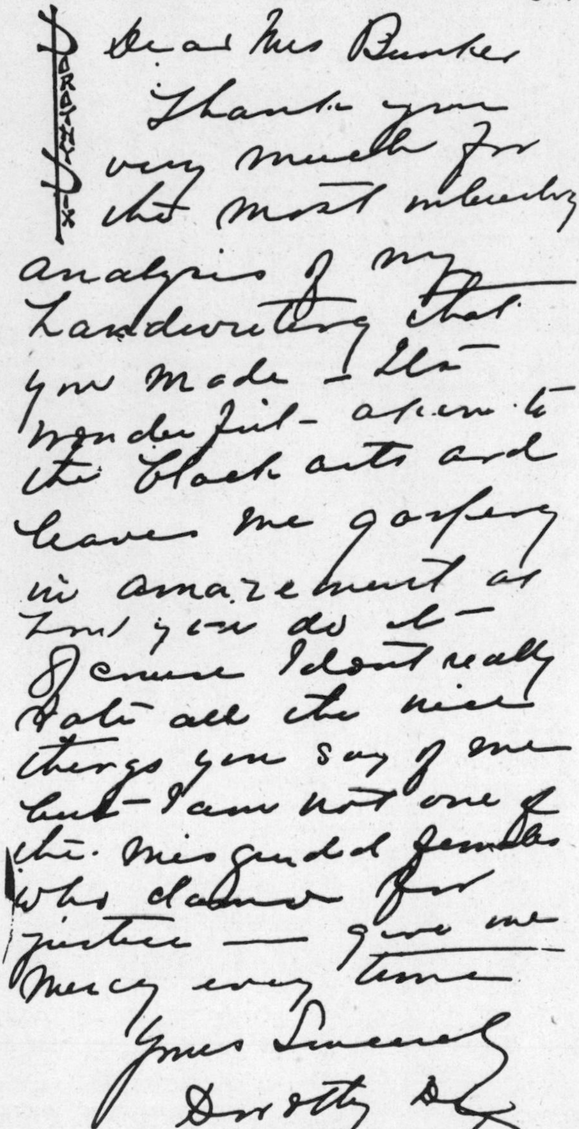
DOROTHY DIX

Dear Mrs Bunker
Thank you
very much for
the most interesting
analysis of my
handwriting that
you made - It is
wonderful - akin to
the black arts and
leaves me gasping
in amazement at
how you do it -
Of course I don't really
rate all the nice
things you say of me
but - I am not one of
the misguided females
who clamor for
justice — give me
mercy every time.
Yours Sincerely
Dorothy Dix

PLATE 139. At one time Dorothy Dix was America's most famous and widely read newspaperwoman. Her m's start large and slope downward, which gives evidence of diplomacy. There is also generosity and determination shown in this handwriting.

had a friendly, neighborly emotional warmth, but her crusades were not
the result of impulse. The down-strokes on her "y's" and other letters
providing an opportunity to use them, are straight, and firm, but she was
completely without imagination. We know this because she made no lower
loops, and her upper ones were so narrow that we know she had little
imagination in the field of spiritual matters. Instead, Carrie Nation was a
realist, she looked at life through very narrow lens, and when she became
convinced that liquor was a national liability she merely picked up a hatchet
and did the thing that she knew would deal with the problem.

On the other hand, Dorothy Dix was a brilliant and a modest woman.
Just starting her newspaper career that was to lead to her place as the
highest paid newspaper woman in America, she was sent to interview and

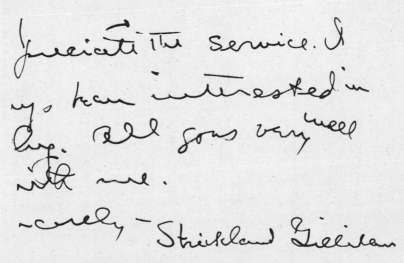

PLATE 140. Strickland Gillilan was a successful newspaper writer. In your
analysis of this writing you will readily see that the slant is that of a non-
emotional personality. The e's indicate a literary tendency.

report on Carrie Nation's activities. How she handled it is something you
can determine for yourself by a study of this letter that Miss Dix wrote me
after receiving her own analysis. Give attention to the way she makes her
"m's". They start large and slope downward to the right, without losing
formation. This is evidence of diplomacy. She had determination that never
turns back, and there is much generosity in this page. Therefore, no matter
what she thought of Carrie Nation and her campaign, it is sure that Carrie
would get generous and kindly treatment. We know the kindly treatment
was sure because the slant of the Dix writing is well to the right. At times
she was very enthusiastic, and like so many newspaper people who have

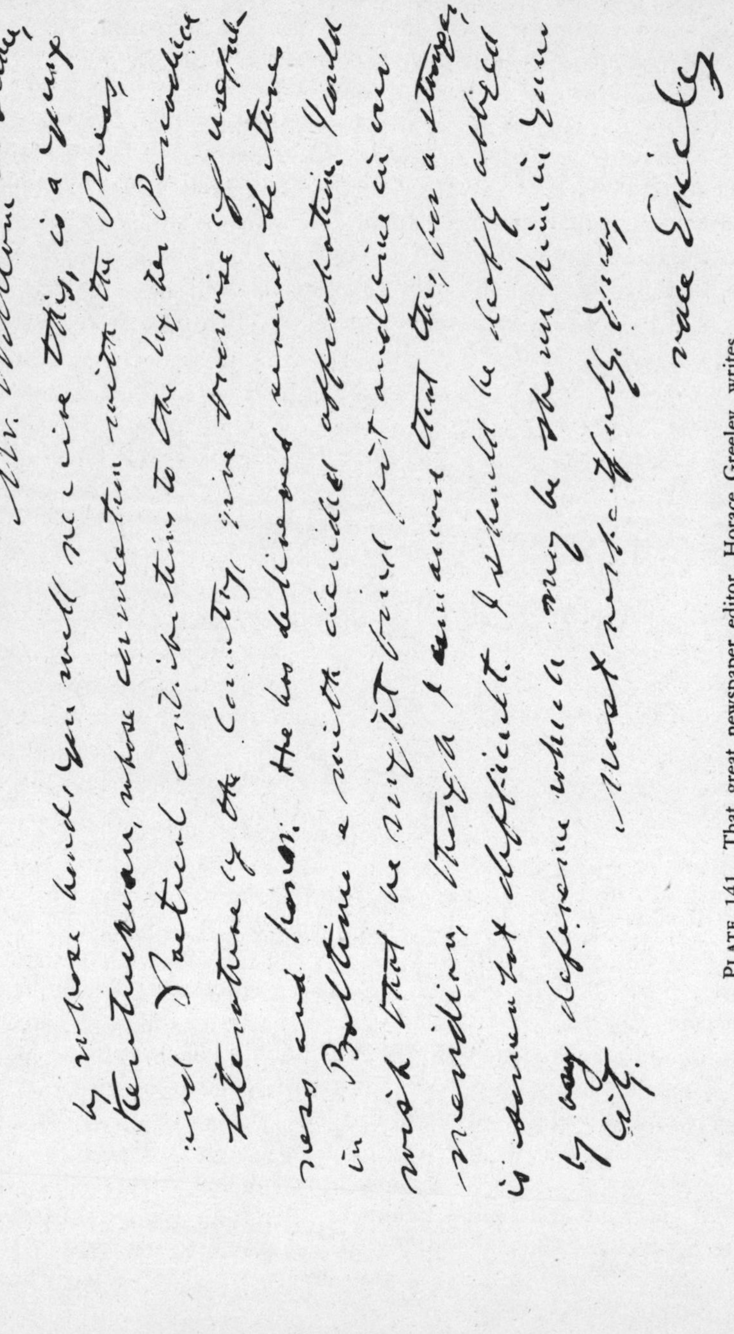

Mr. William Walker,

by whose hand you will receive this, is a young Kentuckian, whose connection with the Press and Practical contributions to the best Periodical Literature of the Country give promise of usefulness and honor. He has delivered several lectures in Baltimore with decided approbation. I would wish that he might find just audience in our meridian, though I am aware that this, for a stranger, is somewhat difficult. I should be deeply obliged by any deference which may be shown him in your city.

Most respectfully, yours,

Horace Greeley

PLATE 141. That great newspaper editor, Horace Greeley, writes t-bars that clearly show his sarcastic nature. Sharp penetrating points, indicating genuine scholarship, are rare in this handwriting.

won top honors she had the ability to pick off the top of any subject just what she needed, rather than exploring it to the end.

Undoubtedly Dorothy Dix won her permanence in American newspaperdom through the combination of these traits. During her lifetime she was tempted many times to give up her newspaper writing, but she never did. She went straight on through, although at times the battle between doing the job and fulfilling what she may have thought were other duties, took courage.

One of the most interesting and friendliest men I have ever know without actually meeting him, was Strickland Gillilan, the man whose verse, "Off agin, on agin, Finnigin" portrayed the problem of the foreman of a railroad section crew. When Gillilan wrote his famous poem, railroads were not what they are today. The section crew labored to get their handcar over the tracks, a back-breaking job. However, Gillilan gave Finnigan a personality that went out and did the job, getting his trains back on the track and certainly and dependably as an eight day clock. As you will discover by studying his handwriting, Gillilan was not a thrifty man. Value slipped through his fingers like water, although his judgment was cool, and his emotional response was almost completely lacking. Instead, he went through life with a smile, never getting riled up, and completely free from emotional storms. You will find his small "e's" made like capitals, indicating his literary inclinations, and though the individual letters are wisely separated, they are well balanced, showing sense of rhythm. As a newspaper man Strickland Gillilan could pick the top off the news, but he was not a digger. He never made a name for himself as a newspaper man who dug deep for his stories. His handwriting shows that he would not.

Another newspaper writer who won great fame was Horace Greeley. At that time the idea of preparing newspaper copy with a typewriter was an unheard of thing, and Greeley wrote his editorials in longhand, to the annoyance of the printers, who had to read and set what they thought he said. There were countless stories of times when they set the wrong word because they could not read his writing. You will find it interesting although you may disagree with the criticism of its illegibility. His t-bars will no doubt interest you, showing as they do his sharp sarcastic nature. He was highly responsive to emotional situations, and when he was emotionally stirred he could use his sharp sarcasm with remarkable effect. He was another of the newspaper men who picked the surface. There is nothing in this writing to indicate a scholar. Sharp penetrating points are rare, and in most cases the letters that might have revealed a brilliant scholar are almost formless.

Teachers who read this book will probably smile when they compare Horace Greeley's writing with that of some of their young folks. After all, there may have been something very valuable in the push and pull exercises of muscular movement. At least it represented discipline, which is important in any field.

Where Greeley's writing was not copybook style by any means, that of

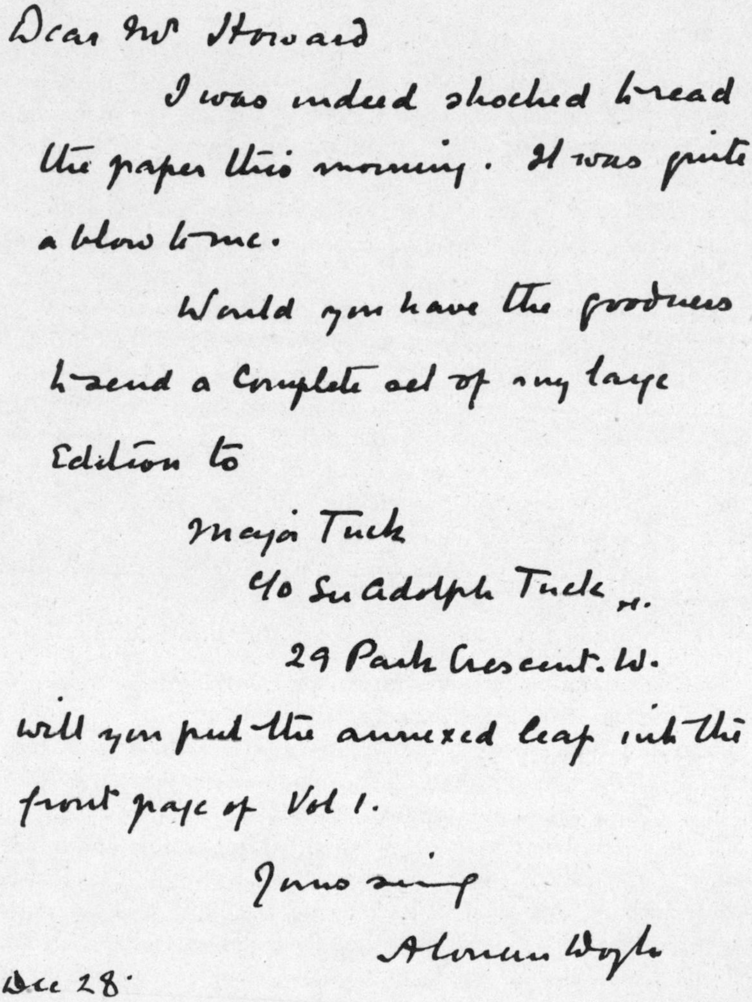

Dear Mr Howard

    I was indeed shocked bread the paper this morning. It was quite a blow to me.

    Would you have the goodness to send a Complete set of my large Edition to

        Major Tuck
        %o Sir Adolph Tuck, .
        29 Park Crescent. W.
will you put the annexed leap into the front page of Vol 1.

    Yours sincy
        A Conan Doyle

Dec 28.

PLATE 142. A. Conan Doyle, creator of Sherlock Holmes and famous for his research in the occult and mystic fields. First thing you notice is that this handwriting by its size shows concentraton. The down-strokes reveal determination.

A. 'Conan Doyle, the creator of Sherlock Holmes, was almost copper plate. You need merely glance at the Doyle letter to see the concentration; small letters that always indicate concentrated effort on the part of the writer. When he does something he does it with all his heart, centering his efforts on one project at a time. You are familiar with the down-strokes revealing determination, the retraced "d's" showing pride and dignity. They are both present in the Doyle writing. Many of the circle letters are open, and there is one trait that is highly important. Take the top line of the note. There are five distinct breaks between letters, registering a strong sense of the intuitive, the musical interpretative sense, the capacity to have hunches.

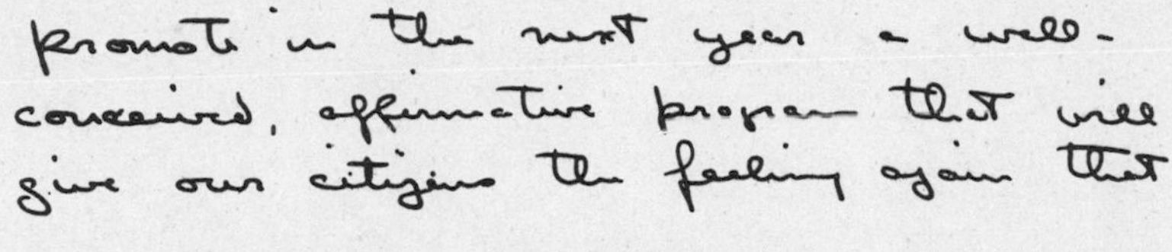

promote in the next year a well-conceived, affirmative program that will give our citizens the feeling again that

PLATE 143. Senator Saltonstall's handwriting shows capacity for making prompt, definite decisions.

These breaks repeated over and over again reveal a psychic sense, and in the case of Sir Arthur Conan Doyle they lead to a very active interest in that age old problem of whether the dead can communicate with the living.

The sharp points on his "m's" and "n's" are not pronounced but when you add the influence of concentration you have more results that you would not have if the writing were much larger. There is irritability here, shown by the t-bars that are written ahead of the t-stems time and again. According to this evidence the famous author who began his professional life as a physician, and ended it as a leader in spiritualistic investigation, while having accumulated a permanent place in literature, could be a very testy gentleman.

● SENATOR SALTONSTALL

One of the most interesting phases of human nature has been the reaction of able men to analyses that said what they considered complimentary things. When I analyzed the writing he submitted to me I gave him the truth as his writing showed it. His writing showed frankness, persistence, and inquiring mind, great determination, judgment, a reasonable amount of concentration, and capacity for definite decisions. The large upper loops revealed a man with a strong sense of philosophy, and his t-bars were strong enough to reveal a man with a clear purpose. You can find all of these traits for yourself, using the rules you know. However, Senator Saltonstall promptly questioned the analysis because he thought it flattered him. You can see for yourself whether it did.

Many of the world's great musicians have sent me their handwriting. During the years many speciments of their writing have come into my possession. But the writing of Julia Ward Howe, the composer of the lyrics of "The Battle Hymn of the Republic", like Horace Greeley's, showed more illegibility than anything else until you started to break down the stroke combinations that made the letters. She could be bitingly sarcastic, was exceedingly independent, and at the same time dignified.

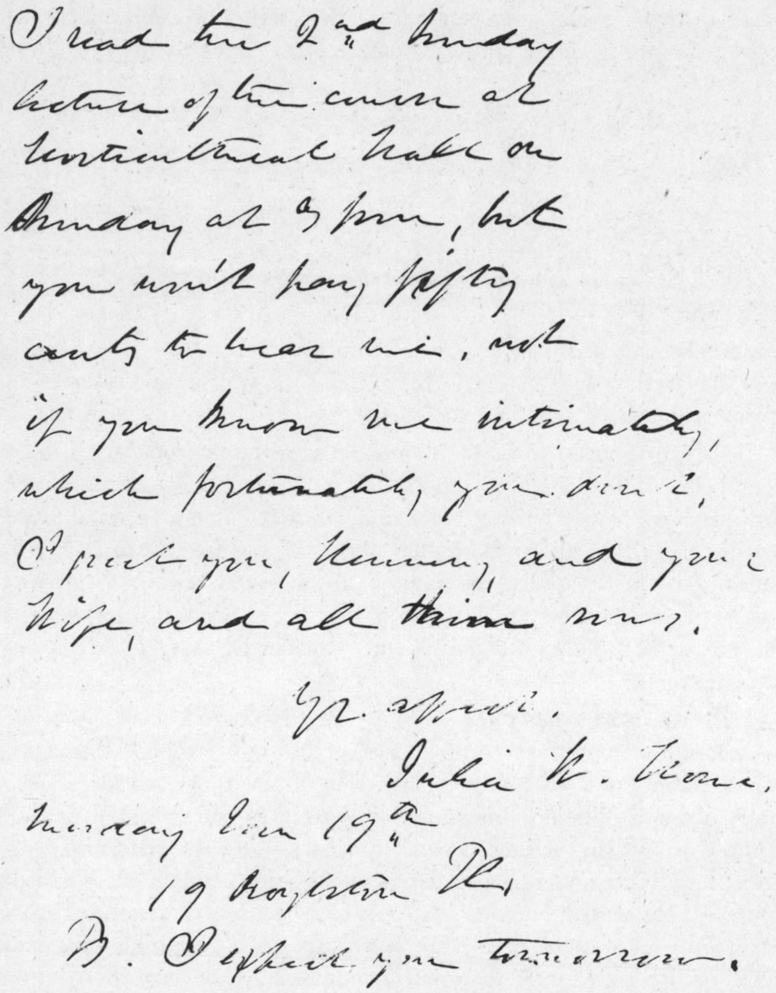
I read the 2nd Sunday lecture of the course at Horticultural Hall on Sunday at 3 p.m., but you won't pay fifty cents to hear me, not if you knew me intimately, which fortunately you don't. I greet you, Henry, and your wife, and all things new.

Julia W. Howe.

Tuesday Dec 19th
19 Boylston Pl.
B. I expect you tomorrow.

PLATE 144. Julia Ward Howe wrote the words to "The Battle Hymn of the Republic." This nearly illegible handwriting is interesting in what it reveals to a grapho analyst.

The shortness of the d-stems, as you know, reveal the independence, and her habit of retracing the stems revealed the dignity. She possessed great determination at times, and at other times her determination faded like the morning dew. You very often find such seeming contradictions, and we might follow through and determine exactly under what conditions Mrs. Howe would have been determined, but her writing is too dim. Too

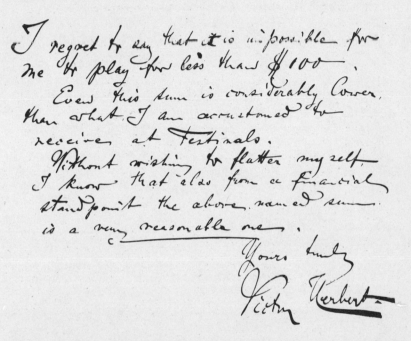

PLATE 14>. Handwriting of the great Victor Herbert shows a musical interpretative sense and a flair for showmanship.

many of the strokes have faded with the years. However, keep in mind that when the writing is not faded it is possible with grapho analysis to handle such contradictions, and come up with the truth.

Another very old handwriting, but one that is very clear and revealing, is this excerpt from a letter written by the great Victor Herbert. The way he drove the pen at the paper to make his i-dots leaves a permanent record of his irritability that at times reached the point of explosion. The flourishes at the finish of words, like in "named", show the flair for showmanship, and his tied "t's" in "flatter" tell us even now that what he started he finished. The breaks between letters in a word give us evidence of his musical interpretative sense, while the heavy ink as it occurs time and again reveals the sensuousness that helped to make him a great musician.

He had imagination that was never put to full use, as his lower loop on "my" shows by not being completed. He was very definite, very decisive when he reached the point of making such a stand. However, there were times when he would do it smoothly, diplomatically. But when Victor Herbert said "no" he meant "NO".

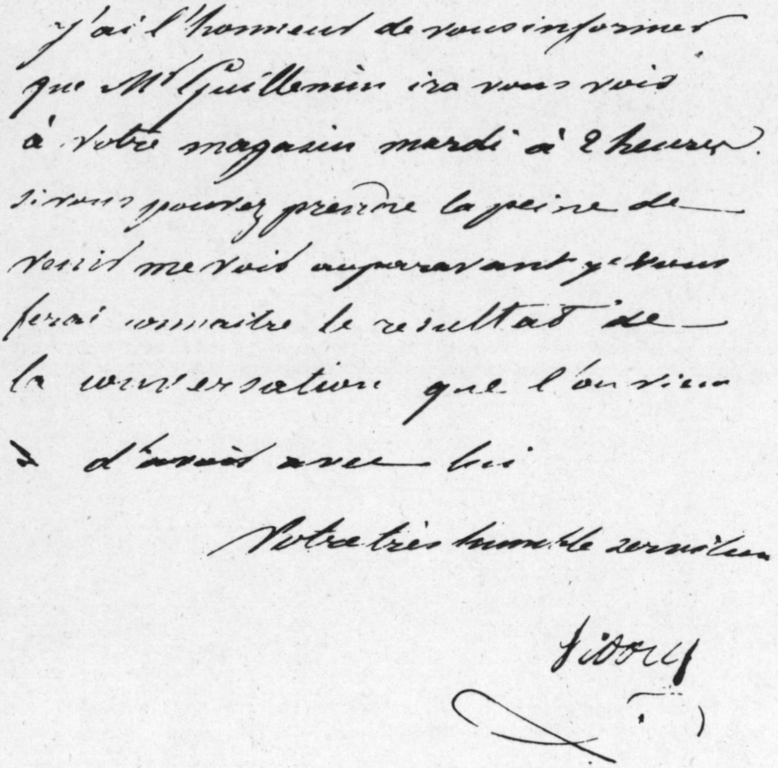

PLATE 146. Reading traits in handwriting—analyzing it—has nothing to do with being able to read the words. You can analyze this French writing of Vidocq, one time head of the French police system, as easily as you can analyze English.

The age of the writing does not matter. The style of it does not matter for all handwriting is made up of strokes, and strokes are combined to make letters, but it is the strokes that count. The writing may be in a language you do not understand. Take, for instance, this page from a letter written by Vidocq, one time head of the French police system. Vidocq started as a criminal and when he joined the sureté he knew almost every criminal in France and nearby countries. He was a great success, and reached a point of world wide fame. This writing shows a man who was ruled by his feel-

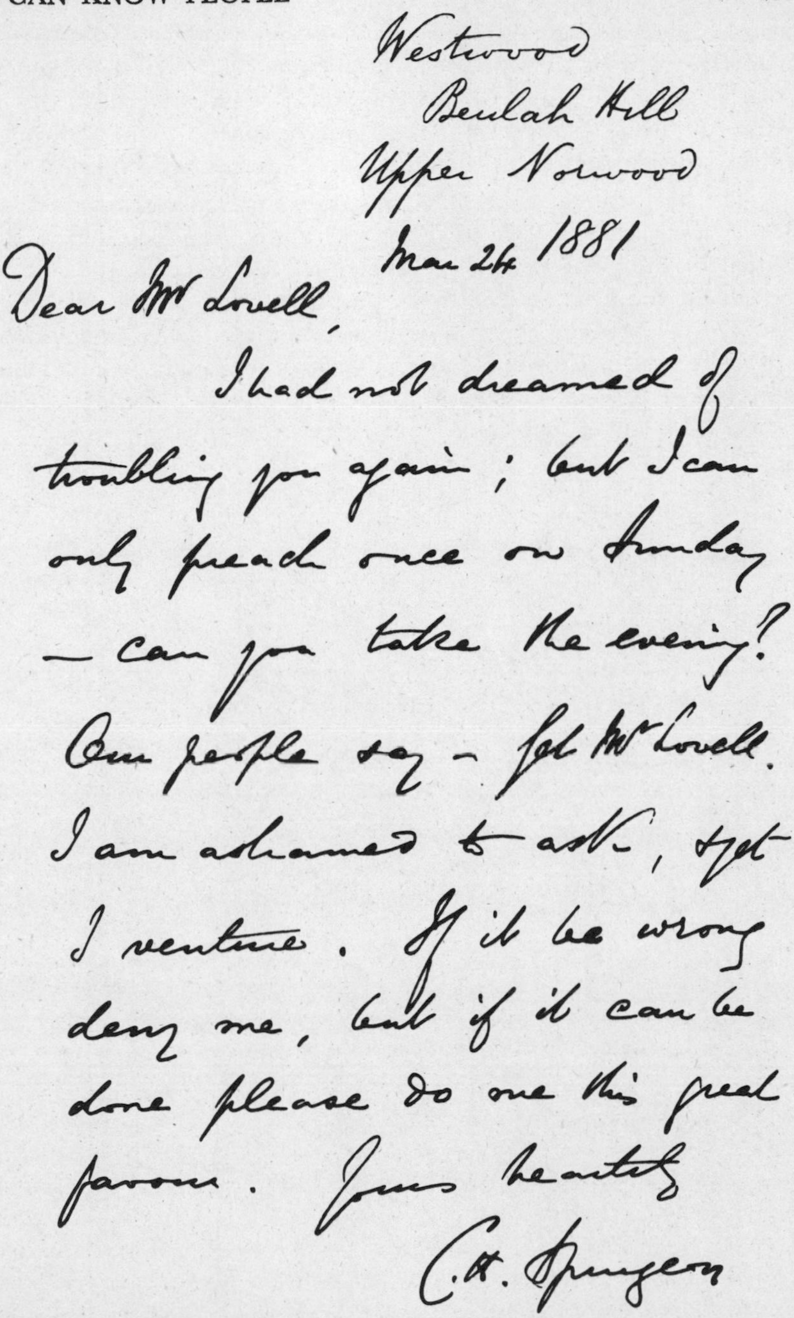

Westwood
Beulah Hill
Upper Norwood
Mar 24 1881

Dear Mr Lovell,

I had not dreamed of troubling you again; but I can only preach once on Sunday — can you take the evening? Our people say — get Mr Lovell. I am ashamed to ask, yet I venture. If it be wrong deny me, but if it can be done please do me this great favour. Yours heartily

C. H. Spurgeon

PLATE 147. The noted evangelist, Charles H. Spurgeon, made tall d's and t's showing great pride in what he was doing.

ings, one who was mentally awake all of the time, and who, when he started to investigate went to the bottom of anything that interested him. Police work interested him, and undoubtedly much of his success was due to his natural ability to explore. He was dignified, given a bit to showmanship, thrifty, irritable, and even in mature years was still self-conscious.

The handwriting of possibly the greatest preacher of another generation in my collection of handwriting pictures of men long gone is a page written by the great evangelist, Charles H. Spurgeon, in 1881. It shows the emotional appeal he used to stir people from the pulpit. His "d's" and "t's" are tall, showing great pride in what he was doing, and in his own personal conduct. He was determined enough to go thru with anything he undertook if it were possible. Sensitive, but this trait was not highly developed. His upper loops and lower loops are very similar in size, so that

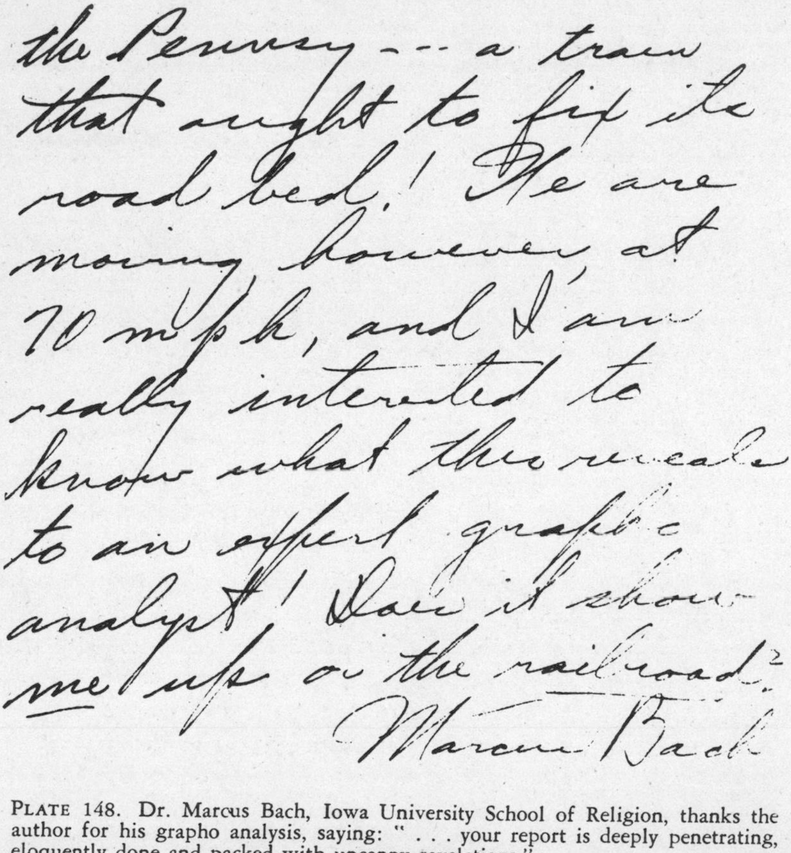
the Pennsy -- a train
that ought to fix its
road bed! We are
moving however, at
70 mph, and I am
really interested to
know what this reveals
to an expert grapho
analyst! Does it show
me up on the railroad?
Marcus Bach

PLATE 148. Dr. Marcus Bach, Iowa University School of Religion, thanks the author for his grapho analysis, saying: " . . . your report is deeply penetrating, eloquently done and packed with uncanny revelations."

we know that the religion he preached was not merely a philosophy but applied to life. You will be able to go on from this point, and really know the man as he was in the days of our grandparents.

The other great religionist with whose name you may be familiar is the very widely read Dr. Marcus Bach of the Iowa University School of Religion. No single author has contributed as much to the study of religions as Dr. Bach, with his explorations into individual groups from Unity to Psychiana.

There are just eight different letters in this signature, but they are revealing. The open-mouthed "a" shows his frankness, while the second "a" shows that he can keep still when it is wise to do so. Neither of these circle letters, however, shows even the slightest inclination toward deceit. He is generous but not extravagantly so. His upper loop on the "h" is tall and generous in size. His interest in philosophy, in a better way of life, is genuine. His two capital letters reveal, by their size in relation to the small letters, that he is not afraid.

His Iowa neighbors probably say of him "he hasn't a tight bone in his body", which is very true when we consider the liberal spacing between the letters. You have had two other rules that apply to Dr. Bach's writing and which you should have remembered clearly enough to determine what stroke shows his willingness to accept responsibility. You will also find from nothing more than a glance that no matter how self-possessed he may be on the speaking platform there is something of the self-consciousness that he had as a small boy.

Dr. Bach's truly monumental studies of religions were introduced to me by a grapho analyst whose handwriting I had analzed. I bought an autographed copy of one of his books, and made an analysis simply because I liked the book. There was not much writing to go on, but here is his letter of comment:

"The truth of the matter is that I have been caught in flying trips to Canada, to the American Southeast, and elsewhere with such uninterrupted regularity that I feel like a flying saucer! This explains, I hope, my unforgivable ingratitude and my failure to reply earlier to your special analysis. You may say for me in any publicity you may wish to use that your report is deeply penetrating, eloquently done and packed with uncanny revelations. This is an unsolicited endorsement of your expert diagnosis of personality through penmanship, and I want to thank you for it very much.

"May you have continued success and find many blessings in your work."

Edgar Wallace, the famous English author of who-dun-its did not hunt for criminals. He created them, so that readers sitting in their easy chairs

PLATE 149. Edgar Wallace, famous mystery-story writer. Notice the blunt strokes in this specimen of handwriting — shows positiveness of his thinking. There is also a color sense in this writing.

halfway round the world could follow their exploits. His bit of writing here is certainly not as legible as it might be, but when you examine it very closely you find out a great deal about the man. Notice how he brings the last stroke in "regards" down bluntly. He does the same with the last stroke in "Wallace", as well as in "kindest" and the final "h" in "with". All blunt strokes and all showing the positiveness of his thinking. If you will

PLATES 150 and 151. An unusual person, Erle Stanley Gardner, has an unusual handwriting. Pay particular attention to the flourishes, the large upper loops, the Greek "e" in the word "best."

turn back to the Maugham writing you will find that the two men had one thing in common. They had the color sense to paint word pictures. Maugham's writing shows more clearly defined literary talent, but if you examine these two lines of the Wallace writing you will find it here too. You have had enough experience now that you should really become well acquainted with the man. It will be interesting.

● **ERLE STANLEY GARDNER**

You may find it interesting to compare Edgar Wallace's two lines with another two lines, written by America's most famous producer of who-dun-its, Erle Stanley Gardner. Gardner, who is now engaged in one of the most remarkable efforts ever made in America to assist those who have been imprisoned through manufactured or other questionable evidence, produces books, string of them. Every one is readable, with an easy fascination that holds the reader. He might give all of his time to the Court of Last Resort, but it is merely another activity, because Erle Stanley Gardner is as restless as an eel. His handwriting shows it, revealing a well developed sense of philosophy in regard to living by his large upper loops. If he has critics who say he lacks literary talent, they get a sharp rebuff from his handwriting, where his small "e" in "best" is the Greek "e" that was accepted by even the graphologists long before grapho analysis was developed. His flourishes reveal his restless energy, his natural ability to do things in a big way, and his final flourish, like the center one in my own signature in Chapter 7, where the "k" is made like a huge hump in the center of the last name, reveals his indifference to criticism, if and when it occurs.

EXAMINATION FOR CHAPTER 13

Your knowledge of grapho analysis will be valuable only as you learn to depend on it. The only way to learn that you can rely on it is to use it whenever and wherever you have any dealings with people. As you use it you will find that you are getting facts that you know are true. Therefore, if this is true, you will get the truth from a handwriting where you may not want the truth. You may be convinced that the facts about the writer you have learned through your use of grapho analysis must be incorrect. However, if you can get the truth from one handwriting and know from contact that it is true you must face the realization that an unpleasant truth you find in the writing of someone you respect or admire is still the truth.

Actually, no one is perfect. You are not. Your friends have weaknesses and you are not using grapho analysis to identify facts about people and then judge them. You are using your knowledge merely to get the truth. This gives you protection. In my years of research and practice I have had many experiences where the handwriting picture of the individual was not a nice one. However, we were on a friendly basis and there did not seem to be any reason for breaking up a friendship. As a result, the writer whose writing had given away secrets did not know that I had made the analysis, or that I had protected myself by knowing what to expect in their actions. Just because you find the handwriting of a friend shows he has the possibility of stealing from you does not mean that you need to drop the acquaintance. You merely protect yourself against his taking anything from you by not providing the temptation. You know the truth and the truth protects you. Use your knowledge every day. Depend on it as you find that you can.

SPECIMEN O

EXAMINATION

1 . . *Check the two or more traits that are prominently revealed in the t-bars of this specimen.*
      a. ENTHUSIASM
      b. LACK OF PURPOSE
      c. VISIONARY
      d. CONSCIOUS SELF-CONTROL
      e. STRONG PURPOSE
      f. SARCASM

2 . . *Does the writing show generosity?*
      YES_____   No_____

3 . . *Will the writer be likely to have strong prejudices?*
      YES_____   No_____

4 . . *What is the basis for your conclusion?*
      a. HEAVY T-BARS
      b. SLANT OF WRITING
      c. WEIGHT OF WRITING
      d. FREQUENT V-BASES

5 . . *Does this writing show irritability?*
      YES_____   No_____

CHAPTER 14

How it Works

CASE HISTORIES SHOW HOW OTHERS USE GRAPHO ANALYSIS AS A CAREER, A SOURCE OF INCOME, PRESTIGE AND A HELP TO OTHERS WHO ARE CONFUSED OR LOST JOB-WISE. HOW TO USE YOUR KNOWLEDGE IN THE FAMILY AND IN BUSINESS AND PROFESSIONAL LIFE.

IF you have learned enough about grapho analysis to protect yourself even in a small way, it has been worth while. In case you have gained knowledge that will help you understand yourself, your friends, people you do not know, then something has been added to the sum total of happiness, and that is worth the time.

You see, I did not undertake the practice of grapho analysis because I had chosen grapho analysis as a career. I merely set out to answer my own questions, and ended up by looking at handwriting, finding how people thought, and telling them the truth when they asked me. The accuracy of what their individual handwritings revealed startled them, and laid the demand for instruction. I did not want to teach grapho analysis. I did not even want to write about it.

● HAD TO WRITE TEXTBOOKS FOR NEW COURSE

However, those early analyses set intelligent men and women at my heels demanding that I teach them. That was done without text books, and without a teaching organization. Writing the text books was a slow, wearing undertaking. In the first place, I did not realize how much knowledge I had gained, and in the early days I failed to put on paper all that I might have done in giving the student the help he needed. This called for frequent revisions of text material. Further, in order to know what the student did not understand, it was necessary to work closely with each student, and

very often to set him right in misinterpretations where my own acquaintance with a principle, through having developed that principle, was clear
to me but not to the student.

Thirty years ago the very idea that analyzing handwriting was anything else but an adjunct to fortune telling was not even thought of. Books
on psychology scoffed at the idea of a handwriting specimen revealing anything about a writer, other than whether he or she could write legibly. So
the going was rough, and if there had not been actual accomplishment on
the part of students here and there it would certainly have been so dis-
couraging that I might have given it up. It was not profitable financially.
And it was a heart-breaking undertaking to handle the multiple details of
organization, teaching, writing and financing. The latter was really the
greatest problem, and yet because editors were kind, it was solved by long
hours at my typewriter. Editors paid well, not for material on grapho
analysis especially, but for almost everything I could grind out of my
machine.

There were only a few students in the early days, but an amazing thing
happened. One woman in a neighborhood who found she could actually
tell the truth about an individual from a handwriting specimen told others.
A business man who possibly scoffed at the start, found that grapho analysis
gave him information about credit applications, or personnel applicants, and
he told other business men.

So the technique and science of grapho analysis has grown until today
it is a profession. Recently a busy housewife called me late at night. She
was vexed, and her first complaint was that she had banked only $25 that
day. In other words, she had spent time with only one client. But when
she explained that she had done her week's baking, and that she had called
on a neighbor for an hour, the twenty-five dollars did not seem so in-
significant.

● *HOW ONE WOMAN MAKES GRAPHO ANALYSIS PAY*
This housewife did not make $25 just by talking. She did not perform
blind magic or indulge in hocus pocus. She actually helped a woman with
a vexatious family problem that was leading to divorce. This woman was
helped to understand something of her husband's disposition, and of how
he annoyed her because she was possibly a bit too meticulous. Also, she was
annoying him by nagging at him for not always picking up his magazines
or his trousers, or shirts.

That housewife-grapho analyst actually rendered a valuable service. It
was a simple service but because she did not know either the woman who
was her client, or the woman's husband, her findings took on great value.

They were objective, not fault finding. She looked at a handwriting, found the answers and told her client what she had found.

● GRAPHO ANALYSIS AS A PROFESSIONAL SIDELINE

A credit manager told me an interesting story about his experience that will show you how the part time grapho analyst renders a service, although he may have studied solely for his own use. This particular man who passes on thousands of applicants for credit, had added public talks on grapho analysis, as a matter of public relations between his company and the area in which they worked. After one particular talk, for which he received a handsome fee, a man took him aside, and explained that he and his wife were considering sending a young son to a military school or turning him over to the state to be sent to an institution supported at public expense. "We can't do anything with him. He's not the least cooperative, and though we think he is capable of doing well in school he's failing right along. After hearing you today, it has occurred to me that you may be able to help us get him straightened out."

The credit manager saw an opportunity to help, not only the parents but the boy, and asked for the youngster's handwriting which was furnished to him by mail. He studied it carefully. Then he telephoned the parents, and asked for the handwritings of each of them. The three handwritings gave him the answer, and he made an appointment for a personal visit.

He had found that the blame did not lie with the boy, but with the parents who had forgotten in their exceedingly busy lives that their son was not something to be merely fed, clothed, and given spending money. The boy wanted to build something, and after that interview he had his chance. An empty building in the backyard was turned into a shop. Instead of simply giving him spending money, the father undertook to be interested in the lad's activities. The mother missed some of her bridge clubs and took an interest in her son. The result was two-fold. The analyst, who had undertaken to clean up a problem out of plain neighborliness and human sympathy, got a fat check, and the boy was headed toward good citizenship.

One of my earliest experiences with juvenile problems had to do with a lad in a southwestern state. He was running away from school. He did not study. He would leave home in the morning for his high school but never get there. The truant officers and the mother were all at their wits end. The boy was picked up and hauled into juvenile court, but fortunately the judge had been analyzed some years before. Instead of giving the boy a sentence of a reformatory, the judge suggested to the mother that she send the boy's handwriting in for a thorough analysis.

The lad's handwriting gave a perfect picture of why he was running away, and why he was not studying while in school. He felt he was being imposed upon, because he wanted a shop of his own. He wanted to tinker. He wanted to use his hands, not his head, and he did not want to study to be a doctor, even if his father had been one. The writing showed very real scientific and engineering possibilities, but not the kind that would be basic with a medical man. The analysis recommended that he be permitted to withdraw from school, and be given enough money to equip a small home laboratory, where he could mix things.

Fortunately the judge knew that his own analysis had been accurate, and he consented. The next fall the boy was back in school and making top grades. He had found for himself that he needed more knowledge, and that the way to get that knowledge was to attend school regularly. He was not a delinquent in the ordinary sense of the word. He was simply the victim of circumstances that were proving too big for him. When he had a chance to adjust himself, he was all right, and his handwriting and what it had revealed about him was the means by which he was set on the road to a happy and successful life.

● *VOCATIONAL APTITUDE AND GRAPHO ANALYSIS*

We hear much of juvenile delinquents today. You can help meet this situation if you will, like the credit manager above. Use the knowledge you have gained from this volume to help youngsters find themselves. In many cases you will not know enough, but use what you do know. When you find that your own knowledge is lacking, you have two choices: either add to your knowledge, or contact a professional grapho analyst. In either case you will be on the way to a solution to not only the difficult problem, but to everyday problems of all kinds that have to do with people. It is one of the basic tenets of grapho analysis that the truth as revealed in the handwriting is the only truth or version to be given the client.

In studying through this book you do have valuable knowledge. Hence you may be interested in some of the comments from others who have put their knowledge of grapho analysis to good use.

Case 13229—"Recently friends from out of the city visited us. Mr. B. who holds his doctorate in physics, and the corporation of which he is president, is doing a great service for this country in the way of research. When I explained grapho analysis to them, Mrs. B. was very enthusiastic, but he gave me a blunt opinion that there was nothing to it. However, they both asked me to examine their handwriting. Mr. B's sample read 'Foo to you too', along with his signature. Fortunately I noted at once a common trait in their handwritings, and pointed it out to them. They admitted the truth of what the handwriting had revealed. This approach stirred up enthusiasm on the part of Mr. B. and before he realized it he was asking me to analyze the writing of two of his men whom he 'just couldn't figure out'."

● **GRAPHO ANALYSIS IDENTIFIES CUSTOMER WITH MUSICAL KNOWLEDGE**

Case 11948—"All credit applications pass over my desk. A brand-new customer unknown to me or to anyone in the department was given' credit while I was at lunch. When I returned and looked over his signature I told the man who waited on the stranger that the fellow was very musical. Our man was amazed and said that while they were talking the new customer had told him of his love for and interest in music and that he led a chorus of 30 voices."

● **DETECTS FORGERIES**

Case 11995—"I recently received a reply to a letter I wrote to a magazine concerning handwriting specimens appearing in the pages of a recent issue. The specimens were accompanied by pictures of women staff members modeling dresses. The specimens slanted from upright to far-forward, were heavy and light, fancy and plain, but the analyses all had a marked similarity. I became convinced they were all written by the same person. I wrote the editor explaining my interest in grapho analysis and told of my findings. My letter in reply admitted that the writing was all done by the same person, which the editor, too, was surprised to discover. The writer of the specimens was a professional penman who was able to change the appearance of the different signatures, but could not free himself from his own pen-picture of himself. I know now that grapho analysis has great value in recognizing forgeries."

Case 11032—"I just recently had proof of the accuracy of grapho analysis in such an outstanding and funny way that I have told many of my friends about it. A new tenant handed me a check. My wife said 'analyze it'. I knew the man was an art teacher, but I was immediately impressed by the strokes revealing literary tendencies. I told him that if he wasn't a writer, he should be. The man has a very forceful laugh, and he howled. 'I've written four books,' he said."

Case 13442—"I was talking grapho analysis to our insurance agent one day and he offered me a signature just to see what I might find. The first thing I noticed was the strong resentment of possible imposition, and I mentioned it. He started laughing, then told me that the writer had blacked the eyes of one of his neighbors only the day before."

● **POLICE INVESTIGATOR USES GRAPHO ANALYSIS**

Case 12425—"I see handwriting all the time in my work as investigator for the police department. It is my job to interrogate people in regards to crimes that have been committed, and to evaluate the information I get.

Also I screen all applicants prior to their taking examinations for the Police Department.

"On one occasion I had a friend visiting who had had his writing analyzed by a professional grapho analyst, and in order to get a comparison he requested that I analyze his writing. I was more than glad to comply although at the time I had no idea what he was doing. At the completion of the analysis he told me that both my analysis and the other were the same. He wanted to know if I was acquainted with the professional, but we had never met. This gives all of the proof of the accuracy of grapho analysis that I can ask."

Case 11730—"I got quite a test of what I know about grapho analysis at a fraternity alumni meeting. Some of those who were there were complete strangers to me. Quite naturally they wanted me to look at their handwriting and tell them what I found. I did one for a man who seemed to be well known, and when I remarked that he was very self-conscious, everyone laughed and said I had certainly missed. However, the evidence was so strong that I was sure I was right, so asked them to put the question up to him. They did and he readily confirmed my statement. Those who had laughed were certainly surprised and I am sure they went away from that meeting convinced that grapho analysis reveals the truth."

● **DEALING WITH CRIMINALS**

Case 12887—"As an investigator for the detective division of the Police Department of our city, I have used my knowledge as much as possible in the field where I work. I have found that where a look at the handwriting of a suspected criminal is possible before talking to him, it has given me ideas on how to deal with the individual, man or woman. This gives me confidence in dealing with the suspect, and I am sure that I get a much more factual statement simply because I know how to approach him."

Case 13580—"I refused to take a check from a stranger who offered it in our place of business. Later I found from the Credit Bureau in this county that he had been giving worthless checks."

Case 11133—"A friend recently asked me to look over an application that he said he had received regarding a position as secretary. I studied the application and told him what I had found. He then informed me that he had played a practical joke by giving me the handwriting of his secretary who had been with him for several years. The point worth while was he said my analysis was absolutely correct in every statement that I made."

Case 10865—"I recently analyzed a man's handwriting and was very much surprised to find that he had a lot of natural musical ability. So much so that as he was a stranger, and I did not want to make a fool of myself, I hesitated to mention it. Imagine my satisfaction when I found that I really knew more than I was willing to admit to myself. He has five musical instruments in his home and plays all of them."

● **GRAPHO ANALYSIS SIMPLIFIES "GETTING ACQUAINTED"**

Case 10887—"Going into a new hospital as a Medical Director is far from easy. I studied the handwriting of the business manager, the nursing supervisor, and the charge nurses. The knowledge I gained of their individual inclinations, and capabilities has proven invaluable in knowing how to handle these people. Now that I am working with them and have been here long enough to know my way around I am amazed and grateful for my knowledge of grapho analysis. I find that the strangers were not strangers at all, that I knew them, and am able to work with them as though we had worked together for a long, long time."

Case 11630—"I learned that the language in which the writing is done has nothing to do with what is learned from that writing. A friend handed me a letter written in French. I examined it and analyzed it for him, only to learn that it was his own writing, because he can write equally well in German, French and English. He had merely put me to a test to see if I was depending on what I read or what I analyzed. You see I do not speak one word of French, so I had to stand entirely on what I found in the handwriting. Now I know that language has no bearing on what the writing reveals."

● **HANDWRITING AS A HELP IN JOB ANALYSIS**

Case 10027—"An outstanding placement that we made was a girl who thought she wanted a job as a receptionist. When I analyzed her handwriting I could not find the personality requirements that are required on such a job, but she had unusual natural ability for analyzing. She was careful, almost precise. I placed her on a bookkeeping job, although she was reluctant to take it. Now she is delighted. So you see my knowledge of grapho analysis helped me make a satisfactory placement, and also the young woman was helped to find her proper niche in business."

● **LAWYER PRAISES GRAPHO ANALYSIS**

Case 7357—"In handling my law practice I make it a point to obtain not only specimens of writing of my client or clients, I also get the handwriting of 'the other side' and frequently I already have the writing of their counsel. If possible I get the handwriting of the judge who is to hear the case. With these handwritings I have a better understanding of the controversy, who may or may not be to blame. Also I know how each party will act under certain circumstances and situations. For that matter, I even gather the handwriting of my own witnesses so that I know which will be precise and accurate in his testimony, which one may be inclined to shade the truth or even lie. All of this 'inside information' is invaluable, and has enabled me to win many cases where lack of this knowledge would have ended up the other way."

● *HOW A DOCTOR USES GRAPHO ANALYSIS*

Case 11330—"My receptionist hands each new patient a scratch pad, giving the data which she will later transfer to the patient's record card. However, this page of writing comes to me before I see the patient. With this advance information it is much easier to understand how to deal with each patient. Also, although we have a requirement that all bills be paid promptly, every doctor knows this rule is not always workable. My receptionist, who also knows grapho analysis, knows who will be trustworthy, and who will not pay a bill unless forced to do it. As a result of grapho analysis and this team work I help more people, and we save more money by having fewer losses. My knowledge of grapho analysis is worth every hour I spent studying it, and I have spent a good many hours."

Case 13311—"There are so many surprises when one can analyze handwriting. An acquaintance of mine, a dignified, white-haired lady, whose breeding and manners were of the lavender and old lace school, gave me her writing. Her p-loops were very prominent, but it is not easy to picture such a person participating in physical activities the way her "p's" indicated she wanted to do. I steered the conversation around to sports, and what do you suppose she said? 'All my life I've wanted to be an acrobat but when I was a girl that was unthinkable. I still want to be one, but the old joints and muscles will not stand it now.' This proves what we have been taught, that it is the mental desire, not always the fulfillment, that shows in a person's handwriting."

● *THIS GRAPHO ANALYST WINS A BET*

Case 6703—"Grapho analysis is not only valuable to me in all of my business relations, but it even gives me a bit of odd fun now and then. I have a 'Doubting Thomas' friend who has always insisted that I have a sixth sense. At any rate, be brought me the handwriting of two brothers, and put up a nice little sum as a wager that I could not pick the one brother who has musical talent. The writing was very similar, but it was like pie and ice cream to win the bet in less than five minutes, and was my friend red in the face? Surely, I've used grapho analysis so long that skepticism on the part of others seems very foolish, and these little incidents give me a terrific kick."

You may say to yourself that such incidents may be for others but not for you. Each of these writers acquired the same knowledge presented to you in the preceding chapters. The incidents were not reported by supermen, who were especially "gifted". Some of them were made by those with high professional training in accountancy, and law or medicine. Others were made by men and women with only an eighth grade education, because formal education is not necessary for a practical use of grapho analysis. Further, these comments were not made by professionals. These experiences are the experiences of men and women just like you who have learned rules, learned to apply them, not in an abstract way, but just as you have had them presented in your studies of people. After all, people are your field. They are the greatest single study in the world, and when you have sound, proven rules, you will be able to really know people.

It is true that today grapho analysis is a profession for an increasing number of men and women who began by learning simple rules and proving them. They desired to know more and as they learned more they found a greater field for their services. A huge volume might be compiled of stories of men and women who are artists, writers, business executives, doctors, and teachers who have made grapho analysis a part or full time profession. They have attended resident classes, and have done work just as in any other profession.

There is an association of grapho analysts representing thousands of men and women trained professionally. They live in small towns, and large cities from the southern most tip of Africa, over into South America, back to the orient, in Australia, and all through North America. Starting in 1939 the first summer school was held, tuition free to all home students of this association. Canada and several states were represented; but it was just a small group.

Then came World War II and a cessation of summer activities, but these were revived in 1950. Now professional analyst students travel across oceans, the provinces of Canada, and the states, all with one purpose—to go back home and render a bigger service to those who consult them on matters of every conceivable nature, except the future. There are love affairs, family problems, juvenile problems that may be presented by either the teacher, the parents, and occasionally by the courts.

Professional grapho analysts deal with human nature in the raw, and their records of accomplisments provide a tremendous backlog of support for the science which started when my curiosity got the best of me, and I began tracking down the cause for my long finals. It has been a lot of fun, long days of punishment when finances were so limited that meals were few and far between. But the physical and financial problems have never been great enough to overshadow an enthusiastic letter from a husband who tells how the truth as revealed to him and his wife reunited their happy home.

Actually such results are naturally to be expected. Ninety-five percent of all our troubles stem from a lack of knowledge of human nature. This could be a misunderstanding of ourselves or of others.

You should have gained a lot from this volume. The more you use what you have learned the more you will depend on your knowledge. This is so basically true that the money you paid for this book, and the time you have spent reading it becomes at least in a small way, an insurance policy covering your happiness and your success in the years ahead. One phase of grapho analysis has been purposely omitted. Your writing defines your natural capabilities in regard to the work you do in life. However, this is not a job for a neophyte. A writer may, for instance, show artistic talent, but he may possess weaknesses that completely overshadow his natural ability. Therefore, in making a vocational determination it is necessary to completely evaluate all of the evidence in, not a few lines of writing, but in pages. From such evidence the analyst can draw a fine picture, although it is not possible to say to a man whose writing shows, as Hoover's did, natural engineering ability or talent, that he will build bridges. The analyst must take into consideration whether the added evidence gained from other strokes shows a tendency toward research engineering, or the actual creation of a project. Each writer is an individual. Each has great strength and also powerful weaknesses that check his upward climb. It takes hours to evaluate all of such evidence.

Grapho analysis has grown. Much of its growth has been accomplished without advertising. It is only in the last few years that magazine space has been used in liberal quantities. However, the reason for the growth is that men and women who have studied have found they can depend on it. They have interested their friends, so that as this book is written it is not difficult to look ahead and envision a resident school. It may be a huge clinic where problem children may be taken by their parents for complete understanding. And under the guidance of experts changes in writing habits will make a change in personality, with strong points being encouraged and weaker ones discouraged.

So it has been worth while. You will be making it even more worth while as you memorize and use these rules, and benefit by doing so. After all, life is worth while—when you understand yourself, and others. This knowledge will give us peace, and prosperity, both financial and spiritual. Our minds, freed from the limitations of quarrels and bickering will grow, and each of us will become a better citizen, a better homemaker, and a better individual within ourselves. Grapho analysis will give you this knowledge, and it will also give you freedom, with all that freedom means without license.

EXAMINATION FOR CHAPTER 14

You have covered a great deal of ground since you picked up this book and started on Chapter 1. Actually, you do not know how much you have done. But now you will have an opportunity to prove to yourself that you have learned and can use grapho analysis. However, you will find it necessary to go back and restudy some of the chapters.

If you cannot be sure on some points in this final test, do not become too worried. Go back and hunt for the answer. You have had very large plates used for illustrations so that you can get a general picture of the writer's character. Actually, most of the illustrations provide plenty of material for you to use profitably all you have learned. Therefore, a full page handwriting plate is not included just to illustrate one or two points, but to provide you with some of the most fascinating laboratory material in the world; the writing of people, some of them famous, others not so famous. All, however, people, and all with some good or valuable traits and all with some weaknesses.

With this approach, you are ready to examine the final handwriting study. You should be able to check at least fifty percent without reviewing. If you need to review you should check out with eight out of ten correct identifications of traits.

SPECIMEN P

EXAMINATION

The above plate to be used for this final test was written by one of the most famous men in America in his field. Do not attempt to guess his name or profession because that is not the object of this test.

Do not attempt to check all the traits. Instead, select only those you find in the handwriting. There are a great many traits and questions listed here and you may find that you will not check more than half of them. This may be true because no man must have all the traits listed.

Check down through the questions one by one. Start with the first and try your best to answer each one where the writing provides a definite answer. If you skip around you are almost certain to make a low rating. Do your best to make a good grade. You have had the principles, now is your chance to use them.

1 . . *What was this writer's reaction to emotional situations?*
    a. VERY STRONG
    b. STRONG
    c. DID NOT REACT
    d. MEDIUM REACTION

2 . . *Did the weight of the writing influence his reactions?*
    YES_____   No_____

3 . . *Would he be friendly, warm hearted and sympathetic?*
    YES_____   No_____

4 . . *Was he generous?*
    YES_____   No_____

5 . . *Do you find any evidence of his ability to make definite decisions?*
    YES_____   No_____

6 . . *Was he enthusiastic?*
    YES_____   No_____

7 . . *Is there evidence of a strong purpose?*
    YES_____   No_____

8 . . *Check below the traits to be found in this writing.*
    a. TIMIDITY
    b. AGGRESSIVENESS
    c. INITIATIVE

9 . . *Do you find any mud in this writing?*
    YES_____   No_____

10 . . *Does the writing show depth of emotion enough to show an appreciation of words and how they sound?*
    YES_____   No_____

11 . . *Is there any imagination revealed in this writing?*
    YES_____   No_____

12 . . *Was the writer*   a. FRANK   *or* b. SECRETIVE*?*

13 . . *Is there any evidence of diplomacy?*
    YES_____   No_____

Answers

ANSWERS TO THE CHAPTER EXAMINATIONS

Chapter 1—No Test

Chapter 2—
    1. YES 2. No 3. YES 4. No 5. YES 6. No 7. No 8. YES 9. No
    10. YES 11. YES 12. No 13. d 14. d 15. YES 16. c

Chapter 3—
    1. YES 2. a 3. a 4. b 5. b 6. c 7. YES 8. b 9. b 10. c

Chapter 4—
    1. No 2. a 3. a, b, c 4. b 5. YES 6. b, c

Chapter 5—
    1a. No 1b. YES 1c. YES 1d. No 1e. YES 1f. YES 1g. No
    1h. No 1i. YES 1j. YES 1k. No 1l. YES 1m. No 1n. YES
    2. No 3. c

Chapter 6—
    1. YES 2. b, c 3. No 4. b 5. a 6. b, d, f 7. c

Chapter 7—No Test

Chapter 8—
    1. b 2. e 3. d 4. d 5. b 6. c 7. b 8. a

Chapter 9—No Test

Chapter 10—
    1. No 2. a 3. YES 4. YES 5. YES 6. No 7. YES 8. YES
    9. No 10. YES 11. No 12. YES 13. No 14. No 15. No
    16. YES 17. YES 18. YES

Chapter 11—
    1. No 2. b 3. c, d 4. c, d 5. c 6. c, d, f

Chapter 12—
    1. c   2. c   3. b, c   4. Yes

Chapter 13—
    1. c, d, e, f   2. No   3. Yes   4. b, c   5. Yes

Chapter 14—
    1. b   2. Yes   3. No   4. No   5. Yes   6. Yes   7. Yes   8. b, c
    9. Yes   10. Yes   11. No   12. a   13. Yes

Dictionary of Graphoanalysis

A

acquisitive Initial hooks. The volume of the desire indicated by the size of the hook. May occur at the beginning of a word, but retains its value wherever found as an **initial** stroke.

adaptable Mental alertness indicated by ability to understand without inflexibility of thought.

adolescent Lack of definiteness. Calendar years do not determine the mental growth of the individual, hence many writers who are grown physically are mentally adolescent.

aggressiveness Last stroke of "g", "j", "y" and "p" carried forward with a strong and vigorous swing.

analytical A v-shaped formation at the base line. This may occur between any two strokes, one written downward at any slant, and the other written upward. The deeper the trough of the v-formation the greater the analytical ability.

minimum

antagonistic Inflexible initial strokes. Usually combined with highly developed analytical sense.

do and ag

artistic May involve many qualities including line values, creative ability, and color sense.

Russell forty orty

C

caustic T-bars made like arrows. This applies regardless of location of the bar.

don't dot it

but get it

change (and variety) Long lower loops running into lines below.

ags you may

for if you

clannish Sharp inverted loop at end of "y", "j", and "g" lower stems.

boy may go

cold Vertical writing, lacking warmth or emotional depth, and sympathetic traits as generosity.

See CREATIVE for stroke formation.

color sense Determined entirely by the heaviness of the writing.

trampled your grasses

comprehension Ability to understand or comprehend is determined by the formation of "m", "n", "r", and the last half of the "h". The more pointed, the greater the mental speed or ability to probe into the matter under consideration.

This is a sample

handwriting

concentration Small writing. The smaller the writing the greater the concentration. This trait intensifies all other traits found in a writing.

at the end of the road and I stop

creative ability Flat top "r's", broad or well-rounded "m's", "n's", and last half of "h" and broad "k".

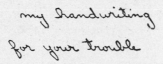

curiosity Sharp pointed inverted v-strokes on "m", "n", "h", or "r". Curiosity is investigativeness lacking the purpose of the latter trait.

D

deceit-deception Indicated by repeated initial half or complete loops at the beginning of the circle in "a", "o", "d", "g", or "q", and by a loop occurring at the same time in the ending of the "a" or "o". Deceit must be intentional in order to qualify under this heading. Many who are charged with lying do so because of lack of attention to details, vivid imagination and talkativeness. Persistent initial loops as indicated, coupled with wide open circle strokes would indicate deceit based in part on volubility.

decisive Final strokes on letters at the end of words firm, ending abruptly at or near the base; may be broader at the finish in which case the degree of decisiveness will be increased.

you can get it

definite Firm letter formations; firm endings for final strokes in words.

more than you

deliberate Upper stems made double. Must be "t" or "d" but evidence may also be found in capitals "W", "M", or "N".

M do this

depressed Writing that turns down sharply at or near end of line.

and may be you

determination Strokes instead of loops for down stroke letters, "g", "y", "j", or "q". Strength and endurance of determination determined by stroke qualities.

high lonely

diplomacy Strokes that taper either at the end of a word or within the word itself. Strokes must taper rather than fade.

discouragement Downward slant of lines. Sharp drop at end of line indicates occasional severe periods of discouragement. Should not be mistaken for emotional depression or disgust. Pessimism.

domineering Cross-bars of "t" slanted downward, arrow-like.

E

egotism Very large capitals in proportion to small letters, frequently accompanied by ostentation.

emotional expression Forward slant. The greater the expression at the time.

emphatic-emphasis Firm down strokes that reach the base line, or by their location give evidence that they should be completed at the base line. Strokes may end in a blob of ink which increases the evidence of bluntness or definiteness.

The Question

enthusiasm Sweeping left to right cross strokes, the longer the stroke the greater the individual enthusiasm. The heavier the stroke the greater the force of that trait.

that raineth

extravagant Extreme finals to words, letters widely separated rather than close together.

it may be so and so

F

frankness Open-mouthed "o", "a", "g", "q", "d", and well rounded "e's". The wider the opening the greater the talkativeness.

only do not talk so fast

G

generous Long finals in body of writing.

some are so

genius Depending entirely on some outstanding traits of a constructive nature. Usually erratic in an outstanding way, but not possible of illustration any more than genius is possible of conformity.

graceful This represents a sense of line values and is registered by graceful lower loops.

going long

H

homosexuality May be determined by too much color, utter absence of color or other combinations that do not show balance. Usually accompanied by extreme clannishness, but this trait must be considered more as a contributing element rather than final evidence. This trait cannot be definitely illustrated because homosexuality presents an endless variety of elements.

humor Flourished stroke as shown before any letter. Usually "M", "N", or "W", but may occur in small letters.

w M W

I

independence Short d-stems.

duly sorely

imagination Inflated lower loops. Inflated upper loops add the influence of imagination to philosophical or visionary habits of thought. The greater the inflation of the loops, the greater the imagination.

g yours truly

initiative Last stroke of "g", "j", "y", and "p" carried forward.

say jag

interpretative See PSYCHIC.

rudiculous

intuition Frequent breaks between letters. Not breaks in the letters themselves.

some are true
urco more for

inventive Usually investigative with creative ability, but many times the creative ability is lacking.

investigative Inverted v-strokes for "h", "m", "n", and "r". Size of letter does not effect the determination regarding investigativeness.

more in din
money dun

irritable Broken or fine arrow-like "i" dots.

J

jealousy Inverted initial loops. Must be small and swung sharply from point of origin backward or to the left.

judgment Poise, emotional balance; affected by other traits.

judicial Poise, provides the basis of this quality; affected by other traits.

K

kindliness Expressive, generosity. Absence of sarcasm or similar hurtful traits.

L

languid Evidence of deliberateness with possible procrastination.

lecherous Frequent and heavy blotches. Corrugated strokes.

line values Loops, either lower or upper. The longer and more slender the greater the understanding or appreciation of line values.

y   y   j

loyalty Small and well rounded dot for "i". Location does not determine loyalty.

possibly it is

M

materialistic Lacking upper strokes for "f"; usually low cross-bars on t-stem. All upper loops short.

f f from

N

normal There is no such writing. Taken generally it will be an absence of striking qualities. Dr. Louis C. Bisch says that normal people are commonplace, and this may apply to the writing.

O

optimism Writing with decided upward slant. Words slanted upward, with following word started at base line indicates short-lived and unhealthy optimism.

organization ability Well balanced "f". Upper and lower loops the same.

ostentation Showy, over-decorated writing.

P

passionate Very heavy writing, likely to have corrugated edges on principle strokes, blotted or blurred, either extremely expressive or lacking expression.

peaceful Letter "p" made with sharp upper point.

peace party fur

persistent Tie stroke regardless of location.

put into form qui

pessimism Downward slant to lines of writing.
See DISCOURAGEMENT. This specimen shows the downward slant of marked pessimism, the pessimist however slanting the entire line downward instead of starting each word on the line.
See under positive. This is also an excellent illustration of poise in spite of the deep emotions also expressed.

philosophic High "l", "t", "f" and "h" stems.

hig for te

physical-mindedness A love or desire for physical activity expressed by lower-loops for "p". Where loops are long and slender the physical activity will be expressed gracefully; when enlarged the physical expression will be more vigorous. A prize fighter can win great success without love of physical ac-

tivity, depending upon initiative, aggressiveness
and other traits.

[handwritten signatures]

poise Well balanced.

positive All strokes made with a firm hand, and
final strokes reaching or intended to reach the base
line are firm and strong.

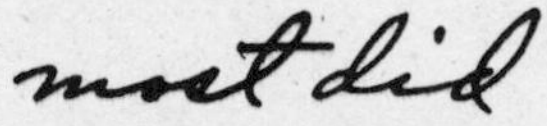

[handwritten: most did]

practical Organization ability; t-bars written **not**
above the point of the t-stem. Degree of practicality
determined by the location of the cross-bar. When
written well down on the stem the writing indicates
a nature that lacks ambition, satisfied with the
primary requirements of life; ie., food, shelter,
and clothing.

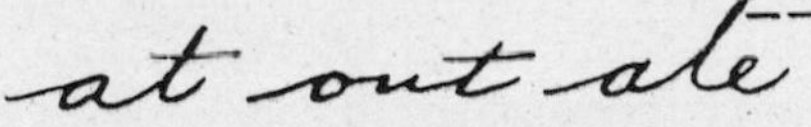

[handwritten: at out ate]

pride Tall d-stems, t-stems, not vertical.

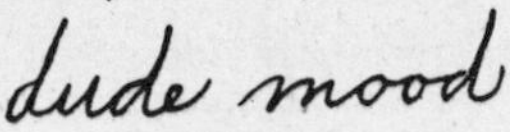

[handwritten: dude mood]

procrastination T-bars preceding the stem. Emphasized by i-dots also preceding the i-stem, when the
t-bar evidence is present.

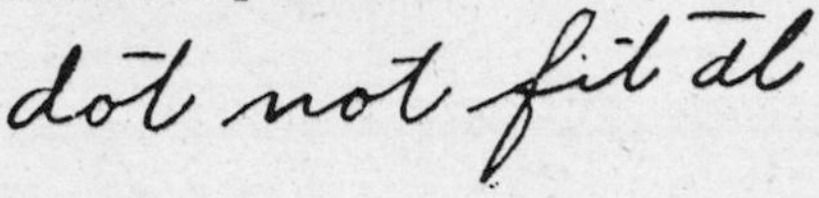

[handwritten: dot not fit dl]

psychic Frequent breaks between letters.

some day

R

repressed Strokes written close together. However, there must be some definite trait expressed in the writing, and which may be repressed.

more more more

resentful-ment See antagonism-antagonistic.
reserved Backhand writing without ostentation; frequently compact.

merely say wary
merely wary so do it

S

sarcasm Arrow cross-bars for "t's". Stroke may be long or short, the sarcasm being registered by the knife-edge ending of the stroke. A short, very arrow-like stem will give great sarcasm; a longer stroke registering modified sarcasm.

tit for tat

secretive Circle strokes tied.

out art bot

selective Narrow lower loops on "y", "g", "j", and "q". See CLANNISH which is extreme emphasis of the selective inclination.

clay day ray may

self-consciousness Last third of "M" or "m", and last half of "N" or "n" made higher than previous strokes.

M N M m

self-interest Writing vertical or near vertical. Absence of generosity.

Will you please give

self-reliance Strong stroke under signature. Strong signature, somewhat larger than body of writing.

Jene

sensitive Looped "d" and "t" stems. The larger the loop in proportion to height the greater the sensitiveness. Short stems may be looped, the heights

of the stem having nothing to do with the evidence
of sensitiveness.

that dot .

sensual Heavy, blotched writing; corrugated strokes.

merely do your part

sensuous Heavy, clean cut writing and smooth
heavy strokes.

Peer Gynt

shallow Weak writing.
See SUPERFICIAL.

spiritual See psychic and philosophical. These traits
combined in marked development.

stinginess Pinched writing without finals to words
or after letter formations.

not in my place

stubborn Inverted v-stroke in "d" or "t". May occur
at the end of word or at any other place.

it did rod

superficial Shallow or dish-like t-bars; usually light

lines and accompanied by erratic stroke combinations. Frequently weak or unformed writing.

tunner fit

suppressed Abnormally close writing, with evidence of some outstanding trait.

do not expect anyone

sympathetic Expressive and generous.

indicative emm

T

talkative Wide open "a", "o", "d", "q", and "g".

at y. ur associu

temper Two distinct strokes, both or either of which may be found.

t t t

t f t h t

tenacity Final hooks; may occur at end of words, or at the end of any stroke combination or stroke when standing alone.

that mate

V

vain High d-stems, vertical or near-vertical.

do fade wade

variable An emotional condition, writing slanting first one way and then another. Variable in interests is the result of desire for change.

say for your so

virtuous This represents a combination of qualities and cannot be determined by any single stroke. Virtue is a mental rather than physical condition from the standpoint of Grapho-Analytical study. Therefore, people of known virtue may lack this quality and reveal the lack in writing.

visionary Cross-bars written above t-stems. If some "t's" are crossed, and others have the cross-bar written above the stem, the influence of the visionary will be determined by the proportion of visionary strokes. Light strokes do not increase the visionary nature, but they determine the permanency or weight of the visions.

t t

W

weak Lacking definiteness. Composite of many traits.

your part it is not

will Cross-bar of t growing stronger.

t t tot

Index